Best Sermons 7

Best Sermons 7

James W. Cox, Editor

Kenneth M. Cox, Associate Editor

HarperSanFrancisco
A Division of HarperCollins*Publishers*

BEST SERMONS 7. Copyright © 1994 by HarperCollins Publishers. All rights reserved. Printed in the United States of America. No part of this book may be used or reproduced in any manner whatsoever without written permission except in the case of brief quotations embodied in critical articles and reviews. For information address HarperCollins Publishers, 10 East 53rd Street, New York, NY 10022.

FIRST EDITION

Library of Congress Catalog Card Number 88–656297
ISSN 1041–6382

94 95 96 97 98 HAD 10 9 8 7 6 5 4 3 2 1

This edition is printed on acid-free paper that meets the American National Standards Institute Z39.48 Standard.

Contents

91879

IV. Ethical

V. Pastoral

VI. Devotional

Epilogue: Eschatological

Preface

This is the final volume in the *Best Sermons* series. It has been a delightful experience as we have read hundreds upon hundreds of sermons, many of them fine sermons that did not win in the competitions. We hope that the challenge of the annual competitions has caused many preachers to evaluate their sermons and perhaps hone their skills so as to lift their regular homiletical productions to new levels of excellence.

Our approach was not reductionist; we did not look for sermons cut by patterns of mere personal preference. Unavoidably our subjective judgments entered into our choices; however, within the parameters of our general and stated expectations we found a significant variety of approaches.

Our personal tastes showed up most definitely in the commissioned sermons, the sermons not a part of the competition. Public acclaim had something to do with those choices: Some of the most outstanding and widely recognized preachers of our time were asked for their sermons. Also, some preachers and lay people not so well known were willing to have their work appear in *Best Sermons,* and many of these sermons compared most favorably with sermons by better-known preachers.

These sermons have been useful to Sunday School teachers and seminary students of homiletics, as well as to pastors. Also, some people have read and meditated on these messages for their private devotionals.

When I preached recently in the church of which I am a member, a fellow member suggested that I publish the sermon. Although I have published numerous sermons in other places, I had not published one in this series. My sermon appears in this volume, as the last sermon, like Alfred Hitchcock's fleeting image in his films. It appears as an epilogue in a new, seventh category—eschatological. The sermon is about hope, and I can think of no more appropriate way to bring this series to a close.

My thanks go to the many who submitted their sermons; to my wife, Patty, who cataloged the sermons as they arrived; to my son Kenneth, who was my associate editor and often read sermons on his lunch hour in his office. I appreciate especially the initial suggestion by HarperCollins editor John Shopp for this series. He and his associates have given encouragement and support all along the way. Also, I am most grateful for the participation of the panel of Contributing Editors for their sermons and for their recommendations of other sermons to be included in the various volumes, and for the careful work of the judges who made the final selections of winners in the annual competitions.

Judges for the *Best Sermons 7* competition were as follows:

Catherine Allen, President of the Women's Department, Baptist World Alliance

Yates Bingham, Director, Northeastern Baptist School of Ministry, Boston Center

James W. Cox, Victor and Louise Lester Professor of Christian Preaching, The Southern Baptist Theological Seminary

John McClure, Associate Professor of Preaching and Worship, Presbyterian Theological Seminary, Louisville, Kentucky

Mark Trotter, Pastor, First United Methodist Church, San Diego, California

Albert J. D. Walsh, Pastor, First United Church of Christ, Schuylkill Haven, Pennsylvania

Preston N. Williams, Houghton Professor of Theology and Contemporary Change, The Harvard Divinity School

JAMES W. COX

I. EVANGELISTIC

1.   What He Left Them
Roger Lovette

John 20:19–23

About four years ago while I was at a conference, my wife decided to drop by and see my mother. While my wife was visiting her, my mother was rushed to the hospital. She told my wife that she had bought me two Gerber daisy plants. She asked my wife to go by her house and pick them up. We were about to move. "Don't plant them now," she said. "Save them for Memphis and plant them there. Give them plenty of water and they will do fine until you put them in the dirt." Like a good daughter-in-law, my wife did as she was instructed. She brought the plants home and passed on the instructions. Three weeks later my mother died suddenly. And so, when we moved weeks later, in early August, two of the treasures I put in my car and took with me were those two Gerber daisy plants. I can still remember that hot August Sunday morning, after the move, when I planted them in the Memphis soil. Heart heavy with grief, I whispered, "Dear God, let these flowers live." They did live. And one morning in October, when the air was cool, I went out to get the newspaper. It was my birthday. One Gerber daisy was blooming. The other followed in a day or two. Bloom after bloom just popped up and flowered all the way until the first frost. But her gift first bloomed on my birthday. This was her final gift.

After Ascension Day and Pentecost, when the early church leaders began stitching together the story, they must have asked

Roger Lovette has served as a pastor in South Carolina, Kentucky, and Tennessee. He is a native of Columbus, Georgia, and a graduate of Samford University (B.A.), the Southern Baptist Theological Seminary (B.D.), and Lexington Theological Seminary (D.Min.). He is the author of *For the Dispossessed, A Faith of Our Own, Questions Jesus Raised,* and *Come to Worship.* He is currently pastor of Church of the Covenant in Birmingham, Alabama.

one another, "What was it that he left us? What legacy did he leave behind?" John gives one account. Acts gives us another story. But John's Pentecost story is less well known. He answers this question: What was his final gift to us?

John writes that it was Easter evening. Don't you find the disciples' response strange after that wonderful, wonderful day? They gathered behind locked doors. They were afraid that they would be either killed or charged with the crime of stealing Jesus' body. John writes that they were afraid. And behind closed doors—carefully locked—Jesus came. He just stood there. The text says *in their midst*. Always, he comes, in their midst. Jesus' first words were: "Peace be unto you." And the Lord showed them his hands and his feet, and maybe he lifted his tunic, as LBJ did once to show his appendix scar. But they saw the wounds and got quiet and wept as they remembered. Perhaps because they were crying softly, Jesus said a second time, "Peace be with you." And he prepared to send them out—breathing on them, John says, and saying, "Receive the Holy Spirit." Then Jesus gave his followers their orders: "Go out and give wherever you go a gospel of forgiveness." That is what he left them. And writing to the church, John would indirectly say: This is what he left us, too.

Dear God, it seemed so hard and so complicated. Life. Its problems. A terrible world. In the middle of it all a little fussy church. All-too-human disciples. Weak as water. Pentecost says that he left them something. And that special something kept them going.

"*Peace be with you*" (20:19). It was an ordinary Hebrew greeting, just as we say, "Hello, how are you doing?" "Peace be with you." But Jesus says it twice, not once. For John is trying to say that this is more than just a greeting. Jesus left them more than just a "Hello."

In Judges 6 we read that it was a terrible time in Israel's history. Israel was invaded by Midianites and Amalekites and people called, ominously, "children of the East." They looted and killed and destroyed crops and families and everything. And in that awful time God calls Gideon. God says, "Peace be with you—do not fear" (Judges 6:23). And the next verse says that in the middle of all that madness Gideon built an altar to the Lord God. They must have thought him crazy. He called that place: "The Lord is peace . . ."

In time, this word, *peace*, became a eucharistic formula. "Peace" is what they gave to one another. William Barclay says it meant "may God give you every good thing." That's God's peace. Surrounded by Midianites and Amalekites, behind closed doors and scared out of their wits, they received something special from him. "Peace," he whispered. He said it twice.

This is the spirit of Pentecost. In the dark, with windows shut so tight that it was hard to breathe, cloth covering the openings, he—speaking only in whispers because the enemy might otherwise hear—gave them this wonderful gift: "In this world you will have tribulation; be of good cheer, I have overcome the world. So be not troubled or distressed or disquieted. . . . Peace." It's here, he says. For Gideon and frightened disciples of every age. *Peace.*

"After he said this, he showed them his hands and his side . . ." (20:20). This was proof of his identity. They knew him by his scars. They looked closely at the hands and feet, and, lifting up that tunic, they saw the place where the sword had left its mark. What was it he left? He left his scars, and that is how they recognized him. Thornton Wilder, in his play *The Angel That Troubled the Waters,* says, "In love's army only the wounded soldiers can serve."[1]

Funny, in the sacrificial system blemished animals could not be offered. No scars, the rule book said. No ugliness. And here, Jesus was holding out his hands, and Simon and Matthew and James and John, who limped and lusted and broke promises and sometimes lied—they pondered the mystery.

Harry Crews is a southern writer who grew up in terrible poverty. In his autobiography he writes that every so often his family's dull, empty lives would come to life. The postman would put in their mailbox the Sears, Roebuck catalog. Crews said they would sit down and open that wonderful wish book and gaze in amazement. The catalog brought mystery and beauty into the lives of those simple country people. He became fascinated with the people in the catalog because they were perfect. Crews says that everybody he knew had something missing—a finger cut off, a toe split, an ear half chewed away, an eye clouded by blindness from a glancing fence staple. If they didn't have something missing, they were carrying scars from barbed wire or knives or fishhooks. The people in the catalog had no such hurts. Poring over the pages for hours, he realized that not only were they whole but they were beautiful—arms, legs, toes, and eyes on unscarred bodies. Their legs were straight and their heads were never bald and on their faces were looks of happiness and even joy.[2]

For years we have preached this gospel for the unscarred: He takes only the unblemished ones—not whosoever will, but whosoever has been successful and made a lot of money and had a good education and won the Miss America contest and who pastors a five-thousand-member church and drives a Mercedes and lives in a big house and cosmetizes away every wrinkle and scar and drugs every pain. Where did we get such a gospel?

A young friend of mine knew better. He called the other night. I had not seen him since he was eleven or twelve. His parents had gone through a terrible divorce when he was very young. Just out of the blue, he called. He is now in college. Working with inner-city kids. He wants to make the world better. "I haven't seen my daddy for a year," he said. What about your mom? "Mom never has gotten over the divorce. I don't go home much. I joined the Baptist church. I'm a liberal Baptist. I even believe homosexuals ought to have full rights. Do you think I'm crazy?" "No," I said. He told me he was six feet tall and weighed one hundred seventy pounds. He had come a long way from that skinny kid across the street. And then he said, "I used to think that divorce just happened and it didn't affect me. I was so little. But now I know it did. A lot. And do you know what I think? Somehow my love for inner-city kids and my concern for the underdog has something to do with the pain of my parent's divorce." I told him that he was using his pain to make the world a better place.

Isn't that the real gospel? Jesus dignified our wounds that Easter evening as the sun was slowly setting when he opened his hands and pointed to his feet and pulled up his tunic. He left them his scars.

"Then Jesus breathed on them and said, 'Receive the Holy Spirit'" (20:22). The word translated as "Spirit" is *pneuma*—"breath" or "spirit." Jesus was giving them his essential being. In Genesis God breathed into man the breath of life and man became a living soul. That's what happened that Easter evening behind closed doors. They were empowered that night. They were given something— they called it life and breath—that kept them going. It's a gift. God's thing. Not just statistics and church history and bulletins and pastors and budgets. Like Ezekiel, the old bones come alive only through him.

Jesus gave them power and energy. Back in the early seventies we did not have much money in the little church I served in Kentucky. Just a small building. A tiny sanctuary. Two bathrooms. A nursery. A pastor's study. Four adult classes in the sanctuary. Vacation Bible School in somebody's basement up the street. Sunday School classes scattered in homes all over town. It was a mess. We needed a new building desperately. For education. More offices. A great big room we could use for socials and Sunday School. But we didn't have any money and we didn't have many people. Finally we got the plans. And one of our members served as overseer. And we built an educational facility. It was so scary. Ten years later they invited me back. We burned the note that Sunday. They said, "We want you to finish what you started." But as the note burned I remembered the words of Paul: "He who began a good work in you will bring it to completion." After we burned the note that Sunday, we broke ground for a new sanctuary.

What he left his followers was this power—breath—spirit. Breathing on us. Empowering us. Keeping us going. Helping us do what we thought there was no way in the world we could do. *He left them his spirit.*

Our Lord then told them, *"As the Father sent me, so send I you. . . . If you forgive the sins of any, . . . they are forgiven . . ."* (20:21, 23). He left them a new authority. A new message. This was the whole point of what he was to be and to do. *Kattalegete*—"Be reconciled."

Could the disciples forgive sins? Of course not. But they could make the announcement. They could communicate the message. They could tell the story. They could let it seep down into their lives until they were released from the terrible, terrible grip of so many things. Then they could begin to live out their lives in the wonder of this great, great power until it spilled over to all they touched. Theirs was a new authority.

The first book that Frederick Buechner wrote after his conversion was a novel, *The Final Beast.* It is the story of a young pastor whose wife has died and who is trying to raise his children alone. The church he serves is giving him a hard time, and he isn't coping too well with his own life. One of the women in the town, sensing his loneliness and his pain, comes to him for counseling. She has committed adultery. And she is barren. She wants to stay with her husband, but there is this awful guilt between them. She does not know what to do. Underneath the surface, she longs for the pastor. Somehow, underneath the surface, he longs for her also. She leaves town in desperation and goes to an inn not too far away. She tells no one except the pastor. She leaves him a note: "I am at [and she gives the name of the place]. No one else knows. Do not come." He is torn. If he goes, he is afraid of what will happen between them. If he does not go she may do something desperate.

In his indecision, he goes to see an old wise woman. She is a Christian. He tells her the story and his dilemma and fears. And when he is through, she tells him to go. Go and help the woman. The old woman says, "Give her what she really wants." And he says, "Give her what, for Christ's sake?" And she says, "For Christ's sake . . . the only thing you have to give. Forgive her for Christ's sake." And he tells her, "But she knows I forgive her." The old woman shakes her head: "She doesn't know that God forgives her. That's the only power you have—to tell her that. Not just that he forgives her the poor little adultery. But the faces she can't bear to look at now. The man's. Her husband's. Her own, half the time. Tell her he forgives her for being lonely and bored, for not being full of joy with a houseful of children. That's what sin really is, you know—not being full of joy. Tell her that sin is forgiven because whether she knows it or not, that's what she wants more than anything else—what all of us want. What on earth do you think you were ordained for?"

Because he does not know anything else to do, he follows the old woman's advice. He goes and finds the troubled woman. They talk. Toward the end of their meeting the young pastor moves toward her.

> With the palms flat against her temples, he tipped her face to him, and raised her own hands and pressed them against his so that each seemed to be preventing the other's escape . . . he heard himself pronounce like a stranger: "The almighty and merciful God pardon and deliver you, forgive every face you cannot look upon with joy. . . ."
> And the burdens of her life, great and small, began to melt away and she was healed. When she got home, the first thing she did was to make love to her husband. And it was at that moment that this woman, trying for years to have a child, conceived and found herself pregnant.[3]

Jesus said that our task is to lay hands on their heads and tell them that God forgives them.

Across the world churches gather to remember Pentecost. It was a scary time. A time when they were afraid. Dark, very dark. Everything was unsure. And a wonderful thing took place.

Jesus came into their midst—always in their midst. And he brought them peace, that peace that really does pass all understanding. He brought his own scars, dignifying the pain of us all, and spirit—breath and empowerment—without which they could not live. And then he gave them an authority so strange and so wonderful that it is almost a dream. We can be forgiven, and all the hurt and pain and sin we have caused can melt away and be gone forever.

This is what he left. Like those Gerber daises, they work their power at the strangest times, when they are needed the most. Thanks be to God.

NOTES

1. Thornton Wilder, *The Angel That Troubled the Waters* (New York: Coward-McCann, 1927), 149.

2. Harry Crews, *A Childhood* (New York: Harper & Row, 1978), 54.

3. Frederick Buechner, *The Final Beast* (New York: Seabury Press, 1965), 114–15.

2. The Great Yes!
Arthur P. Boers

While the classic book *Black like Me* was very famous in its time, few people realized that its author, John Howard Griffin, was motivated by a profound Christian faith to undertake the dangerous and sacrificial journey the book describes.

Griffin was a white man from the southern United States. Born in 1920, he was raised in a racist society. But having experienced blindness for a number of years, he learned to judge people by something other than their color. After he recovered his sight, he began thinking seriously about the problems of racism. However, black people kept challenging him, saying that he could not really understand their situation. "The only way you can know what it's like is to wake up in my skin," they told him.

Griffin decided to try to do just that. Using drugs, dyes, and radiation, he darkened his skin color. He shaved his head and, in his words, "crossed the line into a country of hate, fear and hopelessness—the country of the American Negro." The year was 1959, and he traveled for two months in the deep South. His observations were published first as magazine articles and then in the widely acclaimed book *Black like Me*.

Robert Ellsberg wrote about Griffin in an essay entitled "A Life of Radical Empathy."[1] He notes:

Arthur P. Boers has published three books and more than three hundred articles and reviews in over a dozen periodicals, including *Christianity Today* and *Leadership*. He is a columnist for *Christian Living*, a contributing editor for the *Other Side*, and a columnist and editorial adviser for *Christian Ministry*. In 1990, he received the Evangelical Press Association award for an interview with Henri J. M. Nouwen. He received his M.Div. from McCormick Theological Seminary and is currently pastor of Bloomingdale Mennonite Church in Ontario, Canada.

Griffin changed nothing but the color of his skin—
and that was everything. Suddenly doors closed,
smiles became indignant frowns, or worse. Griffin
describes his experience of the "hate stare":
"Nothing can describe the withering horror of this.
You feel lost, sick at heart before such unmasked
hatred, not so much because it threatens you as
because it shows humans in such an inhuman light.
You see a kind of insanity, something so obscene,
the very obscenity (rather than its threat) terrifies
you. I felt like saying 'What in God's name are you
doing to yourself?' "

Griffin saw that racist hatred not only dehumanized blacks, but also destroyed the souls of oppressors.

Griffin's descriptions of the hate he endured, his vain search for work, his tired walks across town to drink from a "Negro" fountain or use a "Negro" washroom are heartrending. And he endured this for only two months, while African Americans lived with it all their lives.

After his story was published, Griffin received many death threats. He was hanged in effigy in his own hometown. When he eventually died at the age of sixty, one of his ailments was skin cancer—partly the result of temporarily changing his skin color years earlier. He paid a high price for radical empathy.

Once a journalist complimented him on the terrific gamble he took in making himself black. Griffin responded: "What people don't really know . . . is that long before this I took another great gamble—what the French call simply '*le grand oui*,' the Great Yes. The gamble was for God. That means leaping off that cliff and never knowing where you're going to land, but you have the faith that you're going to land somewhere."

Griffin had said *Yes!* to God.

God asks us questions, calling us to answer *Yes!* Ultimately, we are invited, encouraged, exhorted to say *le grand oui*, the Great Yes, to God.

Our questions to God are often an attempt to avoid commitment. We see this in some of the Bible's most famous questions. After he murdered his brother, Cain was asked by God where Abel was. Cain responded with a lie and a question: "I do not know; am

I my brother's keeper?" Unprepared to tell God the truth, he hoped to avoid a commitment by *asking* a question.

A lawyer asked Jesus how to inherit eternal life. Jesus and the lawyer discussed what was written in the law, including the admonition to love "your neighbor as yourself." The lawyer was dissatisfied. According to Luke, he wanted "to justify himself" so he asked a question: "And who is my neighbor?" It is not clear that he really wanted an answer or that he truly wanted to know. He was splitting legal hairs so that he too could avoid making a commitment.

When Jesus stood before Pilate, he did not say much, even though he was on trial and his life was at stake. But at one point, he did say, "Everyone who belongs to the truth listens to my voice." "What is truth?" Pilate asked. He did not necessarily want to know. He was asking questions as a way of blowing fog, making a smoke screen, avoiding commitment.

These three questions are particularly infamous in the Bible: "Am I my brother's keeper?" "Who is my neighbor?" "What is truth?" They were all masterpieces of trying to avoid the call of God, the invitation of God.

Of course, there were even worse questions. Religious authorities often asked questions of Jesus not because they wanted to learn or grow, not even because they wanted to avoid commitment. They asked questions of Jesus hoping to trick and trap him.

But it is a dangerous thing to ask such trick questions. Jesus often turns these questions around or asks us harder questions. When the young lawyer asked, "Who is my neighbor?" he wasn't prepared to hear a story about someone who unexpectedly acted like a neighbor. He was surprised by Jesus' question: "Which of these three do you think was neighbor to the man who fell into the hands of the robbers?"

In Luke 20, the Pharisees asked Jesus, "Who is it who gave you this authority?" Jesus answered with a question about where John derived his authority. The Pharisees were afraid to answer. Jesus therefore said, "Neither will I tell you by what authority I am doing these things."

Asking nasty questions of God can backfire on us. Jesus often turns questions on their head. God often overturns our questions.

I am amazed at how often God addresses *us* with a question.

Adam and Eve "heard the sound of the Lord God walking in the garden at the time of the evening breeze, and the man and his wife hid themselves from the presence of the Lord God among the trees of the garden. But the Lord God called to the man, and said to him, 'Where are you?' " As if to say: How are you doing? Have you been faithful? What happened to you? Are you serving me?

Or, as we already saw, "Then the Lord said to Cain, 'Where is your brother Abel?' "

Or, Elijah came and spent a night in a cave. "Then the word of the Lord came to him, saying 'What are you doing here, Elijah?' " (1 Kings 19).

Or, in Isaiah 6, Isaiah too is addressed with a question: "Whom shall I send, and who will go for us?"

Or, "Now Saul was going along and approaching Damascus, suddenly a light from heaven flashed around him. He fell to the ground and heard a voice saying to him, 'Saul, Saul, why do you persecute me?' " (Acts 9).

Or, when the disciples had "finished breakfast, Jesus said to Simon Peter, 'Simon, son of John, do you love me more than these?' He asked this three times" (John 21).

Or, Jesus "asked his disciples, 'Who do people say that I am?' and they answered him, 'John the Baptist; and others, Elijah; and still others, one of the prophets.' He asked them, 'But who do you say that I am?' " (Mark 8).

In all of these famous Bible scenes, God asks a question, a pointed question, that demands a response of commitment.

Amazingly, the word of the Lord of hosts is often not a statement, not a command, not an order, not even a declaration. No, God's word often comes to us as a question: Where are you? Who do you say that I am? Who will go for us?

God's questions ask of us a response, and not just any response but a *commitment*. These kinds of questions are harder than commands. If God would just tell us what to do, we could decide one way or another whether we will obey. But when God asks a question, we are called to make an open-ended, even risky, commitment.

Our questions often avoid commitment. But God's questions demand our commitment.

God's questions continually burst into our lives and shed new light, giving unexpected perspectives. Over and over, we can hear their meaning, their challenge for us.

In the cartoon Pontius Puddle, King Pontius says, "Sometimes I'd like to ask God why he allows poverty, famine, and injustice when he could do something about it."

"What's stopping you?" his trusty sidekick asks.

Pontius responds, "I'm afraid he might ask me the same question!"

Reading newspapers, we may well reflect on all the trouble and pain in our world. We might be tempted to call God to account. But our questions of God might become God's questions of us. We realize that the fighting, wars, and suffering are aggravated by the wealth of our own culture and society. Pondering these challenges, we might hear God ask *us* why do *we* allow it?

God's questions come in many different forms: in a blaze of light, like what happened to Saul (a blaze so bright and loud and unexpected that it knocked him off his horse); in a quiet voice in the middle of the night, like Samuel's experience (a voice so quiet that Samuel had no idea that it was God); in the innocent question of a child; in the stirrings of our conscience.

Such questions strip us to our essence and pierce us to the heart. They do not allow us to hide. When we take God's questions seriously, we cannot remain the same and we cannot avoid making a commitment. God's questions can shatter all we hold as sacred.

Such a shock to our realities can mean breakthroughs. Paul Tillich wrote of his namesake: "Paul experienced the breakdown of a system of life and thought which he believed to be a whole, a perfect truth without riddle or gaps. He then found himself buried under the pieces of his knowledge and his morals. But Paul never tried again to build up a new, comfortable house out of the pieces. He dwelt with the pieces. How could Paul endure life, as it lay in fragments? He endured it because the fragments bore a new meaning to him."[2]

God's questions shake up and even shatter the meaning of our lives. Legend has it that in a certain European country, when the emperor died his body was carried to the cathedral. His pallbearers knocked on the door. "Who is there?" cried the people from behind the cathedral door.

The pallbearers announced that it was Karl, emperor of such-and-such territories.

Those within the cathedral said, "We know no such man."

The servants knocked again and again heard the question, "Who is there?"

The pallbearers answered, "Karl the emperor."

But once more came the disquieting response from within: "We know no such man."

They knocked again and once more heard, "Who is there?"

"Karl," came the simple response, and the doors swung open.

God's questions do not permit or allow our confusions, our evasions, our pride, our arrogance. God's questions call for commitment to his kingdom, his ways.

Sometimes the cost of that commitment is high. Think of how much the commitment, the great gamble, *le grand oui,* cost Paul and John Howard Griffin. Martin Luther King, Jr., once preached:

> You may be 38 years old, as I happen to be. And
> one day some great opportunity stands before you
> and calls you to stand up for some great principle,
> some great issue, some great cause. And you
> refuse to do it because you are afraid.... You
> refuse to do it because you want to live longer....
> You're afraid that you will lose your job, or you
> are afraid that you will be criticized or that you
> will lose your popularity, or you're afraid that
> somebody will stab you, or shoot at you or bomb
> your house; so you refuse to take the stand. Well
> you may go on and live until you are 90, but
> you're just as dead at 38 as you would be at 90.
> And the cessation of breathing in your life is but
> the belated announcement of an earlier death of
> the spirit.[3]

Saying *Yes!* to God is a matter of life and death. It is of ultimate importance. Taking God's questions seriously is of ultimate consequence. We cannot overestimate its significance.

While God's questions are a challenge to deep commitment, they are also an invitation, an opportunity, a welcome chance: to join the kingdom and the messianic banquet, to be a part of God's covenant people. God's questions are both challenge and opportunity.

Ultimately and finally, God's questions call us to say *Yes!* Mary said such a *Yes!* when she told Gabriel, "Here am I, the servant of the Lord; let it be with me according to your word." We are all called to say such a *Yes!* to God. We might ignore God's questions and avoid the call to discipleship. But the examples of Paul and Isaiah and Mary and John Howard Griffin and Martin Luther King, Jr., call us to a different response.

We are called to make our lives an Amen. *Amen* means *Yes!* It means *Indeed!* It means *So be it!* It is not just a punctuation word at the end of a long and boring pastoral prayer. *Amen* is a commitment to action, a response, a dedication.

When we say "Amen," we say *Yes!* to God. We endorse God's purposes, God's will, God's kingdom. To say "Amen" is not just to utter a ritual word, but to make a serious commitment. God calls us to make our lives an *Amen* to his purposes, lives that say *Yes!* to God.

Dag Hammarskjöld, United Nations secretary-general and winner of the Nobel Peace Prize, lost his life on a peacemaking mission for the U.N. in 1961. He once wrote: "I don't know Who—or what— put the question. I don't know when it was put. I don't even remember answering. But at some moment I did answer yes to Someone—Something—and from that hour I was certain that existence is meaningful and that, therefore, my life, in self-surrender, had a goal."[4]

God calls us every moment of every day. God's questions are all around us: Who do *you* say that I am? Where are *you*? Are *you* acting like a neighbor?

God calls every moment of every day. Are you listening? Will you follow?

Let our answer be *Yes!* Let our answer be *Indeed!* Let our answer be *Truly truly!*

Yes! Amen! Let it be so!

NOTES

1. Robert Ellsberg, "A Life of Radical Empathy," in *Cloud of Witnesses,* ed. Jim Wallis and Joyce Hollyday (Maryknoll, NY: Orbis Books, 1991), 148–55.

2. Paul Tillich, *The Shaking of the Foundations* (New York: Charles Scribner's Sons, 1948), 112–13.

3. As quoted by Richard Rohr and Joseph Martos in *The Wild Man's Journey* (Cincinnati, OH: St. Anthony Messenger Press, 1992), 125.

4. Dag Hammarskjöld, *Markings* (New York: Alfred A. Knopf, 1966), 205.

3. A Fishing Story
David S. Bell

Mark 1:16–22

So you are sitting behind your desk, working on a project that is due by the end of the day, when your secretary tells you that you have a visitor. And the visitor, whom you saw in the cafeteria at lunchtime, says to you, "Forget about that project. Come follow me, and I will give you some human-need projects." You desperately try to make up some reason for leaving. You inform your secretary that you forgot about this appointment with your so-called new golfing partner. And you immediately rush out of the office.

You are retired and in the midst of your annual drive to Florida for a few weeks of relaxation. You've just arrived at the Holiday Inn in Wytheville, Virginia. Someone approaches you wearing a cross and says, "Why don't you put off your trip to Florida? Come follow me, and I will bring real excitement into your retirement years." So, you quickly try to get a refund from the front desk, making some lame excuse that the air-conditioning doesn't work well. Then you immediately jump into your car and follow this apparent prophet down some red-clay road.

David S. Bell was Minister to Youth at the United Methodist Church of Summit, Ohio, for two years, and is currently Minister of Christian Education and Youth Ministries at Rocky River United Methodist Church in Ohio. He received his M.Div. from Drew Theological School in 1990 and has been honored with the John Lennon Memorial Award for Christian Education (1992) and the East Coast Conference Outstanding Christian Educator Award (1992). He has also been featured in *Who's Who in Religion* (1992, 1993).

You are home from college for the summer, sitting in the family room, like a couch potato, watching TV. The doorbell rings. You assume it's someone wanting a donation. But instead the person says, "Why don't you leave your parents, and come follow Jesus and me?" You try to call your mom at work, but she's out to lunch, so you leave a note by the telephone, forget to take a house key, like always, and walk down the street with this pied piper.

You make your living by catching fish in the Sea of Galilee. It's a family tradition that has carefully been taught from one generation to the next. You leave your home before sunrise, get in your boat filled with fishing nets and other equipment, and row to the nearest reef to begin today's work. As you're throwing your net over the side of the boat, you happen to notice this man walking along the shore. You can barely see who it is. Yes, you have seen this person around town lately. He's a street preacher. He seems to be waving his arms, trying to get your attention. He's shouting something, but you can't quite hear him. He's saying it again. OK, now you can understand him: "Come follow me, and I will make you fish for people." And immediately you leave your net and follow him.

These stories are crazy. They are absolutely absurd. Yet one of them is completely true, and it's not the story about the college student! I have wondered so many times why these disciples left their fishing enterprise and followed Jesus. Mark's account of the calling of the first disciples is simply remarkable:

> "As Jesus passed along the Sea of Galilee, he saw Simon and his brother Andrew casting a net into the sea—for they were fishermen. And Jesus said to them, 'Follow me and I will make you fish for people.' And immediately they left their nets and followed him. As he went a little farther, he saw James son of Zebedee and his brother John, who were in their boat mending the nets. Immediately he called them; and they left their father Zebedee in the boat with the hired men, and followed him."
> (Mark 1:16–20, NRSV)

I often use this passage of the Bible at camps or on youth retreats. And I encourage the kids to come up with all the possibilities for why Peter, Andrew, James, and John might have left their boats—in fact, their careers—to follow this person Jesus. They had seen and heard of Jesus. They knew that he was a teacher, a street preacher, a person who was trying to bring about change. However, they certainly did not know that Jesus was the Christ, the Messiah, God's son.

So, why would they leave their boats? The youths' first answer sounds like a typical teenager's response: Probably they weren't catching any fish, and they were bored. So, they figured, why not check this guy out? If they didn't like him, they could always come back to their fishing business.

Another good possibility is that they knew that Jesus was attracting a lot of people. He was definitely "a man on the move." Now they had the opportunity to be close to him as he became even more powerful. Perhaps, if he somehow could become a leader in the synagogue or in government, they would, in turn, get a special position as well. So, a second possibility is that they were motivated by their own greed—their greed for power, recognition, and even money.

Amid all the other possibilities, another good one is that they were simply moved by the Spirit of God to follow Jesus. If we were able to ask them why they chose to leave their boats, perhaps they wouldn't really be able to give us an exact reason. In fact, they might even recognize that it was not a rational decision. Yet, they just knew from within that this was a call from God, which they didn't fully recognize until much later in life.

So now let us raise the question with ourselves: What motivated us to follow Christ? Or let me ask a more practical question: What motivated you to come to church today? Maybe you came to church today because you have for the past seventy years; it's a habit, a duty, a routine. Maybe you came to church today because you have several friends who worship here whom you wanted to visit with today.

Maybe you came to church today because you have discovered that this is the only time during the week that you can just go "Ahh!"—that you can reflect through silence and prayer on your life and become refocused for another week. Or maybe you came to church today because you are lonely, or you have questions with no answers, or your life is a wreck. Maybe you came to church today because you're church shopping—looking for a new church home.

Or maybe you came to church today because you thought my colleague was going to be preaching. Sorry for the disappointment! But maybe you dressed for church today and are sitting in that pew because in some unexplainable way the Spirit of God has brought you here to renew your faith in Jesus Christ. You are here because God has called you to be here, and you don't even know it yet!

So, if I may be so bold as to say them, hear those two words of Jesus Christ, the Lord our God, as Mark recorded them: "Follow me." Jesus says to you and me again and again, "Follow me—the way, the life, and the truth." To meet Christ, in Mark's understanding, is to be faced with the dilemma of either following Christ or abandoning him. When you encounter Jesus, there is no avoiding that some commitment is to be made. You are faced with a choice that must be decided. You must leave "your fishing nets" and pursue his path. Commitment is required.

It was the final night of freshman orientation at the College of Wooster. It had been an interesting week of getting to know each other, even amid the jitters of being a freshman. We all had walked (in huddles of people, of course, since no freshman wanted to appear a loner) to McGaw Chapel for the Freshman Talent Show.

I will never forget the person I will name Jamal Washington standing on the stage with his soprano saxophone, playing "Somewhere over the Rainbow." He was so talented. He was without doubt the best saxophone player I had ever heard up to that point in my life. He played his last note to a standing ovation and five hundred college students screaming for more.

I became acquainted with Jamal pretty well during my four years at Wooster. Everyone knew him from the talent show, which led to countless other performances. Jamal was voted by his peers as the Outstanding Senior Male, and he rode in the homecoming parade around town. And, in fact, he was an outstanding guy—except from what I knew about him, he lived a lifestyle that never would have indicated that he was raised in the church. He was a party animal—and all types of parties!

That's why I was so shocked to read in our alumni magazine that Jamal had completed seminary, was ordained a minister, and serves the three-thousand-member California Christian Center as their Minister of Music. I immediately got his phone number and called him up. He has his own production company, called Anointed Horn Ministries, and has just released his first solo recording. He told me that he came from a very faithful family, but that in college he really lost touch with his faith. It was only after some bad experiences with some touring bands that he again turned to his childhood faith. He is now married, and he and his wife have a two-month-old baby girl.

For whatever reason Jamal began playing his saxophone, he only recently discovered the real reason that God gave him this musical gift—to lead others to Jesus Christ. And in the process of discovering his real purpose, he has left "his nets" behind and continues to hear those words: "Follow me!"

So why did you come to church today? I believe we are all here to be renewed in the faith of Jesus Christ. If we are to meet Christ, we may face some changes, like Jamal did. There are some nets to be left behind and some new tasks to be done. I can't tell you what those nets are in your life. But I don't need to. Jesus Christ stands on the shore and calls you and me to be his disciples, just like he called those first disciples. And our response to Christ is far more important than watching a TV show, or traveling to Florida, or completing a corporate project, or even catching a fish that was "this big."

4. Star Struck and Travel Ready

Richard Andersen

Matthew 2:1–12

They were star struck and travel ready, those Wise Men of the East. We can only speculate as to the nation from which they traveled, as well as their religious affiliation and professional background. Matthew seems to suggest they were Zoroastrians—those who worshiped fire, including the fiery brightness of the stars. They may have been priestly astronomers from Persia. Possibly they were Median astrologers. Evidently they were well-off financially, and highly educated, since they could afford to travel a long distance for an extended period of time and were important enough to consult with a king. They brought expensive and lavish gifts that undoubtedly brightened the hopes of Herod the Great.

These Magi continue to baffle us, as does the star. *Newsweek's* end-of-the-year edition speculated whether the Guiding Light was a star . . . or planets.[1] A dozen years ago David Hughes, in his book *The Star of Bethlehem,* came to the same conclusions.[2] It's an exercise in scientific speculation that has puzzled astronomers for years.

Richard Andersen began a three-year ministry as Lutheran pastor of the International Church of Copenhagen in Hellerup, Denmark, in August 1993. He is founding pastor of Community Church of Joy in Glendale, Arizona, and has served senior pastorates in Long Beach and San Jose, California. He received his M.Div. from Wartburg Theological Seminary in Dubuque, Iowa, and his Ph.D. from California Graduate School of Theology in Glendale, California. He is a former columnist for *Clergy Journal* and is the author of numerous articles, sermons, and books. This sermon was preached for the Epiphany of Our Lord.

There are many star scenarios to choose from, but Matthew makes it clear that the Magi were struck by whatever celestial light it was and sought out the king for whom such a star was an omen according to their astrological conclusions.

We may not be stargazers, but there is something to be learned from the Magi as we embark on a new year. It would be well for us to be star struck also and travel ready in the sense of the Magi, for the wisdom of the Wise Men is as needful in this age as it was then.

As they were *caught* by a vision, so let us catch the bright vision of hope God has for us in this new year. As the Wise Men of the East *sought* the Messiah, so let us seek him. As they *brought* their gifts, so let us place before him our gifts also. They surrendered their old religion for a new one and opted to return home by a different route, forsaking the evil Herod and his devilment. As they *wrought* a new life out of the old, so let us set our course for a new destiny as well—one that begins with Jesus and ever remains loyal to him. In short, let us be star struck and travel ready for the year that lies ahead.

Preacher John Killinger reminds us, "Life isn't rootedness, and it isn't settledness. It is journey, movement, going from one place to another."[3] Thus, star struck and travel ready, let us move with the rhythm of the Wise Men and their determination to "pay . . . homage" to the King who is the Messiah, the One Micah foretold, Jesus, the Babe of Bethlehem (5:2). Let us journey to the future with hope intact and faith assured.

I.

Star struck and travel ready, the Wise Men caught a magnificent vision. Have you caught a vision for the year before us?

America is in the doldrums, we're told. This recession is not as bad as the last one, say the economists, and yet hope seems to have eluded the large majority. There is little confidence in the economy. The old pioneer spirit, the zeal for new enterprises and plunging into new possibilities, seems to have evaporated. But if we can learn something from the Wise Men of the East, it is to catch hold of a vision, the *right* vision.

They saw a brilliant, unusual star! They researched its meaning and planned to do something about it. Maybe that's our need . . .

your special need for this new year. You may have the vision, but not the gumption needed to achieve it. Think of good old Abraham. "By faith," says the writer to the Hebrews, "Abraham obeyed when he was called to set out for a place that he was to receive as an inheritance; and he set out, not knowing where he was going" (Heb. 11:8). It is because the call came from God. God used astrology, so it would appear, to call these scholars from the East to the house where Jesus dwelled. They caught hold of a vision, and so must we.

John Killinger says the Wise Men rode "across more miles for Hallmark and American Greeting Cards than they ever rode to get to Bethlehem!"[4] Still, it was no easy trek traveling across the wilderness for a minimum of twelve hundred miles. It took weeks, months . . . and Scripture seems to suggest years! The point is this: They caught a vision and kept on going until they found it. Says the King James Bible, "Where there is no vision, the people perish" (Prov. 29:18). Therefore, where there *is* vision, people can thrive. Abraham proved it before the Wise Men, and they proved it even more so. It is still the need of this end of the twentieth century: vision! Catch it! God has a vision for more than greatness for you: satisfying service, salutary sacrifice, and simple success. Catch it and follow it!

Some people remain only star struck, but the Wise Men were star struck *and* travel ready. Are you?

II.

They caught the vision and sought the Messiah!

Writes Fulton Sheen:

> God spoke to the *Gentiles* through nature and philosophers; to the *Jews*, through prophecies. The time was ripe for the coming of the Messiah and the whole world knew it. Though they were astrologers, the slight vestige of truth in their knowledge of the stars led them to the Star out of Jacob (Numbers 24:17), as the *Unknown God* of the Athenians later on would be the occasion for Paul preaching to them the God whom they knew not, but simply desired (Acts 17:16–34).[5]

Surely the Wise Men encountered difficulties in convincing the religious and national authorities of their intentions. Undoubtedly there must have been warnings of robbery and bloodshed along the caravan route from the East. Admittedly the Wise Men heard of dangers of windstorms and fast-flooding ravines from mountain rains as they traveled the desert way toward Israel, but they did not relent. They persisted. The cost did not dissuade them. The duration of time involved did not discourage them. Are you able to persist in the face of criticism and catcalls, in the midst of naysayers and gloomy prophecies? Are you able to keep on when others draw back and flounder in their own negativism? Then you will seek out the Messiah in the vision God gives you . . . and you will find him. You will kneel before him in adoration.

We are uncertain what resources these stargazers used to conclude that a king was born in the East. It must have been more than astrology. Is it possible that a remnant of Jews remained in that Babylonian region where so many of them had been taken captive centuries before? Is it likely that in this Jewish diaspora the prophecies of Isaiah and Micah were known, perhaps not in detail, but in substance—for they sought the King *of the Jews?* We do not know what prompted their urge to seek the new king except the star, but these scholars probably left no stone unturned in concluding that their trip was essential. When you journey toward the vision God gives you, seek out Jesus, but do it thoroughly and not halfheartedly. Do it with determination and zest. Do it with faith. Even if you don't know him as well as you would like, keep searching, for you will find him in the daily march toward the goal God puts before you. You will see him in the eyes of others and hear him in the words of those along the way; you will see and hear enough so that you know you are moving toward God's grand plan for you.

Says David Farmer:

> This story reminds us that Jesus is someone to be sought. He neither invades our lives nor overtakes us. When something within draws us out of ourselves toward greater spiritual and personal fulfillment as well as the service and the ministries that are inevitable as a result of such genuine fulfillment and maturity, we too must have the courage to seek. The voice that calls us may be

> God's. The road on which we travel may be the
> road to life. And that to which we are drawn may
> be Christ who in ways we have yet to understand
> is our King.[6]

Friend, as the Wise Men caught the vision and sought the Messiah, follow in their spirit to where Christ is. Be not simply star struck, but also be travel ready.

III.

And they brought their gifts, these Wise Men. We have no idea how many Wise Men there were. The number is not mentioned in Scripture, although carols and Christmas cards always seem to depict three, as well as do the legends about them. People probably concluded there were three Wise Men because there were three gifts: gold and frankincense and myrrh. Fulton Sheen speculates that "gold was to honor His Kingship, and frankincense to honor His Divinity, and myrrh to honor His Humanity."[7] The golden casket said to contain their remains is above the high altar in Cologne Cathedral, where fanciful tales are told of the three—including their names, their races, their ages, and where they died.

No matter the number of presents, they brought gifts. Let us bring him our gifts also—our equivalents of gold, frankincense, and myrrh. But let us emulate the Wise Men even more than that. Let us bring something better than material gifts. Let us bring ourselves, for that is what Jesus truly wants . . . what our vision requires and our seeking demands. Bring your possessions, your valuables, but also bring your heart, your faith. Bring yourself. Your talents; your personalities and uniqueness. They brought their peculiarity as scholars and foreign leaders. A prophet had foretold that kings would worship the Christ child; thus we think of them as having sovereign power largely because of their kingly wealth (Isa. 60:3). But also they were able to gain an audience with King Herod without any difficulty. All of their skills, their knowledge, and their rare qualities as priests of a foreign religion and scholars of importance they laid before Jesus and worshiped him. As did the shepherds before them, they gave the Messiah themselves. God expects no less of the Wise Men and women and youth of this age.

King Herod sent another gift. He sent soldiers to murder all the male children of Bethlehem who were two years of age and under (Matt. 2:16ff, RSV). Even in childhood, Jesus knew the threat of the unbelieving. He faced it again at Nazareth when his fellow synagogue worshipers wanted to throw him off a cliff (Luke 4:29). He met it again on Calvary in mortal brutality (Matt. 27:32–44; Luke 23:26–49; and so forth). Jesus wants and deserves something more.

The Wise Men brought their gifts; so must we! What gifts will you offer Jesus in this new year? Or will you give excuses instead? Will they be gifts given in love, or gifts extended in anger, ugliness, and disbelief? You know the kind he prefers. He would have you champion noble goals and earnest efforts. He wants you and me to bring our best so that he can multiply its effectiveness. If we sow seeds of discontent, we will reap its pain. If we sow seeds of kindness and concern, we will experience the beauty of it. The promise is in the purpose, and the purpose must never be less than love.

They were more than star struck, those Wise Men, for anyone can be momentarily dazzled by the rich and famous, the sparkling and the glittering. Those Magi of the East were star struck and travel ready . . . and ready to give themselves totally to the Lord Christ. Says Matthew, "On entering the house, they saw the Child with Mary His mother; and they knelt down and paid Him homage. Then, opening their treasure chests, they offered him gifts of gold, frankincense, and myrrh." That homage giving was the giving of themselves to him who was not only the King of the Jews, but the Messiah promised to the whole world. By so doing, they defied Herod and rejected an earthly monarch's favor for the heavenly peace the little Bethlehem King afforded them. They were truly *wise* men—star struck and travel ready.

IV.

Those Wise Men caught the vision God gave them; sought the Messiah God promised as their King; and brought their gifts by giving themselves. But they did even more. They wrought out of the past a new life for the future.

"No one whoever meets Christ with a good will returns the same way he came," observes Fulton Sheen.[8] The Wise Men returned to their homeland by another route, for God gave them a warning in a dream, as he did Joseph in safeguarding Jesus to Egypt. When you've encountered the Christ of God, life changes. Bitterness evaporates. Resentment melts. Hatred dissolves.

When you meet ugliness, you can be sure those you confront are not returning from a visit to the Messiah. They are still traveling in the wrong direction, right back to the palace of Herod and right into the midst of deviltry. Make sure you dream of the new way of courageous helpfulness and insistent sacrifice.

Augustine was stuck in the mire of lust and looseness, but once he truly met the Christ he did not go back into the old rutted route. Lars Olsen Skrefsrud was a thief until, while in prison, he made the spiritual journey to the Jesus of Bethlehem and never went back. He sailed on to India, where he began a missionary work that continues to thrive even today. He died in 1910 having, like the Wise Men, wrought a new life that changed the world. Forty-eight years ago, Kaj Munk, the great Danish poet, patriot, and playwright, who also happened to be a pastor, was murdered by the Gestapo because he refused to turn down the roads that led back to the Herod of that time, to Hitler, and instead went the way God opened to him. He had seen Christ, and there was no turning back to the hindering road of hate. Charles Colson was prominent in politics, but was dashed to despair in the Watergate affair. While in prison, he worshiped the child Jesus, so that he could write: "My lowest days as a Christian (and there were low ones—seven months' worth of them in prison, to be exact) have been more fulfilling and rewarding than all the days of glory in the White House."[9] God wrought a new life for Methodist pastor Gerry Phelps—an intellectual, an economist, and a university professor who got wrapped up in illegal demonstrations during the Vietnam War that found her sentenced to prison. There she found the same wonderful Christ before whom the Wise Men knelt, and she took a different road too. What would Bakersfield or San Jose be without the missions to aid the homeless families that she began? Love took over from anger, and mercy replaced vindictiveness.

Let God fashion, like wrought iron, a new life for you by going a new way in this new year. It may not be free of pain or difficulty or heartache, yet it will be full of joy and satisfaction and peace in serving. Shaping metal to new forms requires heat and force, yet the resulting beauty makes it worth it. Bruce Johnson tells of an Anglican cleric who gave a cross to a dying woman to hold. "When fear comes, take this cross and hold it tightly in your hand because this is the sign of love that will not let you go," assured the priest. She held on so tight that the cross became twisted by the pressure. Says Johnson, "The cross had in part assumed the shape of the woman's hand. It is only a pretty symbol until it does."[10] That is to be star struck and travel ready: heading homeward changed and chastened, molded to the shape of Christ's own triumph!

In the film *Black Robe,* we view the arduous sacrifices of Jesuit priests and their assistants in bringing Christianity to the Algonquin and Huron Indians of Canada several hundred years ago. One French assistant became momentarily convinced that the Indian pagan ideas were better, until he was put to the test and discovered he could not turn back down that road again. He had met the Christ, and his life was to be wrought of faith, not fanciful legends.

Conclusion

The Wise Men were caught by a vision, sought the Messiah, brought their gifts, and wrought a new life. They were star struck and travel ready.

Dr. Stockmann, a character in Henrik Ibsen's play *An Enemy of the People,* was only trying to help his town when he announced his discovery that its water source was poisoned and its beaches polluted, but the townspeople decried his findings. The majority were overwhelming in their rejection.

"Was the majority right when they stood by while Jesus was crucified?" he asked the crowd. "Was the majority right when they refused to believe that the earth moved around the sun and let Galileo be driven to his knees like a dog? . . . The majority is never right until it *does* right," he said.[11]

He had chosen to go a new way. He would not retreat to the Herod of his community—his brother, the mayor—nor would he go back on his findings. The next day, as bricks shattered his windows and his daughter was dismissed from her job and his boys were hounded out of school, his wife asked, "What's going to happen? Tom! What's going to happen?"

All Dr. Stockmann could say was: "I don't know. But remember now, everybody. You are fighting for the truth, and that's why you're alone. And that makes you strong. We're the strongest people in the world . . . and the strong must learn to be lonely!"

Jesus had said, "If you continue in My word, you are truly My disciples; and you will know the truth, and the truth will make you free" (John 8:32).

The Bible records no more about the Wise Men than these words of Matthew. They may have dwelled in loneliness when they returned with their startling findings, but at least they went the way of truth. So must we: Nineteen ninety-two can be a different year for us and our world, for this parish and our community, if we are not just star struck, but travel ready . . . ready to travel with God's Spirit to the furthest goals of Christian ministry and Christian love in this world. Begin now at the altar. Take the bread and wine as the Wise Men ate of the good news and drank in Christ's incarnation. Then resolve to go a new way into life, the way that goes with the truth of Jesus and the joy of the gift he gives us— forgiveness wrapped in love and the promise of life everlasting.

NOTES

1. Sharon Begley, "The Christmas Star—or Was It Planets?" *Newsweek*, 29 December 1991, 54.

2. David Hughes, *The Star of Bethlehem* (New York: Simon & Schuster, 1979).

3. John Killinger, in a sermon entitled "Losing the Star," in *Christmas Spoken Here* (Nashville: Broadman Press, 1989), 116.

4. Ibid., 114.

5. Fulton J. Sheen, *Life of Christ* (New York: McGraw-Hill, 1958), 32.

6. David Albert Farmer, "The Courage to Seek," *Pulpit Digest* 70, no. 501 (Jan./Feb. 1990), 32.

7. Sheen, *Life of Christ*, 33.

8. Ibid., 35.

9. Charles W. Colson, *The Ministers Manual, 1991* (San Francisco: Harper San Francisco, 1990), 22.

10. D. Bruce Johnson, *The Ministers Manual, 1976* (San Francisco: Harper & Row, 1975), 256.

11. Henrik Ibsen, *An Enemy of the People,* adapted by Arthur Miller (New York: Penguin Books, 1979), 94–95, 124–25.

II. EXPOSITORY

5. The Courage of Conviction

James Ayers

Daniel 3:13–18; Romans 9:1–5; Acts 21:7–14

In the year 587 B.C. the Babylonian army captured the city of Jerusalem. The results were not pretty. The invaders tore down the buildings, stole everything worth stealing, and dragged every reasonably healthy man, woman, and child off to become a slave in Babylon. This began the period in the history of Israel known as the Exile, or the Babylonian Captivity.

The Book of Daniel tells us that among the Israelites taken as slaves there were three young men. Their names were Hananiah, Mishael, and Azariah. Their new Babylonian masters told them that they would have to get used to the Babylonian way of doing things from now on. They would have to learn to walk and talk and think Babylonian. They even gave them Babylonian names.

Now, the king of Babylon, Nebuchadnezzar, liked being king. He liked the power it gave him and the deference everyone paid to him. He liked the fringe benefits. He liked it all so much that he decided he wanted even more of it than he got as king; so he decided he wanted to become a god.

Perhaps you have discovered, if you've ever tried to become a king, that it is not such an easy thing to do. It helps if you get yourself born to the right parents, and it helps to be in the right place at the right time, but then it's kind of an iffy shot. You might well imagine that becoming a god would be even more challenging.

James Ayers is pastor of South Frankfort Presbyterian Church in Frankfort, Kentucky. He is a graduate of the University of Albany and Gordon-Conwell Theological Seminary, and received a Ph.D. from Boston College. His sermons have appeared in *Best Sermons 4* and *Best Sermons 6*.

Nebuchadnezzar recognized that it would take some planning. His plan to become a god went like this: He had an image constructed, sixty cubits high—that's about as tall as an eight- or nine-story building. He had it set up in the open fields, just outside the city limits. You could see it for miles.

Then he called in every government official to a special meeting, and this is what he told them: "From now on, everyone has to worship my image. Anytime anyone plays any music, on the bagpipes, on the harp, or any other musical instrument, everybody who hears it has to fall down and worship my image. I want every herald in the land to proclaim this notice." And because he recognized that people might be a little reluctant to accept this right away, he also told them one more thing: "Anybody who doesn't fall down and worship my image will be burned alive in a furnace."

It seemed to work pretty well. The heralds went out and proclaimed. The music played. Everybody in the land fell down and worshiped. Well, almost everybody. Hananiah, Mishael, and Azariah did not. They knew that the God of heaven had created the earth and everything and everyone in it; and they knew that no image fashioned by human hands was going to replace the God who had fashioned those humans. No king, no matter how arrogant, could claim the place of Yahweh. Not in fact; and not in their hearts.

King Nebuchadnezzar felt distressed by their refusal. To me it seems like a pretty harsh attitude on his part. If a person got stuck being the ruler of the biggest empire on the face of the earth, I guess one of the negative features would be that you wouldn't have much chance for advancement. Most of us could live with that. But suppose you decided that even though you were already right at the top, you still wanted a promotion. Suppose you decided you wanted not only to be a king but also to be a god. And suppose you had got nearly everyone in the empire going along with you. Tell the truth, now: Wouldn't you would feel pretty well satisfied with yourself? Why would you even bother to notice a conscientious objector here or there?

But Nebuchadnezzar was not satisfied. Three exceptions were three exceptions too many. He had Hananiah, Mishael, and Azariah arrested. "Weren't you guys listening?" he said to them. "Do you think I was just kidding about this furnace? You guys will do what I say or you're charcoal. You'd better decide to worship me, because there isn't any other god that's going to rescue you."

We find their reply here in the third chapter of the Book of Daniel. Their response is instructive. "We do not know," they answered, "whether our God will rescue us or not. But whether he does or whether he doesn't, we will not worship your image."

It's the kind of line you'd expect to hear at the movies: defiance in the face of danger. The difference is that as we watch the movies, we know that the heroes aren't really running much risk. Harrison Ford may get beaten up, and he may have to face impossible situations, but we know he always wins in the end. We know the movie is not going to end with the hero dying as the villain laughs. By the end of the movie, the good guys are going to triumph despite all odds, and we know that, and so we don't worry too much about them.

But in real life, people get hit by cars and they die. People get cancer and they die. People work as hard as they know how to work, and they still lose their jobs. And their homes. And their self-respect. And their hope.

"We believe," said Hananiah, Mishael, and Azariah, "that our God has the power to work miracles. We believe that our God has the power to rescue us from your hand, King Nebuchadnezzar. But we do not know if he will. We do not know if we will live or die. We do not know. But we still are going to worship him, instead of you."

About six centuries after these events would have taken place— which is to say, in about A.D. 55—the Apostle Paul left the city of Corinth, where he had been doing his missionary work, to return to the city of Jerusalem. There had been some crop failures in Judea and the surrounding countryside, so the local people didn't have much food, or much money to buy food from folks in the caravan and shipping business. Paul had taken up a pretty good collection from the churches of Greece and Macedonia, to help the people of Jerusalem buy groceries.

You must understand how much he loved those people. They were his countrymen, his cousins, his nieces and nephews, his high school buddies and his college classmates: They were his people. Some of them believed, as he believed, that all the hopes of his nation, down the long reaches of the centuries, had been fulfilled in the Messiah Jesus. Others scoffed. Indeed, many of them burned with a great hatred for the followers of Jesus, and for Paul in particular, for he had once been a scoffer along with them.

And he loved these people who hated him. As he got ready to leave Corinth to go back to Jerusalem, he wrote his letter to the Christian community in Rome, and in it he revealed some strong feelings. "I am speaking the truth in Christ," he told them; "I am not lying; my conscience bears me witness in the Holy Spirit, that I have great sorrow and unceasing anguish in my heart. For I could wish that I myself were accursed and cut off from Christ for the sake of my brethren, my kinsmen."

What might a person do, for the sake of someone you love? What risk might you run? "I would give my right arm," you can sometimes hear a person say. Perhaps, to try to rescue someone you love, you might even dare to run into a burning building. "I would do anything," Paul suggests. "Whatever it would take. Even if it cost me my life, even if it meant that I myself would end up cut off from Christ, I would do it."

So Paul and his companions left Corinth, the Book of Acts tells us. They traveled north up to Philippi, and then sailed east across the Aegean Sea to western Turkey, and then south through all those Greek islands until they found a ship headed for Syria. They bought their tickets and voyaged to the port city of Tyre. There was a community of Christians in Tyre, and Paul and his friends stayed with them for a week; and those Christians discerned, in the wisdom the Spirit had given them, that Paul would be in danger if he went on to Jerusalem. They warned him not to go.

But he was determined to go. The travelers got back on the ship, and continued their voyage south to the port of Caesarea. At this point they were only about fifty miles from Jerusalem. While they were staying there, in the house of Philip the evangelist, a prophet named Agabus came down from Judea. Moved by the vision he had seen, Agabus had journeyed those fifty miles, desperate to make good speed on the road so that he would get to Caesarea before it was too late, and yet having to check each caravan and each traveler going the other way in case Paul might have already left for Jerusalem. I don't suppose Agabus took the time to check into his room at the Caesarea Shores Holiday Hotel, to take a shower and change into his clean suit. Instead, he marched right into Philip's house; travel grime streaking his face, he marched right into the room where everyone was having church; he marched right up to Paul, right in the middle of the sermon, probably, and looked him right in the eye. Then Agabus reached down and unwrapped Paul's belt sash; and he tied up his own hands and feet with it. And he said, "The Holy Spirit has told me that this is what they're going to do to you when you get to Jerusalem."

Sometimes prophecies are hard to understand. But not his one. No one felt uncertain about what this prophecy meant. After the work and sweat of the journey down from Judea, pressing along, mile after mile, to get to Caesarea in time to issue his warning—after all that, Agabus did not offer up a hesitant or ambiguous prophecy that people might interpret four or five different ways.

The message was clear. It was clear to Paul's companions. It was clear to the church in Caesarea. Everyone begged Paul not to go to Jerusalem. But the message had already been clear to Paul. It had been clear to him before Agabus arrived. It had been clear to him as he considered all the warnings his friends had offered, all during the journey. It had been clear to him back when he was in Corinth, writing his letter to the Romans, as he set down his heart's sorrow and anguish over his kinfolk back in Jerusalem, as he set down his resolve that he would run any risk—life, death, suffering, even being cut off from Christ if that would do it: anything.

And Paul dared to believe that maybe, just maybe, if their friend and kinsman Saul of Tarsus came to the people of Jerusalem just once more with this message of the gospel—and if he came to them with the gift in his hand from the gentile Christians of Greece and Macedonia, with this tangible demonstration of how the love of God had transformed the lives of those people, so that they gave generously to sustain the lives of people they had never even met—maybe, just maybe, the people of Jerusalem would listen this time. Maybe, just maybe, they would see that the gospel is real. And so Paul told his friends, "I am ready not only to be imprisoned but even to die at Jerusalem for the name of the Lord Jesus." And they could not persuade him that the danger was too great; for he had resolved that he would make this effort no matter the risk. And so they said, "May the will of the Lord be done."

We do not know, said Hananiah, Mishael, and Azariah, if God will rescue us from the burning fiery furnace; we do not know if we will live or die; but we will follow our God and do what is right, no matter the cost. Paul might have said the same thing: I do not know if God will rescue me from imprisonment by the leaders of Jerusalem; I do not know if I will live or die; but I will follow my God and do what is right, no matter the cost.

Our God is able to work miracles; our God does work miracles, right in our midst, calling to us in the midst of our darkness and fear, and inviting us to become children of God, filled with the light of Jesus Christ; and so we will believe that our Lord just might work the very miracle we need. But we do not know. We do not know how the power of God will be shown. We do not know whether the power of God will be shown by transforming our present circumstances, or by transforming our lives to make us people with the courage to remain faithful, no matter the cost, to the vision our God has given us.

Many years ago I saw a poster on the wall of a friend's room. The poster said, "Never doubt in the darkness what God has shown you in the light." It's good advice, at least most of the time. But what if the thing you have seen is dark? What if your best wisdom, your best insight, tells you that it's going to be chains? What if the vision and discernment of your trusted friends comes out the same? "You're heading into trouble," they say; and you have to respond, "Yeah, I expect you're right."

I believe that in the gracious, transforming love of our Lord Jesus Christ, he has equipped us to be people with the courage of conviction. To be people with the courage to believe that no matter the circumstances, we will be kept safe: both in life and in death. To be people with the courage to believe that God's will shall be done, that the lives of our beloved enemies will be transformed because of what God has done in and through us; and even if not all of them are changed before our very eyes, to be people with the courage to believe that the will of the Lord shall be done.

We do not know the details. We do not even know, for tomorrow, whether we will live or die. But we do know the love with which our God has loved us. We do know that the will of the Lord shall be done. And we know that in the courage of that conviction, we will dare to follow the vision that our God has given us, no matter the cost.

6. The Fear of Faces
Gary D. Stratman

Jeremiah 1:4–10

Sometimes people are honest enough to tell me their objections to the Bible. They will quickly add that they know the Bible is important, but it doesn't seem to speak to them. It *is* hard for us to see ourselves in the stories—written in "primitive" times, in "strange" cultures—that we hear on Sunday mornings. Yet, hidden in this "strangeness" is a call to us with an unrelenting familiarity.

In this morning's scripture, we hear of "the call" of Jeremiah to speak the word of the Lord in Josiah's reign (627 B.C.). Surely these words to an ancient Hebrew prophet have little to do with our time or circumstance. But let's look more closely. Let us see Jeremiah this morning not only as a prophet, for not all of us have been called to be prophets, but also as a believer, who is called to be a witness. How can we see ourselves in that picture? A believer, yes, but we are not comfortable with just going through the motions. We want our lives to point beyond ourselves to something lasting.

Someone said to me this week, "I just wish I knew what I was supposed to do with my life." Someone else said a short time ago, "Wouldn't it be nice if God spoke to me the way God seems to speak to other people?" God does speak. If God is to speak to us, does it mean it must be in ecstatic visions? It was so with Moses, and it was true with Isaiah and Ezekiel. Yet, there are other ways in which the living Lord says, "I have a purpose for you." Counter to what some of us have experienced this week, life is not sound and fury signifying nothing. You are called with a purpose. God spoke

Gary D. Stratman is senior pastor of First and Calvary Presbyterian Church in Springfield, Missouri. He holds degrees from Wheaton College, Miami University in Ohio, and Earlham School of Religion and a doctorate from Vanderbilt University. His published writings include contributions to numerous periodicals and to *The Ministers Manual,* and a book, *Pastoral Preaching.*

not in a fiery vision but in a conversation to people like Samuel, Amos, and Jeremiah. Hear again what God says to Jeremiah, and what I believe God is saying to us: "I formed you." It was long before you drew breath that God formed you in your mother's womb. Here we have the same word that is used in Genesis 2:7, the Creation account, where God makes humankind from the dust of the earth. You are formed by God. That means that you and I are created in the image of God. *Imago dei* ("in the image of God")— I.D.; thus our identity is formed. When you are oppressed with feelings of worthlessness, remember that you *are* a person of worth created in God's image. Before we disparage any person or denigrate any group, the word comes again to us: "They too are created in God's image."

I had a friend who dealt with teenagers in deep trouble. He had an inelegant sign in the place where he worked, but it spoke volumes about being created in the image of God. It said, "God don't make no junk." I apologize to all grammarians, but I suggest that we need to hear it, and hear it again. In this scripture God says to Jeremiah, *I formed you.* God says, *I knew you,* and "knew" does not mean just a meeting or an acquaintanceship. It literally means loving approval. The truth is that not only are we created in God's image, but it is good. There are people here, within the greater community, and around this world who hunger for loving approval. We, too, get ourselves into all kinds of trouble because we try to find that loving approval in ways that will not last or satisfy. Yet the word comes not to Jeremiah alone but to us: "Before you were born, *I consecrated you.*" It means that He has set us apart as witnesses. It is not only prophets and priests who have been called to be witnesses. What you do with your life is important.

Hear the call of God to you: You have been set apart for an important task. Your life is important. "*I have appointed you.*" God is speaking to Jeremiah, who was a prophet. We may not all be called to be prophets, but we are all called to be witnesses. The word *prophet* means "one who announces." Whether you have the specific gift of "prophet" or not, you are a witness of God's grace called to be an announcer of good news.

We are all announcing something. We are announcing gloom and doom or those painful episodes of the past that have not been healed for us. Despite our personal and corporate pain, we can announce the glad tidings of the gospel to others: you're valuable, you're created in the image of God, Christ died for you and has a place for you in His kingdom. How do we respond? How did Jeremiah respond? He said, "Well, ah, wait a minute, Lord, I ah, I ah, I ah, don't speak so well." When we hear this call, it corresponds to the deepest desires of our heart, yet we say we are inept. I say, "If you give me a little more training then maybe I'll be your witness in the place where I work; then maybe I can speak a word against racial injustice in my community, but not yet." Jeremiah says he's a child. We say, "I'm too young"; "I'm too old"; "I'm single"; "I have a family." There's always a reason, yet God's call is not burden but possibility. Admitting our limitations does not disqualify us from being witnesses; it is a part of being qualified. In our weakness, we find God's strength.

What is it then that Jeremiah fears when he is called? God cuts to the heart of the matter: "Do not be afraid of them . . ." (Jer. 1:8, RSV). If you read the Book of Jeremiah, it's clear. There were people who made him a laughingstock. There were people who mocked him all day long. Wasn't it natural for him to be afraid of the faces that would reject him, ridicule him, count him as not acceptable? (Who said anything about faces?) Hold on to your prejudices; this is a place where the King James Version gives us a more haunting picture than the New Revised Standard Version: "Be not afraid of their faces." Each of us would do well to get in touch with his or her own gallery of faces that keep us from being a witness. We are afraid of the faces in the crowd, our peers; faces from the past. I know this fear has often been the barrier that prevents me from speaking a good word for Jesus Christ. It is in the conclusion of verse 8 that all of us have hope as we seek to be witnesses: ". . . I am with you to deliver you, says the Lord."

7. In the Storm with Jesus
Eduard Schweizer

Matthew 14:22–33

The story of the sinking of Peter is reported only in Matthew's Gospel. In the earlier account of the disciples' ship in the storm in chapter 8, Matthew makes it clear that he sees this as an image of the church for all times. Thus it is not important that we consider at length what actually happened then and how it may have taken place, but rather that we let Matthew tell us the application for the followers of Jesus today, and so for his church.

Beloved of our Lord Jesus Christ:

The story begins with the disciples, who are in desperate need. We do not have to dwell on that; we know that. We row and row, we work and worry, and it amounts to nothing. "The wind was against them." There are such times, when we can do everything and make no headway. "They reeled and staggered like drunken men," says Psalm 107. So it is Jesus himself who "made the disciples get into the boat," and that is a very strong expression. Thus he has already, for the second time, driven them into such a storm. They could gradually become skeptical. Evidently this Jesus is no guarantor for quiet and peace and a bit of ease in life. Our church is, of course, not exactly afflicted by storm. We are not under persecution. The question is only whether great indifference is not just as dangerous. As long as we do not directly take up political or economic questions, no cock crows after what we say. "[Jesus] went up on the mountain by himself." Jesus does not place himself at the

Eduard Schweizer was born in 1913 in Basel, Switzerland. He was educated at the Universities of Basel, Marburg, and Zurich. Dr. Schweizer, a member of the Reformed Church, served as a pastor and as professor of New Testament at the University of Zurich until he retired in 1979. He is the author of more than twenty books and two hundred essays. A number of his sermons appear in *God's Inescapable Nearness*. "In the Storm with Jesus" was translated from the German by James W. Cox.

disposal of the disciples. He is "by himself." In that, something of the mystery of God, whom we can never possess, becomes perceptible. He always remains strange, beyond our reach, distant. He keeps his plans to himself. Yet that is exactly how Jesus is present for his disciples.

What happened already in prayer is now taking shape: "In the fourth watch of the night he came to them walking on the sea." That is to say, Jesus has been on the way to his disciples for a long time already, long before they notice it. "But when the disciples saw him walking on the sea, they were terrified, saying 'It is a ghost!'" That is just how it is: Even if we get a glimpse of something, we do not for a moment notice that he is the one who is coming. We have just expected him in an altogether different way. As a young man I was once, for a year or so, in the depths of despair, as one can experience it perhaps only in one's youth, because God obviously did not want to give me the one I thought just had to be my wife. And I did not notice that God was already on the way to me and had arranged things ten times better than I had ever imagined. So it is in our text. Jesus has seen his disciples for a long while already, but they do not see him. That is to say, they see that something is happening, but they do not perceive that Jesus is coming to them in it.

"But immediately he spoke to them, saying, 'Take heart, it is I; have no fear.'" It is his word that now really brings help. That is something of the beauty of sermon preparation (in which, incidentally, my wife plays an essential role). We busy ourselves for a long time over the printed word before it comes alive, and then all at once we hear his word, Jesus' word, in it or indeed have an inkling of it, even if we can surely never bring it under our power.

And here the story could properly come to an end. But that would be a storybook ending, the happy end. The disciples are together with Jesus again. In his comforting word he is already present, and soon the storm will subside. "He commanded the waters and brought them home in his faithful keeping." So we have sung of "those in storm and waves."

"And Peter answered him, 'Lord, if it is you, bid me come to you on the water.'" So here is one of the disciples for whom it is not enough to hear "Have no fear!" He wants more than that: ". . . if it is you . . ." Ah, but we also know how that is. We believe, but we are again unsure. When I was a candidate for confirmation,

I prayed again and again for a long time, "God, if you exist, then . . ." Does Peter therefore have to have an extra proof? Or does he perhaps think, on the other hand, that one has to do something also to live out of one's faith? In any case, he ventures something unprecedented. He steps over the edge of the boat into the storm. He disembarks from the relatively safe boat into the completely unknown—thus, in a way, out of the "institutional church" into the very stormy and baffling world. Obviously, this is what is needed: disciples who for once step across the borders, even the borders of the institutional church. Of course, in these cases pure and less-than-pure motives are mixed together, as with Peter. Nevertheless, he steps out. Yet he remains under Jesus' direction; but Jesus says to him, "Come!" Jesus accepts the challenge. He needs people in his church who are willing for once to venture the inconceivable. Jesus could, on the other hand, object on many counts. "This, surely, does not benefit anyone; at most, all it benefits is your self-confidence." He could also say, "So now you are going too far. You are indeed definitely not God himself." But he says nothing like that. "So Peter got out of the boat and walked on the water and came to Jesus." For one brief moment Peter is the mighty hero of faith.

"But when he saw the wind, he was afraid and beginning to sink . . ." In one moment a fantastic experience of faith is bestowed on him, and in the next moment comes its complete breakdown. He sees nothing but the storm. We too know what that is like—situations in which we really experience God and in which, immediately afterward, doubt returns and everything again seems dead. "When he saw the wind . . ." He sees that; he has lost sight of Jesus. But the decisive thing is that "he cried out, 'Lord, save me.' " This is exactly what belongs to every experience of faith; that we see that even personal faith does not suffice, that there is actually no one and nothing more—not even our strong faith—except Jesus, and we expect everything from him. "Jesus immediately reached out his hand." He does not keep him in suspense. He does not say to him, "You braggart. I could have told you that already!" At this point, there is no moral lesson, and Jesus applies none of the disciplinary actions that we are so eager to apply in just such cases. Jesus takes our efforts seriously, even if everything goes wrong. Indeed, this is a necessary part of all faith experience—that is, that through failure we gain the assurance that we expressed in our first hymn: "He is my defender and subdues storm and tempest and whatever brings me woe." So we have sung. But do we also live this way?

That is the first thing that Jesus wants to say to us today. There are tensions in the life of the church. We should learn to be completely open to new ways and, for a change, even to dare the almost impossible. At the same time, we must know in the deepest sense that this is never simply "practicable," that we therefore can only pray and hope that he will bless our venture, our starting out, our work. Perhaps that will become clear to us if we think about our churches today. The temptation of the Catholic Church used to be to believe that God wants all peoples—he has promised that to us and we are supposed to believe it—that it has already ventured into the world, but that it then believes in the "practicable" instead of in Jesus, who many times comes so differently than we can imagine. Then it moves church politics up to the choice of bishop and attempts it occasionally even with forced conversion. The temptation of the Evangelical Church has been to dare for once to step out of the boat, even into political and social problems and needs, even when the wind was against it. But this church then suddenly expects everything of the social program or political party for which it has decided, without letting itself be corrected again and again by its Lord. And in one way or another everything sinks down with such a faith in the "practicable."

But now a second matter comes before us. Jesus said to Peter, "You of little faith, why did you doubt?" Was Peter's losing sight of Jesus, then, little faith? Indeed, Jesus once said that if our faith were as tiny as a mustard seed, we could remove mountains! But *to doubt* means in the Greek, "to be double." The Epistle of James puts it even more graphically: We ought not to be "double-minded." There is something very wrong with it. This does not mean that we live in illusions, blind to realities, or that we fold our hands and expect miracles. Nothing is wrong with Peter's seeing wind and waves. What we read in Psalm 107 certainly does not tell us that there is no danger. It is rather a matter of our seeing Jesus throughout all these realities; not seeing the waves at one time on the left and then again Jesus on the right, but rather seeing him there behind all that threatens. That is what we find at the beginning of the Book of the Wisdom of Solomon: ". . . seek him [the Lord] with sincerity of heart." He stands behind the peril, and he determines how it is to turn out.

And now the last thing: "And when they got into the boat, the wind ceased." Even the outsider Peter may get into the boat again with Jesus. Together with those who remain in the boat, he throws himself down before Jesus, saying, "Truly you are the Son of God." But even with this glorious confession that the daring one and the more sluggish ones come to speak, all is not yet over. Now all the disciples row on—with this difference: Now their action is worthwhile, since they have again found the only one with whom one wins through. We want to join together in the concluding hymn and in spite of "the waves wild roaring": "We live for you, to be your dear little people."

Who lives like this? Dietrich Bonhoeffer had been able to remain in England in 1935 and again in North America in the summer of 1939; but he climbed over the side of the boat into the storm—and what an extraordinary blessing came from that! Now to add a prayer by Jeremias Gotthelf to today's text: "Yesterday nothing was yet visible, today not much, but tomorrow it is brought to completion, and now for the first time we are becoming aware, looking back, how you bring about quietly what we do not achieve with great clamor." We are no Bonhoeffers and no Gotthelfs. We are apparently supremely happy that we can remain seated in the boat and have our fill of storm and waves. With us things do not happen in such a spectacular way. But we want to be very thankful also for those who dare for once to climb over the side of the boat, even when we do not really understand what they are doing. And we want to row, trusting in the one who will at last bring the boat to land. We want to help by our more modest gifts and more modest means of assistance in the collection and our offering of money, and by taking up into the boat the one who has dared to expose himself unprotected to the storm in the company of Jesus.

8. Gift Wrapped in Swaddling Cloths

A CHRISTMAS EVE SERMON

Robert S. Crilley

Luke 2:1–7

I recently heard a rather amusing story about a woman who, just two days before Christmas, suddenly remembered that she had yet to send out any cards. Without so much as a moment's hesitation, she hastily arranged a select list of all those friends and relatives to whom she wished to extend the greetings of the season, and hurried down to the nearest store. Sprinting through the almost depleted shopping aisles, she finally located a box of cards picturing the peaceful serenity of a Bethlehem stable and bought it immediately. In a flurry of panic, she raced home to address and stamp each envelope, rushed over to the closest mailbox, and minutes later found herself again at the kitchen table—her fingers now steepled in a posture of prayerful relief.

A relaxed smile slowly began to soften her exhausted expression, and with a silent nod of approval, she secretly congratulated herself for having completed the chore with such efficiency. As she sat there quietly nursing a cup of coffee, however, she happened to notice a few remaining cards still lying in the box and realized

Robert S. Crilley is senior pastor of First Presbyterian Church in Grapevine, Texas. He received his B.A. from the University of Michigan and his M.Div. from Princeton Seminary. He has received several awards, including the John T. Galloway Prize in Expository Preaching from Princeton Seminary in 1987. He is currently working on a book of sermons based on the Old Testament lectionary passages for the last third of Pentecost. He and his wife, Judy, have three daughters.

that, in all of the hectic confusion, she hadn't actually bothered to read any of them. To her unexpected horror, the cards consisted of but one line: *"This simple note is just to say . . . a little gift is on its way."*

Of course, part of what makes this particular story so humorous is that we all recognize that those aren't exactly the sentiments that this poor woman intended (much less desired) to express. And yet, it seems to me that, for those of us already attuned to the sacred strains of this season, the message of that card does indeed echo the equally unexpected announcement of a holy and silent night long ago. For on that hallowed evening, when the angel first appears and the glory of the Lord shines around that small band of startled shepherds, the proclamation is also one of a surprising gift soon to be on its way. Now, to be sure, those glad tidings are initially heralded in a rather soft and unsuspecting manner—with the hushed whispers of a single heavenly courier. But then others are summoned, and still more swiftly arrive; until suddenly, it is as if a celestial choir has set the entire Judean sky ablaze with anthems: "Glory to God in the highest, and on earth peace and good will among all people . . . for to you is born this day in the city of David a Savior, who is the Messiah, the Lord."

Tonight is Christmas Eve, and the familiar story just read from the second chapter of Luke's Gospel invites us, once more, to be astonished by the mysterious and miraculous nature of such amazing news. For many of us, tonight is a night filled not only with worship but with an overwhelming sense of wonder—for on this night meet the hopes and fears of all the years, and life itself is again illuminated with the radiant light of God's redeeming love. It is a scene so vast in scope, so immense in meaning, that it threatens to spill beyond the borders of even imagination's canvas; and much as did Mary herself, we are sometimes able only to ponder such things in our hearts. Indeed, with every passing season, our frail attempts simply to restate the sacred significance of this night seem more like a thimble dipped into the ocean's depths.

Still, there is one curious aspect of this passage that has always sort of puzzled me. Namely, why it is that, when Joseph and Mary finally reach Bethlehem, there's "no place for them in the inn." Amid the accounts describing the birth of our Lord, few words appear so clearly prophetic of his entire existence as does this short, cryptic phrase. One almost wonders whether Luke actually sensed, when he first wrote it, the dramatic relevance of this line to everything that is to follow ... the fitness of the fact that Christ begins his life by being crowded out—for sadly, much the same will happen throughout his ministry, and, for that matter, throughout all history.

However, it's precisely this part of the story that continues to strike me as somewhat strange. I mean, here Luke is declaring the glad tidings of the glorious coming of the Messiah! And yet, when that joyous moment—which has for so long been eagerly anticipated—finally arrives, there isn't any place prepared for Jesus' birth. Have you ever questioned why that is?

The most widely offered suggestion, at least in my hearing, has always been that on that night Bethlehem is crowded. After all, Caesar Augustus's imperial degree "that all the world should be enrolled" requires everyone to return to his or her own town. A registration ordered by Rome will, no doubt, flood the narrow highways of Palestine with a steady stream of people; throngs of tired pilgrims will pour into that tiny village; and one inn after another will start flashing No Vacancy signs. Perhaps, as Christian lore has traditionally held, the holy couple arrive late into the evening—long after most others have already secured accommodations for the night. (Even in our modern world of mass transit, the ninth month of pregnancy is hardly a time conducive to hasty travel!) And so, with Joseph weary from the day's journey and Mary now beginning to experience the pangs of birth, the two finally reach Bethlehem only to discover the little town filled to capacity.

There are, however, a few difficulties with this familiar explanation of the passage. As accustomed as we have all become to picturing the scene in this fashion, it doesn't exactly fit the text. For starters, Luke never really says that Bethlehem is crowded. In fact, with the much larger city of Jerusalem just an hour or two away, anyone coming from a considerable distance will likely spend the evening there. Furthermore, the Gospel writer makes absolutely no mention of the expectant couple arriving at the last minute, or, for that matter, even late at night. The scriptures state only that "while they were there, the time came for Mary to deliver her child"—as if both of them had already been staying in Bethlehem for a while.

But of far greater significance is the fact that if this, indeed, is Joseph's hometown (being "descended from the house and family of David"), there are surely friends and relatives still living there. Only shortly before this, Mary has traveled to visit Elizabeth in a nearby village. Moreover, considering that the primary purpose of Rome's registrations is to access property taxes, some have suggested that Joseph may even own some land in the region. At the very least, the birth of any child is always an occasion of great joy—especially for such small, close-knit communities as Bethlehem—and it is almost unimaginable that, in their time of urgent need, Mary and Joseph would be forced to seek the shelter of a commercial inn.

Of course, the most compelling evidence in this regard is that there's not a single reference to any innkeeper refusing the couple lodging. Actually, the innkeeper is absent from the account altogether. The text simply says that "there was no place for them in the inn," and even here, many scholars argue that the original Greek word translated as "inn"—*kataluma*—may very well be mistranslated. It's worth noting, for example, that in the well-known parable of the good Samaritan—when the wounded traveler is, indeed, taken to a hostelry—Luke uses the more accepted and accurate term *pandokheion*.

In fact, the only other two instances in the entire New Testament where the word *kataluma* occurs are in the story of the Lord's Supper. There, as you may recall, Jesus instructs Peter and John to go into Jerusalem and follow a man carrying a jar of water until they come to a certain house, where they are to say the owner, "The teacher asks, 'Where is the *kataluma*, where I may eat the Passover with my disciples?' " In this case, *kataluma* is clearly meant to refer not to an "inn," but rather to a "guest room."

Obviously preferring this interpretation, Dr. Kenneth Bailey has gone on to point out that, in the peasant homes of first-century Palestine, the large family area will often double as a guest room.[1] Adjacent to this chamber, but at a slightly lower level, stands a rough, outer terrace into which the animals are sometimes brought at night. Usually, feeding troughs, or mangers, will be cut into the floor at this end of the raised family room, so that the animals may feed without actually being able to come into the house. Now, if you read the story with that understanding, it seems to shed new light upon the entire scene: "Mary gave birth to her firstborn son and wrapped him in bands of cloth, and laid him in a manger"— that is, in one of the feeding troughs of this large family area. Well, why doesn't the owner of the house just offer the family chamber as a guest room? Ah, the text goes on, "because there was no place from them in the *guest room*."

As convincing as this theory sounds, however, it doesn't really resolve the original question—namely, Why is there no place for them in the guest room? Some have suggested that perhaps, with others in the house, the guest room simply doesn't provide enough privacy. More likely, a family of higher social status or greater wealth than this young, peasant couple is already staying there. And yet, from a Christian perspective, is this not a night of *sacred* status? No matter how poor Joseph and Mary may have appeared at the time, certainly the early church will come to recognize that they have been blessed with a richness beyond any worldly standard. Luke himself is apparently already willing to take some historical liberties concerning the precise dating of Augustus's census, in order to reflect the conviction that although unknowing, the great Roman emperor will still ultimately serve the purposes of God.[2] And so, even if the guest room is actually occupied on that particular evening, it still seems strange to me that years later, when the Gospel writer begins to consider the miraculous nature of this night, he does not, at the very least, also find a place there in the family chamber for our Lord's birth.

Of course, Luke may very well have a theological strategy for telling the story in this way. After all, the scene is entirely stripped of any of the elaborate splendors that might possibly remove the Christ child from the lowly, the poor, and the marginal of the earth. Here, cradled in God's arms, the Savior of the world is carried down heaven's stairway and softly laid to rest upon a bed of straw—almost as if, more than anything else, this Gospel writer wants his readers always to remember that Jesus is the one who takes upon himself the humble form of a servant. And thus, the King of Kings arrives surrounded not by soldiers, but by shepherds; born not in a mansion, but in a manger; wrapped not in silk, but in swaddling cloths!

Still, if the crowded accommodations are simply meant to serve a theological agenda, that explains only why it's significant *for Luke* that there be "no place for them in the guest room." Mine is a deeper question: Why, indeed, is it so important for God? I mean, after all, the Creator is intimately involved in almost every aspect of this drama. Far from being an impassive observer casually gazing down from some celestial balcony, the Almighty is constantly dispatching angels, at crucial points in the pageant, to cue the actors onstage and remind them of the larger story line.

Consider Mary, for example. She is just an adolescent girl, hardly old enough to have a child at all—let alone *this* child! Nevertheless, Gabriel is sent out to find her and, perhaps unable to contain his own enthusiasm, arrives with all the subtlety of an obstetrician on his first case who is as eager and excited as the parents. Seemingly flustered by the eternal significance of this encounter, he dispenses with the formality of even a polite introduction, and suddenly declares the surprising news: "Greetings, favored one! The Lord is with you. Blessed are you among women . . . for now, you will conceive in your womb and bear a son . . ." And while these are obviously words that might very well have startled a young woman even if they hadn't come from an angel, it is the timing of this unexpected announcement that proves particularly awkward—for by her own admission, Mary is still a virgin (far more accustomed to being regarded as her mother's child than as a child's mother). Small wonder that she is both perplexed and greatly troubled.

But though the message has now been revealed, it has not yet been received. And in the hushed silence that surely follows this sacred invitation, all of heaven must wait for Mary's reply. Perhaps, as Frederick Buechner so insightfully suggests, Gabriel himself secretly hopes that she will not notice that beneath those great, golden wings he, in fact, is trembling with the thought that the whole future of creation will ultimately hang upon the answer of this young girl.[3]

It is the first crucial point in the story of our Savior's birth, and in steps God with whispers of angelic assurance: "Do not be afraid, Mary, . . . for the Holy Spirit will come upon you, and the power of the Most High will overshadow you; therefore the child to be born will be holy . . ." At the precise moment when guidance is required, guidance is given!

Or think about Joseph. Here he is—engaged but not yet married, the invitations already in the mail, a hefty down payment made on the reception hall, perhaps even a few counseling sessions taken with the local rabbi. On the one hand, you can hardly blame him for initially considering divorce when he discovers that, through no fault of his own, his fiancée is suddenly pregnant.

According to Matthew, Joseph is a just man, but in the society of his day, "justice" will insist that all the facts be made known and the guilty parties promptly punished. To violate the bonds of betrothal is a great evil in first-century Palestine, and the law specifically demands that both the woman and the man involved be stoned to death.

On the other hand, if he decides to take Mary as his wife, he will submit himself to the shame of inevitable speculation, and surely expose the entire family to the humiliating gossip of endless rumor. But I believe there is a matter of even greater significance, for if Joseph commits himself to this relationship now, he must, in fact, accept what any stepparent already knows to be a fulfilling and yet frustrating task—that of loving a child who shares your life but nevertheless will always, rightfully, call another "Father."

Apparently, he is unwilling to do either. True enough, the wedding is canceled, but also the public vindication traditionally associated with acts of adultery. Here, faced with the most indelicate of personal crises, Joseph resolves simply "to dismiss Mary quietly"; and in so doing, he freely chooses to suffer the consequences of what he assumes to be another's sin, in order to spare the life of the one he still loves. Not exactly the justice required by Jewish law, but certainly the justice ultimately required of the child who is coming!

Again, however, it is a crucial point in the story, and by way of a dream, in steps God once more, to confer the comfort of heavenly counsel: "Joseph, son of David, do not be afraid to take Mary as your wife, for the child conceived in her is from the Holy Spirit. She will bear a son, and you are to name him Jesus, for he will save his people from their sins."

Throughout the story, each time guidance is required, guidance is given . . . *except* when Mary and Joseph actually arrive in that tiny Judean village and begin to search for a place to stay. Here is the one moment when guidance is perhaps most needed, and yet, strangely enough, there are no angels awaiting the holy couple's approach, eager to escort them to a room already reserved. In a drama so filled with divine intervention, why does heaven fall silent now?

Some years ago, I happened to hear a Christmas Eve sermon on the radio, in which the preacher scolded the listening audience for what seemed to him to be a seasonal, sentimental, and absurd infatuation with the sweet babe of Bethlehem. "Away *with* the manger," he thundered—intending, I suppose, to question the Hall-mark theology of mawkish romanticism that is too often content with only cooing over the "little Lord Jesus." At the time, I almost agreed with him, but now I am starting to think differently.

To stand in the stable and behold the Messiah's birth does not reduce the majesty of the Incarnation. On the contrary, here the miraculous nature of that event is truly revealed. The mystery of this night is that the Almighty actually chooses to meet us first as a baby—surprisingly willing to initiate the redemptive activity of re-creating humanity from the womb onward. William Willimon is absolutely correct when he asserts that there is nothing quite as frail or fragile as an infant. Indeed, what other religion is bold enough to affirm "the possibility of its God appearing in so vulnerable a form"?[4]

Although it happened almost four years ago now, I can still remember standing in the maternity ward holding my daughter, Katherine Ann. Anyone who has ever cradled a newborn child knows that those first precious moments of life cannot help but make a claim upon our own. Perhaps it is because little ones are so utterly helpless. Infants depend upon us for almost everything. They can't feed themselves; they can't dress themselves (and as one with prior experience in such matters, let me assure you that they need to be clothed with staggering regularity); often they are unable even to get to sleep by themselves. And precisely because of this vulnerability, a baby inevitably summons a deep and demanding commitment from us.

While I can only assume that the intentions of that radio preacher were honest ones, I believe he is mistaken. The church must never do "away with the manger," for here is found the incarnation's most amazing quality—the helpless, trusting, and utterly dependent vulnerability of the Christ child.

All year long, we speak about *our* need for God, but the beckoning mystery of this night is that the Almighty comes into the world as an infant—filled with needs, reaching out to *us* for love and acceptance. Perhaps that is the reason there is no place already prepared for the Messiah's arrival. The voice of heaven falls silent and the guiding angels are hushed because, along with Mary and Joseph, it is now up to us to find a place for Jesus' birth.

Dr. Thomas Long, my homiletics professor at seminary, once told a delightful story about a Christmas pageant that was presented in the fellowship hall of a small, rural church.[5] One of the cast members that year was a seventh-grade boy named Wally. Noticeably shy and reserved by nature, Wally was the kind of youngster for whom you might deem the word *awkward* an apt description—his tall, lanky frame forever seeming to strain against the stretched limits of his clothing. While his peers liked him well enough, Wally was often overlooked and, unfortunately, just as easily excluded—the sort of person who, whenever teams were chosen, was always picked last, and then only with painful and obvious reluctance.

In fact, even on this occasion, it was merely with modest enthusiasm that Wally was selected to play the innkeeper at Bethlehem. If the truth be told, he was ill suited for the role. After all, the scene required someone stern, forceful, and resolute—a hardnosed proprietor whose sole act of hospitality for two weary, and now desperate, travelers seemed to be the meager offer of a manger to serve as maternity ward. Poor Wally, though, was about as abrasive as a jar of cold cream!

Nevertheless, he was given the part, primarily because it consisted of but one line, containing all of two words: "No room!" While it was hardly Academy Award material, Wally spent hours practicing *that* single line over and over again, varying both voice and volume, and struggling to sound as determined (and, for Wally, uncharacteristically authoritative) as possible: "No room! No room!"

When the actual night of the pageant finally arrived and the members of the church family had settled into their folding chairs with eager anticipation, the event was, like all such Sunday School presentations, filled with unintended (although not entirely unexpected) moments of lighthearted humor. In a tempo sure to torture those sensitive listeners of the congregation who happened to be musically inclined, a second-grader slowly pounded her way through "O Little Town of Bethlehem" on the piano; and with the closing chords still challenging the ears of all but the tone-deaf, the curtains were abruptly pulled open.

There, bathed in a blue spotlight, stood a befuddled flock of shepherds in oversize terry-cloth robes and worn sneakers, shuffling around with makeshift staffs and looking, quite frankly, as confused and dumbfounded as the sheep over which, supposedly, they were keeping watch by night. For their part, a noisy herd of kindergartners—complete with shoe-polish noses and cotton-ball ears—milled nervously about the stage.

Minutes later and with a sudden shift of lighting, in fluttered a festive (albeit feisty) chorus of fourth-grade angels—a heavenly host of bed sheets and gilded cardboard wings. Hovering here and there, they quickly adjusted their coat-hanger halos and collectively began to search, in vain, for the correct pitch of "O Come, All Ye Faithful"—giving everyone present a new reason for being "sore afraid."

At long last, now came Wally's big scene. Joseph and Mary hobbled wearily across the stage, knocked on the door, and pleaded for lodging. Determined to stay in character, Wally grumbled to his feet and dutifully recited his line: "No room!"

"But, sir, my wife is having a baby."

It was an improvisation that poor Wally obviously did not expect. After all, he only had the *one* line. Slumping toward the couple, Wally peered into their faces, with a vacant stare, as though studying a museum portrait. "No room!" he finally stammered again, stamping his foot on the floor in the hope that it would add emphasis.

"Please, kind sir, won't you reconsider?"

Wally shifted uneasily, not sure how to answer. He knew what he was supposed to say, but it just didn't feel right anymore. Unable to speak, Wally sadly looked down and simply shook his head.

Joseph and Mary turned, and reluctantly started back across the stage. As Wally watched them, however, his eyes began to fill with compassion. Suddenly responding to a grace that, though not part of the script, somehow seemed to embrace the moment, he startled himself, the holy couple, and the entire audience by calling out, "Wait a minute. Don't go. You can have *my* room."

Now, admittedly, that wasn't part of the Christmas story, but it is surely part of the Christmas spirit. In fact, though that poor woman never intended to send cards with that message, I think the message contained in those cards is also part of the Christmas spirit—for on this night there is, indeed, a gift on its way. Surprisingly enough, it is God's gift of a child who, like all infants, comes filled with needs—reaching out to us for love and acceptance.

No wonder there is no place for the birth: All of heaven now waits for us to find a place!

NOTES

1. Kenneth E. Bailey, "The Manger and the Inn," in *Presbyterian Outlook*, 4–11 January 1988, 8–9.

2. Fred B. Craddock, *Luke-Interpretation: A Bible Commentary for Teaching and Preaching* (Louisville, KY: John Knox Press, 1990), 34.

3. Frederick Buechner, *Peculiar Treasures: A Biblical Who's Who* (San Francisco: Harper & Row, 1979), 39.

4. William H. Willimon, *On a Wild and Windy Mountain* (Nashville, TN: Abingdon Press, 1984), 25.

5. Thomas G. Long, *Shepherds and Bathrobes* (Lima, OH: C.S.S. Publishing, 1987), 42–43.

9. How Wise Were the Wise Men?

Edmund S. P. Jones

Matthew 2:1

Of all the Christmas stories, none is more romantic and colorful than the story of the Magi. With its ingredients of intrigue, double cross, and murder, it soon became more popular than the rather pedestrian story of shepherds keeping watch over their flocks by night. And as it caught the imagination of the faithful, so it inspired their devotion.

Now, royals, even when misbehaving, are more interesting than academics. So the Wise Men became kings. The monarchs of medieval Europe used to attend Christmas Mass dressed as the Biblical figures. The travelers also received personal names— Balthazar, Melchior, and Gaspar. Once you have got a name you also acquire a life history. So it was believed that Balthazar came from Ethiopia and was black, that Gaspar was the youngest, and that Melchior offered the child thirty gold coins.

In later tradition, the kings meet St. Thomas, who teaches them the Lord's Prayer and the Mass, after which they all go to India and have another job change: They become archbishops. When they

Edmund S. P. Jones was pastor of New York Avenue Presbyterian Church in Washington, D.C., for four years, and Queen's Cross Church in Aberdeen, Scotland, for eighteen years. He is a graduate of the University of Dublin, Cambridge University (England), and St. Andrews University (Scotland). He has published numerous articles in journals and in the British press on contemporary issues, and he has frequently spoken on religious issues on BBC television and radio broadcasts. He is currently working on two books, one on preaching and one on prayer.

were all over one hundred years old they died, and because they are the best loved of all the saints in the New Testament, it was believed that their bodies never saw corruption. So in A.D. 1164, remains that were said to be the miraculously preserved bodies of the Magi were transported from Milan to the Cathedral of Cologne in Germany and laid to rest in a special shrine. It became a great tourist attraction for Christians in the Middle Ages. Today, the devotional appeal of the story remains.

The Bible doesn't actually say how many travelers there were. Frescoes in the catacombs of Rome depict four. St. Augustine said there were twelve, to correspond with the tribes of Israel. A pope in the second century said the number should be three. Looking around at all the nativity scenes today, I reckon he was right!

Now, the nativity stories in Matthew and Luke are confessions, not documentaries. They deal with the *why* of his life rather than the *where* and *how.* That does not mean that they are less true. They convey the deepest faith of believers about the meaning of Jesus' whole life. So what was Matthew declaring when he wrote the story of the mysterious travelers?

One of the oldest interpretations was that the Magi were really Persian astrologers. In the seventh century A.D. when a raiding army of Persians, having sacked Jerusalem, descended on Bethlehem, it spared the Church of the Incarnation because a frieze over the doorway showed one of the Magi clothed in Persian dress. The soldiers did not want to commit sacrilege by disturbing the spirits of their ancestors. That tradition continues to modern times. As late as 1947 a new church in the Iraqi city of Kirkuk was dedicated to the Wise Men. So too the Feast of Epiphany commemorates the revelation of Christ to the Gentiles, and the story of the Magi is usually read at that time.

It all makes sense until we realize one thing: Nowhere else in the New Testament are the Magi regarded as good men. Quite the opposite. They are sinister figures engaged in sorcery and black magic. In the Book of Acts they are the archenemies of both Peter and Paul: "Paul set his eyes on one such and cried, 'Thou child of the devil, thou enemy of all righteousness, wilt thou not cease to pervert the right ways of the Lord?' " (Acts 13:10).

By the time Matthew came to write his Gospel some forty years later, had the sorcerers become saints? Or could the truth be that Matthew's Magi were never the wise men of our Christmas cards at all? That they were what they had always been—namely, professional magicians and dabblers in the occult. Could it be that, far from being introduced to the story as examples of saints, Matthew's intention was the very opposite? That they are the bad guys. If so, then Matthew's witness is that sinners are there from the very beginning, that the halo of this radical new faith has nothing whatever to do with moral uprightness, but with the amazing love of a holy God who falls passionately in love with unholy people. The God of the cradle reveals himself first to the humble and ignorant. Then to the honorable and learned. He reveals himself first to the poor and the unimportant. Then to the rich and influential. He reveals himself first to the East and then to the West.

Now, in the first century there was a widespread belief that the stars controlled human destinies. A nationalist leader whose movement died in a bloody retribution even called himself Bar-Cochba, "Son of the Star." Impersonal sinister forces determined human life: "The fault, dear Brutus, is not in our stars, / But in ourselves, that we are underlings" (*Julius Caesar,* 1.2.140).

Astrology influenced even Jewish religion. Jewish catacombs uncovered in Rome depict the signs of the Zodiac, as do recently excavated Palestinian synagogues. The veil of the temple was embroidered with stars. Today many people still have a pervasive belief that the stars determine their destiny. Nero and Napoléon, Adolf Hitler and Nancy Reagan all had a lively interest in astrology.

So the faith of Matthew's Gospel is that the coming of the Christ child is not simply the assurance that our sins are forgiven. It is the declaration that the One who was born in the night sets us free from those mysterious forces that seem to control our lives. As an early theologian called Ignatius of Antioch wrote: "A star shone in the heavens beyond the light of all stars . . . and from that time all magic and all sorcery ceased."

When Martin Bucer, the great Swiss reformer, lay dying in Cambridge, his friends spoke to him in great alarm of the unfavorable conjunction of stars during his critical illness. The dying man raised himself on his bed, pointed upward, and cried out, "It is He, it is He that ordaineth all things in Heaven and on earth." So if anyone should tell you at this season of the year that poverty, homelessness, and hunger are here to stay, that there's nothing you can do to change the way things are because that's how human nature is ordained to be, I tell you this: "It is He, it is He that ordaineth all things in Heaven and on earth." We are not the playthings of fate or fortune, but women and men set free from the powers of the Evil One by a cradle as well as by a cross. So Matthew's Christmas is not about religious feeling, but about religious action. It is not about sentimentality, but about service. It's not about consumption, but about costly conduct.

The story tells us that the mysterious travelers came from the East to Jerusalem. But where is the East? If you're on the West Coast, the East means New York or Boston. If you're in Rome, the East means Persia. But as Ken Bailey points out, if you stand in Jerusalem and say, "So-and-so is from the East," you mean that the traveler comes from across the Jordan.

In the first century, "the East" referred to all the land from Jordan to Saudi Arabia. Justin Martyr, who was born shortly after New Testament times and lived in Nablus, close to Bethlehem, says on three different occasions that the Magi came from Arabia. That is the earliest reference outside the Bible to the Christmas story. And southern Arabia is the only Middle East area to produce frankincense and myrrh. Could it be, then, that our travelers are in fact Arabs—tribal sheiks from the desert? If they were, is not here another amazing declaration of the Gospel, that at the manger one of the most ancient and most modern of all enmities is reconciled at the crib of the Prince of Peace. There is a tribe in Jordan that has an ancient tradition that long ago its ancestors visited a prophet called Isa—which, translated, means "Jesus."

"And when they saw the young child with Mary his mother they presented unto him gifts, gold, frankincense and myrrh" (Matt. 2:11). How inappropriate for a baby! Is this just another dismal example of letting men do the Christmas shopping? Christians quickly got over the incongruity of the gifts by giving them spiritual significance: Gold stood for love, frankincense for prayer, and myrrh for suffering. So these gifts could point to the mystery of the cross. Perhaps that's one way that faith can interpret the story. On the other hand, if these guys were so lost that they didn't even know that the town they were looking for was a mere six miles down the road from Jerusalem, I wouldn't rely too much on their accurate grasp of events thirty years into the future!

Could it all be simpler and more down-to-earth? For the storyteller, worship means handing over our special interests to the Christ child.

Gold is our economic interest. The Magi place all their wealth, gained by tricks and sorcery from the fearful and the gullible, at the feet of the newborn child. And maybe that's what Christmas is really about in the twentieth century. It is the call to surrender our greed and obsession with material things so that we will find life's treasure in a different place.

Frankincense reflects our religious interest. Some churches use incense as part of their worship. It stands for the institution where power bases are real, where forms can be stronger than compassion, where rituals can be more important than people, and where creeds can end up being valued more than faith. As the great theologian Karl Barth pointed out, we must surrender our religion as well as our secular life to the Christ of the New Testament.

Myrrh stands for our power interest. Myrrh preserves things as they are. It is the symbol of the status quo, the barrier to new ways of thinking, new ways of speaking, and new avenues of caring. Whatever the Christmas message is about, it implies the coming of a new age into an old world.

But myrrh stands for something else. In ancient times as well as modern it was used in embalming. It represents our mortality. Each Christmas we are further along in our pilgrimage, which will some day come to an end. Indeed, for someone today within this building, this will be the last Christmas. As he came to give his life to us, so at this festive season we too offer our life back to him.

The true Christmas season for the writer and reader of the Gospels is one that leads not to consumption but to consecration. In the words of an old prophet at that first Christmas: "Lord letteth now thy servant depart in peace, for mine eyes have seen mine salvation." That is what all our life's journey is about today. And it sums up the deepest truth about the journey of these mysterious travelers so many centuries ago.

10. Taking Life Seriously
Robert McClelland

Luke 16:19

The parable of the rich man and Lazarus in Luke 16 reminds me of the time I attended an evangelism workshop offered by our denomination that was intended to demonstrate the latest techniques for saving souls. A team of experts had come to town intent on training us in the art of making cold calls—door to door—seeking converts for Christ. I was assigned to one of the experts as an observer. The idea was to watch and, thereby, learn the technique. We sallied forth armed with two memorized questions that sooner or later were to be introduced into the conversation with our intended converts. The first question was "If you were to die tonight are you assured that you would go to heaven?" "Yes," "No," or "I don't know" were tolerable answers. The second question, however, was the important one: "On what does your assurance rest?" The only acceptable answer was "Faith in Jesus Christ."

We made our first stop and rang the doorbell. A gracious and charming couple opened the door and invited us in. After the pleasantries were exchanged, in which we learned that the husband was a professor of psychology at a large university, I settled back in my chair to observe. I wanted to see how this was going to unfold. Eventually, the first question—the one about dying and going to

Robert McClelland has served pastorates in Missouri and Illinois and is currently pastor of Gibson Heights Presbyterian Church in St. Louis, Missouri. From 1962 to 1970 he was assistant professor of religion at Illinois College. He is a graduate of San Francisco Theological Seminary and McCormick Theological Seminary, and was awarded the Merrill Fellowship of Harvard Divinity School in 1980. He has published several books, including *God Our Loving Enemy*.

heaven—was introduced into the conversation. "If you died tonight would you go to heaven?" asked the evangelist.

"I don't know," replied the woman pleasantly, "and neither one of us really cares." That was *not* one of the rehearsed answers. It fit none of the anticipated categories and pretty well finished the subject. All that was left for the expert to do was either to accept the fact that the matter was a dead issue as far as our hosts were concerned or to argue with them, trying to convince them of its importance. In any case, the second question was never asked because there was no way it could be inserted into the conversation. My companion was frustrated, and we soon left.

This method of evangelism was based upon the erroneous assumption that if heaven is our home, all of us must surely be homesick. Furthermore, it assumes, we can get there only if we have faith in Jesus Christ. The professor and his wife, however, were focused on life in this world, and the would-be evangelist had nothing to say to someone who had no interest in faith or the life hereafter.

The Church frequently seems preoccupied with the next life and assumes that faith in Christ is required to avoid eternal torment and gain heaven's bliss. Our first reading of this parable, therefore, focuses on the judgment after death. Good guys will win; bad guys will lose! Believers will be rewarded; nonbelievers will be punished.

But this reading of the parable—like the traditional method of evangelism—misfires on two scores. First, according to the parable, faith in Christ has nothing to do with eternal rewards and punishments. Our destiny is determined not by our faith in a savior—but by our attitude toward others. The rich man walked past Lazarus every day, but he had no compassion for him. Lazarus's needs were obvious, but the rich man felt no sense of obligation in meeting them. It was not his lack of faith in Christ that was his problem, it was his lack of regard for Lazarus.

Second, the parable's focus is on life, not death. As with the professor and his wife, the concern is with this world, not the next. Religion has led us to believe that life in the next world is what really matters. Heaven and hell are where the real action is; everything else is secondary and preliminary. Our actions here are of importance only insofar as they determine our eternal destiny. We do good in order to get to heaven. As a result, Christian spirituality has often discounted life in this world, and those who benefit from our charitable activities become mere pawns in the self-centered game of salvation. D. H. Lawrence labeled such apparent charity "greedy giving." We are good for ulterior reasons—because life here is only a means to a greater end.

I mean to suggest that the point of this parable is instruction not in how to make it in the next life, but in living well in this one. It draws its meaning from the surrounding teachings recorded by Luke, which make it clear that Jesus wants us to live in this world wisely, responsibly, and charitably. The issues that Jesus sets before us are larger than putting stars in our individual crowns. Human suffering is not a matter of indifference to God. Indeed, it is a matter of *eternal* importance. God's concern for the well-being of others here on earth follows us to the grave . . . and beyond. In this parable God is less concerned with our sinful bumps and warts than with the needs of those around us.

The question the Bible continually asks is, What is the focus of your life? Do we live for ourselves—our comfort, our security, our salvation—or for others? Micah, the prophet, prompts us with the correct answer: "He has showed you, O man, what is good; and what does the Lord require of you but to do justice, and to love kindness, and to walk humbly with your God?" (Mic. 6:8). That demand remained unchanged through all the years separating the Old from the New Testament. Jesus merely gave it visibility and clarity when he told his followers to feed the hungry, visit the prisoner, and clothe the naked. To love God is to love the neighbor—who, it must be noted, is not only the person living next door but any needy person in the world. That covers a lot of uncomfortable ground. The eternal question to be asked—here and hereafter—is simply, How are the neighbors doing? Their welfare must be of genuine concern to us because it is to God.

So too, life on our planet earth. Its creation was an act of God. But its destruction could well be our doing: polluting the earth with our waste; cutting down rain forests; killing off species of wildlife; punching holes in the protective ozone layer. The photograph of the earth taken from the moon should make it abundantly clear that we are all part of an intricate and delicate ecosystem. This morning as I was putting on my suit, I reached into the breast pocket of the coat and pulled out a slip of paper that read: "This garment has been inspected by number 46." Even the clothes we wear are part of a social network on which we depend.

The question that the parable raises for us is, What are we going to do with our world? How are we going to shape its history? What legacy do we leave for the neighbors who come after us? Dietrich Bonhoeffer argues that for Christians the only ethical question is, How shall the next generation live? We are stewards of our time and place in history whether we construe it globally or locally. We are responsible for the estate that is passed on to others.

The purpose of the parable, then, is to direct our attention to the serious business of living in this world rather than pointing to the next. Indeed, the parable warns about allowing our attention to wander. We do not have all the time in the world to be about it. A sudden turn of events reminds us that we are not immortal: a serious accident; the discovery of a lump while taking a shower. Our lives are bounded by birth and by death . . . our death. Søren Kierkegaard proclaimed the earnest thought of death to be life's greatest ally. When we begin to do the arithmetic of life, it brings a sense of urgency with it. No one can do our living for us. We get threescore and ten years, the Psalmist says; even if by reason of strength (and the luck of the draw) we have fourscore to get it right, yet we are soon gone. We fly away like a sigh. This awareness of limits means we can take up a conscious stance with regard to our inevitable mortality. We can avoid squandering our time.

A woman in the hospital was weeping after being told she was terminally ill with cancer. When a friend sought to console her she replied, "I'm not weeping because I'm dying. I'm weeping because I never lived." Her remorse came from missed opportunities to live—a failure to discover the unique miracle of her life and take it seriously.

Kurt Vonnegut's lines catch the amazement and delight of the miraculous opportunity we all have by virtue of our birth.

> God made mud . . .
> God got lonesome . . .
> So God said to some mud, "sit up! . . .
> See all I've made," said God, "the hills,
> the sea, the sky, the stars." . . .
> And I was some of the mud that got to sit up
> and look around . . .
> "Lucky me, luck mud."[1]

Yet with our lives comes a sense of responsibility for fulfilling the unique opportunity to live them. We realize that if we do not find purpose in our living, no one can do it for us. The opportunities that life offers me, of course, are different from the ones it presents to you. Lazarus is not at my doorstep, nor is he probably waiting at yours . . . but someone is! I cannot drink the rich man's cup of responsibility, but I can drink mine. Indeed, no one can do it for me.

In my younger days when I was learning to fly I had to practice takeoffs and landings. After one particularly rough landing— something on the order of a controlled crash—I commented ruefully to my instructor, "That was a terrible landing." His reply contained the wisdom of the ages: "It's a good landing if you can walk away from it."

I suspect God is not interested in the style of our landings . . . or our lives. Onlookers may roll their eyes and the Pharisees may cluck and comment. But not God. When we stand before our Creator to render an accounting of our days, God's concern will not be with our sins or shortcomings. They are foregone conclusions. They are simply part of the cost of living the great adventure. No, God's concern will be with our ability to walk away from our lives with some sense of appreciation for occasions to love seized, chances to care taken, and opportunities to leave the world a better place attended to.

Jesus' parable heightens our sense of responsibility for living well. We have only one shot at the landing, one go-around. As the selfish rich man woefully found out, we have only a few years to make this planet a better place, or the life of our neighbor more bearable. The lesson to be learned is that we need not be actively evil to miss resting in the bosom of Abraham; we need only be inactively indifferent. We do not have to kick the person who is down—only step over him.

As followers of Christ we are to share ourselves and our blessings with others—not because heaven follows, for that would imply that this life is not as important as the next, but because it is the only opportunity we will have to responsibly live in the time and space in which we have been placed. Jesus warns: "If you save your life, you will lose it. Only if you give it away, will you find it." We can debate the economics and the logic of his teaching, but we ought to be clear that this is what he believed . . . and taught. It is in this dying-living, living-dying that we find meaning for our lives.

As human beings we can choose how to live and, sometimes, how to die. The cross of Christ reminds us that Jesus chose to die. He was not a victim of circumstances, nor was he a tragic hero. He could have died in bed of old age. But instead, Jesus chose to die. "My hour has not yet come," he kept saying during the days leading up to his final journey to Jerusalem. Then suddenly, during the last meal with his disciples, Jesus uttered the words that must have popped their eyes open: "The hour has come!" (John 17:1). The words burst forth, not as a death knell, but as the glorious climax to life intentionally lived.

When Jesus invites us to take up our cross and follow him, he invites us to live for a cause and die for a reason. We go around only once, and Martin Luther King, Jr., put it well when he said, "Until we are willing to die for something, we're not fit to live for anything."

"Okay! Okay! But heaven! What about heaven?" someone is probably asking.

In Jesus' view, heaven is the projection forward—into God's time and space—of a life lived wisely, responsibly, and charitably here. Apparently, self-consciousness survives death and we live either with regrets over our lack of responsible stewardship for the years allotted to us, or with joy at new opportunities offered. To be found trustworthy in our custodial responsibilities is to be promoted to larger responsibilities. To whom much is given, much will be expected. The point is graphically made by Jesus in the parable of the talents (Matt. 25:14–30). To one person ten talents are given, to another five, and to another one. The distribution is not equal, yet each is expected to invest the resources for the benefit of the landlord. Those who do are put in charge of greater wealth. The one who fails in his stewardship by hiding his wealth discovers that even that which he has is taken from him. The good news is that if God finds us trustworthy in carrying out the loving concern of the Creator for the planet and its people, we are entrusted with even greater responsibilities in the life to come.

More than that we dare not say. It would be nice if we could add, ". . . and they all lived happily ever after." But Jesus—always the realist—was not in the business of telling fairy tales or parables with happy endings. He knew that we live by the choices we make.

The ending of the story, therefore, is ours to write. Jesus simply said, "Those who have ears to hear . . . let them hear!"

NOTE

1. Kurt Vonnegut, *Cat's Cradle* (New York: Dell Books, 1963), 149.

III. DOCTRINAL/ THEOLOGICAL

11. Commencement Address
M. Vernon Davis

I am honored to have this opportunity to speak to you today. On behalf of the faculty I want to salute you who graduate and commend you on your accomplishment.

The father of one of our graduates here today (whose bumper sticker says, incidentally, "I'd rather be fishing") heard that I had been asked to speak. He came to me and said, "You've had your chance at these people for years. What more could you possibly say to them that will do any good at this point? Why don't you just congratulate them and let them go? Let us all go." He wanted me to put it to a vote of the graduates. That was a temptation—but one that somehow, some way, I have found the strength to resist. I trust that there will be value in this one last word, and that it will not keep us too long from where we might rather be.

When James Sanders published his book *God Has a Story Too*, he dedicated it in a quite unusual way. On the dedication page are these words:

> For Sisters Agnes and Iris and my sister, Nell,
>   women who told me the tomb was empty,
>   and
>   for Ruth and Joe Brown Love,
>   who told me my head need not be[1]

The dedication expresses Sanders's gratitude to the three women (two Pentecostal preachers and his own sister) who were responsible for his becoming a Christian as a young boy during a holiness revival meeting. He was also grateful to a couple who as campus ministers years later helped shape his vision of becoming

M. Vernon Davis is Vice-President for Academic Affairs and Dean of the Faculty at Midwestern Baptist Theological Seminary in Kansas City, Missouri. Dr. Davis served for twelve years as pastor of the First Baptist Church in Alexandria, Virginia. He is a graduate of Baylor University and Southwestern Baptist Theological Seminary, where he received a doctorate. This address was given at Midwestern Baptist Theological Seminary on May 22, 1993.

a Christian scholar. The book became an opportunity to acknowledge gifts that he could never pay back but only pass on. The dedication speaks of two basic convictions that guide James Sanders's life: The tomb is empty; his head need not be. The gospel is true; all of the gifts God has given us are required in our stewardship of it.

Perhaps these final moments before unleashing you onto an unsuspecting world may be best spent in affirming the experience that brought us here and acknowledging the responsibility with which we leave. Commencement day is an appropriate time to reflect on the convictions that are basic to our lives as Christians and the competence that we need to become good ministers of the gospel. When we seriously engage in doing that, most of us inevitably bring to our minds the names and faces of people to whom we are indebted—those who first introduced us to Jesus, those whose lives and witness made it possible for us to be where we are today on the journey of discipleship.

We entered this process of theological education because we came to believe that the tomb is empty and to know the risen Christ who lives within us and who continues to go before us. We came to that conviction in varied ways. For some of us the dawn of that day of transformation came up like thunder; for others it silently stole into our souls almost unnoticed, like the awareness of light that can come after a struggling and sleepless night. Some of us were introduced to Jesus in ways that now bring smiles to our faces because of their naiveté and even their ineptness. Yet, however we came to know the living Christ as more than a historical fact, we are forever grateful to those who told us that the tomb was empty! Let none of us condemn the bridges that brought us across.

Today we celebrate both the convictions we have been given and the competence we have gained. The two are not mutually exclusive, although some at times seem to want to choose one and abandon the other. Conviction and competence need not be strangers, much less engaged in civil war within ourselves.

As never before, the world needs to hear the conviction that the tomb is empty. People need the Lord—the living Lord. People need to see the difference in those of us who have heard and believed the gospel proclamation. People need the witness of those who have discovered in Jesus the most dependable fact in the universe, the clue that unlocks the mystery of life. People need to look on life from the vantage point of the empty tomb and in the energizing power of the living Christ.

I do not know how you first heard the authentic voice of Jesus out of the babble of all the rest, but today is a time for gratitude that the Christ of the empty tomb walked into your life and you heard that enduring challenge to discipleship: "Follow me!" The shape of your obedience to that call has brought you to this place. The sovereign freedom of the Spirit of God means that none of us can know where our response to that invitation will lead. We only know that the journey will be in the company of the One we can trust to work in us each day, molding us into the image of the Son. We go also from this place with the conviction that what the living Christ is doing in us he wills to do through us for people who need the wholeness and hope found in the gospel.

We go as people who are convinced that the tomb is empty— and that makes all the difference in the world. We also go as people who believe that our heads need not be and must not be. The gospel of resurrection is not an easy word to hear and believe in the world where you go to minister. Millions have not heard it at all; millions who have heard it live as if it were not so. With the materials available in the culture of every age, people seem intent to fashion new crosses on which to crucify Christ and carve new tombs into which they can inter him. Tragically, this can be done by those who claim to be Christ's friends, as well as by his enemies.

To go to minister with hearts full of conviction but heads empty of any idea of how to share that conviction effectively in this world is to experience failure and frustration. The goal of your education has been "a way of education that joins the mind with the heart."[2] All of God's gifts in creation can be used in the service of God's gift in redemption. Indeed, this is the highest use of our knowledge and skills. As Parker Palmer has reminded us, there is a knowledge that is gained in pursuit of control and a knowledge that is gained as a result of curiosity; but the knowledge we seek is that which is produced out of compassion.

We search for truth in the service of love. Without compassion, what is in your head may destroy rather than create. It may serve your self-interest in the world as it is rather than become the instrument for producing the world that can be.[3] What has been put into your heads and hearts has been placed there to serve the foundational affirmations of the Kingdom of God: Christ has died! Christ is risen! Christ will come again!

When we fail to use the best we know in the service of what we believe, *we fashion new tombs for the Christ.* In the marketplace of competing ways of life, how often we have reinterred the living Christ in work that is unworthy of him. Too often we have abandoned the pursuit of excellence. This is the day that demands competence in the handling of things holy, excellence in the doing of God's work.

Your theological education has sought to give you tools with which you can work effectively in any circumstance to which God calls you. We have done what we can do for you. Today we are like parents watching their children leave home, hoping that we have prepared you for all that is out there, but certain that we have not. We hold the bandages and ointment ready.

We send you forth in the hope that you will be able to remember what you know. We watch you go with the prayer that you will be good stewards of all that is in your minds. As you go, we trust that the scriptures will never have reason to sue you for exegetical malpractice.

We send you forth to read the Bible for all its worth, through a hermeneutic of the Resurrection. The best place to read the Bible is in the open doorway of an empty tomb. The best light in which to read the Bible is that provided by the inner witness of the Spirit of the living Christ.

When the Bible is read through the Resurrection, it reveals a liberating gospel. We send you to use its words not to bind but to set free. Go not to be primarily proclaimers of judgment, but to be heralds of grace; not to add burdens to the people's already backbreaking load, but "to bring good news to the afflicted, to bind up the brokenhearted, to proclaim liberty to the captives, and freedom to prisoners" (Isa. 61:1). We send you forth to proclaim the gospel in the liberating power of the Risen Christ to all who have been denied full participation in the Kingdom of God.

This gospel demands the best you can offer. We send you forth with the challenge to do your best and to stand by your words of witness.[4] Shoddy workmanship in the service of the Risen Christ can carve new tombs and cause the world to wonder whether this story is really true.

I have learned of a quite interesting building practice in ancient Rome. When a Roman arch had been completed and the scaffolding was being removed, the engineer on the project was required to stand beneath it. This obviously created a significant "tremble factor." If the arch came crashing down, the engineer would be the first to know. He had a personal concern that the materials used be the best available and that the workmanship be characterized by excellence. Is it any wonder that so many Roman arches have survived?[5] Perhaps we would give more attention to our proclamations and programs if we had to "stand under" them. Too often we find it easy to send out our résumés even before the scaffolding comes off.

In this difficult and demanding world you will need all that is in your head to be effective witnesses to the empty tomb. Do not shrink back from the challenges or fail to believe in the new light that is able to break forth from God's word. In these words of an ancient prayer: "From the cowardice that dare not face new truth, the laziness contented with half-truths, and the arrogance that thinks it knows all truths, O Christ deliver us."

We carve new tombs for the Christ when in challenging times we take refuge in a narrow dogmatism. Dogmatism closes too soon on truth and sweeps stubborn facts that will not fit our theories under the rug. Dogmatism closes too soon on an experience that otherwise would allow new times and places to expand our understanding of the truth we know. Dogmatism closes too soon on what is meaningful to us and denies us the fruit of another's discoveries of Christ. Dogmatism frames the picture of the truth with the view from our window and does not acknowledge there are other vistas from which to experience the reality of the living Christ.

When we think straight, we treasure the insight we have received from others and what we have experienced for ourselves. Even then, however, we acknowledge that our vision is partial. If the Apostle Paul felt it important to say that he saw through a glass darkly, it is rather presumptuous for us from our vantage point to exclaim that we have it all figured out for ourselves and for others.

> Strong Son of God, immortal Love,
>   whom we, that have not seen thy face,
> By faith, and faith alone embrace,
> Believing where we cannot prove;

> . . .
> Our little systems have their day;
> They have their day and cease to be;
> They are but broken lights of thee,
> And thou, O Lord, art more than they.[6]

When we become too enamored with the ways in which we have come to say the gospel, we have difficulty hearing it in the accents of another. We need to pray for the grace of humility and the gift of listening as well as speaking. This is never easy.

When he was running for president in 1952, Adlai Stevenson said, "The sound of tireless voices is the price we pay for the right to hear the music of our own opinions . . . . Everyone has a right to be heard; but no one has the right to strangle democracy with a single set of vocal cords."[7]

In times when we are tempted to deny to another the liberty of conscience because we have deified our own, we need to remember that God just may not have spoken the last word on the subject to us. In the grip of our own strongly held convictions, we need to remember that more people believe that the Bible is the Word of God than can ever agree on a doctrine of inspiration. More come to kneel at the cross "just as they are" than can ever agree on a theory of atonement. More celebrate the reality of redemption in taking the bread and cup than can ever agree on just how Christ is present in the experience.

> There's a wideness in God's mercy,
> Like the wideness of the sea,
> There's a kindness in God's justice,
> Which is more than liberty.
> . . .
> But we make God's love too narrow
> By false limits of our own
> And we magnify God's strictness
> With a zeal God would not own.

We carve new tombs for Christ when we fail to be good stewards of our own heritage. One of the greatest dangers you will face as ministers is the temptation to think according to the secular assumptions that dominate our culture. To many today the past is irrelevant, and the future is uncertain. In living for the present, for success in the "now," we are tempted to jettison the lessons learned from our forebears—lessons often learned through personal sacrifice. In so doing we may achieve success as celebrated by our culture but fail to measure up to Jesus' criteria of true discipleship. Evangelicals must avoid the errors of an earlier liberalism that accommodates the culture for the sake of relevance while losing the heart and soul of the gospel.

Much in our Baptist heritage can serve us well in such a time as this. As Wendell Berry has said, "Culture preserves the maps and records of past journeys so that no generation will permanently destroy the route."[8] Place in your heads and hearts the gift of those who have gone before; it may serve you well in times of wandering in the wilderness.

We have a heritage of freedom, a legacy of liberty. It is not the gift of an easy way or one of pious permissiveness. It does not encourage everyone to do as one pleases. It is not a heritage that shows us how to avoid sacrifice; rather, it calls us to self-sacrifice in response to the self-giving servant Christ whom we follow. At the same time, it proclaims that the sacrifice we make must be our own and that we must resist sacrificing others on our own altars, however holy or worthy they seem to us to be.

There will always be endless and enticing arguments to give up your freedom. Certainly we are not called to crawl up on every cross. There are many causes worth not dying for. But the danger we face is that we will find it too easy to rationalize our desire for self-preservation. When we do, the call to deny ourselves, take up our cross, and follow the crucified Christ who has been raised from death will come to sound like hollow words echoing in our own souls.

With all that is in your heads and hearts, go to serve Christ in the world of common life. *We carve new tombs to inter the Christ when we seek to keep him in the church rather than among all the people for whom he died.* Yet it is to this kind of incarnational ministry that he has called us.

You have learned the language of the church. You have acquired the skills to lead in the work of the church. You have discovered security in the fellowship of the church. You will be tempted to live out your ministries inside the walls of the church and look out on the world through stained-glass windows.

To go into the world as incarnations of the love of Jesus Christ is to meet the same kind of opposition that he encountered. Yet this is precisely what discipleship involves. As Dietrich Bonhoeffer has taught us so well, to know Christ is to know him in the world or not at all. Often when we issue Jesus' invitation, "Follow me," to others, we give them the impression that he was primarily going to church and is bidding us to follow him there. Usually he wasn't. The call to follow is a call to discover the path of Jesus into the world. How much easier it would be if we could avoid the implications of the Incarnation for our own ministries.

On August 1, 1964, *Ranger 7* was on target for its mission to the moon. The *Ranger* series was designed to send unmanned spacecraft to photograph the moon's surface and to send back to earth visual detail that scientists had not been previously able to acquire. The project had been plagued by six previous failures, or, as NASA said, only "partial successes." I watched television with millions of Americans as *Ranger 7* neared its goal. The cameras were turned on, and across the vast miles of space came images of high resolution far superior to any we had ever seen. The people in the Rockwell laboratories sent up a cheer of victory and relief. A proud nation was in awe.

Several days later I read an interesting story about something that happened in the aftermath of that event. The officials in California took the pictures from the mission that night and flew across the continent through the night to show them personally to President Johnson at the White House the next morning. Everything was in readiness in the screening room. The people had come in according to protocol, and when the president entered, the lights were turned out. Then the projector malfunctioned. (I have always thought that the best demons were assigned to audiovisuals.)

I smiled at the story. People could transmit clear images from the moon's surface to earth. They could take the pictures across the continent in one night on a jet airplane. But they could not get the images the last few, critical feet from the projector to the screen. I smiled, until it turned into a painful parable related to all we have talked about here today.

Through grace God gave the definitive revelation to us in Jesus Christ the incarnate Son and Risen Lord. His life, death, and resurrection form the heart of the gospel. People who have followed him through the centuries have borne witness to this good news across the barriers of time and culture. Faithful witnesses to the truth that the tomb is empty continued telling the story until some-one told me. Why is it that I have such difficulty in getting that revelation the last few feet from myself to others? Why is it so difficult to bridge the gulf between the study and the pulpit, the pulpit and the pew, the pew and the pavement, Sunday and Mon-day? Why is it so difficult to project that saving image of the living Christ to those nearest and dearest to us? This is our enduring challenge—to incarnate the witness to the living Christ in the world for which he died.

The future is uncertain, and contemplating it can fill us with fear. In "Epistle to a Godson," W. H. Auden wrote to his godson, Philip Spender. He wrestled with the futility of one generation seeking to give helpful advice to another in a world that was rapidly changing. He said:

> In yester times it
> was different: the old could still be helpful
> when they could nicely envisage the future
> as a named and settled landscape their children
> would make the same sense of as they did,
> laughing and weeping at the same stories.

Today the challenge is even greater. Our confidence does not lie in our being able to know the "named and settled landscape" of the future. Nor does it lie in a mistaken assumption that we have given you an inexhaustible supply of generic answers guaranteed to be effective in every time and place. Our confidence rests solely in the glorious truth that the tomb is empty and in an enduring hope that your heads and hearts are not.

NOTES

1. James Sanders, *God Has a Story Too* (Philadelphia: Fortress Press, 1979), v.

2. Parker Palmer, *To Know As We Are Known* (San Francisco: Harper San Francisco, 1993), x.

3. Ibid., 6–8.

4. See Wendell Berry, *Standing by Words* (Berkeley: North Point Press, 1982).

5. John Silber, *Straight Shooting*, 163–64.

6. Alfred, Lord Tennyson, from "In Memoriam."

7. Adlai Stevenson, *The Wit and Wisdom of Adlai Stevenson*, 10.

8. Wendell Berry, *What Are People For?* (Berkeley: North Point Press, 1990), 8.

12. On Being a Baptist

Bill Moyers

It is providential to me that Marion Hays is here this evening. Many Baptist heroes stirred my imagination when I was young, from John Bunyan and John Milton to Roger Williams and William Carey, from Adoniram Judson and Annie Armstrong to E. Y. Mullins and George Truett. But they were dead or distant heroes, admired from afar. Marion's husband, Brooks, was the first Baptist hero I met face-to-face. Brooks's courageous stand during the 1958 school-desegregation crisis cost him his seat as congressman from Little Rock, but it won for him a place in legions of hearts. "This is Mr. Hays," said Martin Luther King, Jr., when he introduced Brooks to a friend. "He has suffered with us."

For Brooks, Christianity was about challenge, not comfort, and politics was a parish where one tried to serve the poor and powerless. Senator Sam Ervin said Brooks possessed an "understanding heart." It overflowed with a love that embraced even his enemies—even Orval Faubus and Richard Nixon. And he was a cheerful crusader, with humor for a lance. Like many of us he resisted the handcuffs of ideology. During his last campaign he pointed to the dog at his side and said, "Old Fergus here, who goes with me every day, is a liberal when he's sniffing through the bushes looking for a rabbit, but a conservative when he buries the bone."

Bill Moyers is executive editor of Public Affairs TV, Inc. He was born in Hugo, Oklahoma, and was educated at the University of Texas, Edinburgh University, and Southwestern Baptist Theological Seminary. He was Special Assistant to President Lyndon Johnson (1963–66) and served as Press Secretary to the President (1965–66). His publications include *Listening to America, Joseph Campbell and the Power of Myth, A World of Ideas,* and *Healing and the Mind.* These remarks were delivered at a midnight prayer meeting at the First Baptist Church of Washington, D.C., on the eve of the inauguration of President Bill Clinton and Vice President Al Gore, and were published in *Religion & Values in Public Life: A Forum from Harvard Divinity School* 1, no. 3 (Spring 1993).

I met Brooks when he was president of the Southern Baptist Convention and spoke in chapel at Southwestern Baptist Theological Seminary, where I was soon to graduate. I maneuvered to be the one who drove Brooks and his wife, Marion, to the airport after his speech. When he learned that I had studied journalism at the University of Texas and worked for Senator Lyndon Johnson in both Austin and Washington, he put his hand on my shoulder and said, "When you finish seminary you ought to give thought to government; public service can be a calling, too." He admitted that politics could be hell sometimes, but—and he grinned that long snaggly grin of his—"after working for LBJ it should be a pleasure to wrestle with the devil."

I never forgot his hand on my shoulder, never forgot his counsel; and often through the years I have been reminded of that favorite passage of his from Isaiah, where "you who pursue deliverance, who seek the Lord," are urged to "look to the rock from which you were hewn, and to the quarry from which you were digged." Or as my own rough translation from the Hebrew says, "Remember your roots."

This is what brings us here tonight. We come not as Democrat or Republican, male or female, black or white, politician or journalist, but as members of an extended family of faith. And we are here to remember our roots. Baptists hold dear the contention of that early forbearer who said that "the magistrate is not by virtue of his office to meddle with religion on matters of conscience, to force or compel anyone to this or that form of religion or doctrine, but to leave religion free to every individual conscience." That conviction is sacred to us. Yet we do not believe that separation of church and state means the hermetic exclusion of religion from politics. We believe Harvey Cox got it right when he said that in secular society "politics does what metaphysics once did, it brings unity and meaning to human life and thought." And we agree with Jim Wallis that "the relationship between politics and morality is absolutely vital to the future," that our challenge is to take the rhetoric of "values," "vision," and "new covenant" that pervaded our recent election and see if there is common ground for action.

Baptists have much to offer the conversation of democracy, beginning with candor about our own diversity and raucous history. Baptists have been to the left of the American establishment—and to the right. Jesse Jackson is a Baptist; so is

Jesse Helms. Baptists defended slavery, and Baptists agitated to end it. Some black Baptist churches today are precincts of the Democratic Party, while in some white churches GOP stands for God's Own Preserve. Some Baptists read the Bible as if it were a Triple-A road map to Armageddon; others find it a spiritual codebook to the mysteries and miracles of the Kingdom within. Millions of Baptists see American culture as the enemy. Millions of others joyfully proclaim that we are part and parcel of the show. Onlookers shake their heads at how people so disputatious could be defined by a common name; those of us who wear it shrug our shoulders at the anomalies and schisms and go on punching (usually each other).

We are Baptists for many reasons. The experience is so much a part of my story that I would be unable to explain myself to my grandson without it. Newman McLarry's ringing call to repentance took me into the waters of Baptism when I was twelve, and Brownlow Hastings's quiet appeals to reason took me back into those waters six years later. Between Bible drills the burly contractor who doubled as our Sunday School teacher, Bill Price, let us slug him in the stomach to prove that hard work produced a hard body. One of our sopranos sang off-key to the entire church, but no one cared because she brought the best custard pies to dinners-on-the-ground. These may seem banal recollections, but I learned about humanity in that Baptist church, learned about frailty and forgiveness and fellowship, and if the anecdotes are unremarkable, the journey wasn't.

I also learned about democracy in that church. It was the very embodiment of home rule. In deciding church affairs every believer had an equal voice. Every leader called to office—whether pastor, deacon, or teacher—was subject to a vote of the congregation; and leaders were expected to be servants, not rulers. It was the pew, and not the pulpit, that we thought should be exalted. This leveling meant we fought a lot. My father said Adam and Eve must have been the first Democrats because only Democrats could mess up Paradise, and he was certain Cain and Abel were the first Baptists because they introduced fratricide to the Bible. But faith called us to a public stand, and there was no place in our politics and religion for bystanders. It never occurred to us to ask the Irishman's question, "Is this a private fight, or can anyone get in it?" We knew from our past that politics is where liberty is saved or lost, where issues are decided, justice mediated, and values defended. Neither church nor state is served by anemic democracy. So Baptists plunge into the thick of the fray. And we do so with an ardor for equality that springs from the hot coals of faith.

At the core of our faith is what we call *soul competency*—the competence of the individual before God. Created with the imprint of divinity, from the mixed clay of earth, we are endowed with the capacity to choose, to be (as my brother James Dunn puts it) response-able, a grown-up before God—making my own case, accounting for my own sins, asking my own questions, and expecting in good faith that when all is said and done I'll get a fair hearing and just verdict. At last count there are twenty-seven varieties of Baptists in this country; the brand that appeals to many of us holds that while the Bible is our anchor, it is no icon; that revelation continues, truth is not frozen in doctrine but emerges from experience and encounter, and continuity is found in the community of faith that includes both saints and sinners. In Jesus we see the power of the living Word over tired practice and dead belief. In his relationships with women, the sick, the outcast, and the stranger—even with the tax collector—Jesus kept breaking new ground. The literal observance of the law was not to quench the spirit of justice. "The Sabbath was made for man and not man for the Sabbath."

These beliefs do not make for lawless anarchy or the religion of Lone Rangers. Nor do they mean we can float safely on the little raft of our own faith while the community flounders. Our beliefs form the ground of personhood. They aim for a community with moral integrity, the wholeness that flows from mutual obligation. Our religion is an adventure in freedom within boundaries of accountability. Governor Clinton and Senator Gore, it may be that this inbred tendency in free church life is one of the best gifts you bring to high office at this most pluralistic, fragmented, and perplexed time in our history.

There is in the tide of affairs what General George Patton called "the unforgiving minute." Decision and choice force fate. Opportunity lost is lost forever. The road not taken disappears. The unforgiving minute allows no second chances; at such a moment in our nation's life the gridlock becomes permanent, the cleavage between classes irreversible, the injustices fixed, the fiscal profligacy immutable; millions give up on the system for good, and the dream of forging a single American nation from our separate realities dies.

So this unforgiving minute—this fullness of time—begs from us, citizen and politician alike, a renewed sense of religion and politics as challenge and service. But of our leaders it makes the most severe demands. Vaclav Havel writes that while politicians are indeed a mirror of their society, the opposite is also true; society is a mirror of its politicians. It is largely up to the politicians which will suppress, whether they rely on the good in each citizen or on the bad. As we move toward the twenty-first century, Havel says, we need politicians who trust not only a scientific representation of the world but also the world itself; who live not only in sociological statistics but in real people; who trust not only the summary reports that cross their desk each morning but their own feelings; not only an adopted ideology but their own thoughts; not only an objective interpretation of reality but their own soul. The ancient Israelites had a word for this: *hochma*—the science of the heart. Intelligence, feeling, and perception combine to create the moral imagination. The science of the heart.

Thirty years ago, when I was young in this town, I would not have understood this. I possessed far more energy than wisdom, and craved facts, information, and action. But time and experience, love and loss, round the rough edges of pride, zeal, and partisanship, and I see now that it is not just knowledge alone—not just facts and reasons—that will transform our lives or bring about a just society; what we also need is truth, the truth of the competent soul. It is this that enables us to respond as Gloucester does when asked by Lear: "How do you see the world?" And Gloucester, blind Gloucester, replies: "I see it feelingly."

Tomorrow at noon the real struggle begins. I can tell you that rarely is it a titanic, heroic, winner-take-all battle. It is rather a series of daily, often small, sometimes subtle battles. Because of the persistence of what Reinhold Niebuhr called "the sinful pride and self-deception" that afflict us all (what Baptists know as "original sin"), the hardest struggle of all is the one that is waged within. The character of a government is forged every day in the soul of its leader as he chooses for power or for justice.

So I conclude where we began—with our friend Brooks Hays, and something you may have heard quoted by him over the years, something he held fast even though it cost him the office he served so well among the people he loved so much. Remember?

"It is only religion reaching the ultimate solitude of the soul that can create the unpurchasable man, and it is only man unpurchasable by any society that creates the sound society" (William Ernest Hocking).

13. God with Us
Jan M. Lochman

John 1:1–14

I.

My dear brothers and sisters, some time ago I took part in a celebration in which the late writer Friedrich Dürrenmatt gave a notorious speech. In it he compared Switzerland to a prison in which the prisoners also reciprocally play the role of warden. The image was hotly disputed. Some listeners seemed amused; most were rather angry.

I have been compelled since then to think about this image often, even while preparing this sermon—of course, not just in special connection with Switzerland, but in the sense of a comparable human situation to which the biblical message of Christmas is related. Indeed, it is striking that some of the most beautiful Christmas songs speak of prison; of the lot of prisoners. Since my youth I have sung the song of the Bohemian Brothers in which the coming of Christ is celebrated with the words "You have visited us, miserable slaves, in prison." And in a German Christmas song especially dear to my heart, a song by Paul Gerhard, are these impressive words: "Our prison, where we sat, where grief beyond measure gnawed at our very heart, is broken open—and we are free."

Jan M. Lochman, a native of Czechoslovakia, is a member of the Swiss Reformed Church. Dr. Lochman has been Professor of Systematic Theology at the University of Basel since 1969 and is the author of a number of books, most recently *Christ or Prometheus: A Quest of Theological Identity.* This sermon was translated from the German by James W. Cox.

No doubt about it, the message of Christmas has to do with imprisonment, with literal imprisonment, with the need of prisoners, the tortured, the outcasts. The author of the Czech song we have selected for this service, Bishop Jan Augusta, was one of them. He spent twelve years in the most horrible prison on account of his faith. But we must also consider the other captivity, the figurative captivity that Paul Gerhard speaks of. We are all of us meant. We who are prisoners of trouble, people whose hearts are eaten away by anxiety, plagued by self-made troubles and external troubles—even we are addressed in those words. It is dark on the horizon of Christmas; on *our* horizon of life.

Dear friends, the word about the *darkness* is also in our text, impossible to miss. It appears twice. But this darkness is not its real theme, but rather its background. The message of the Evangelist is this: *the light.* "And the light shines in the darkness" (John 1:5). The prologue to John's Gospel witnesses this event. From its inexhaustible riches I would like, above all, to emphasize its beginning and its middle—these sentences: *"In the beginning was the Word"* and *"The Word became flesh and lived among us."*

II.

"In the beginning was the Word"—with this sentence John begins his message. He begins with the beginning. Recently I read this sentence in a piece of writing where I, at first, had not expected it. It was what Václav Havel had said about the Word in a speech. He delivered it some time ago—therefore, not yet as a famous European statesman, but rather as a more or less unknown writer, fresh out of prison. It is a moving piece of writing, this speech, a poignant confession of the value of the free word. Havel reflects on the ambiguity of human words: "The Word is a mysterious, ambiguous, treacherous manifestation. It can be a ray of light in the realm of darkness, yet it can also be a deadly arrow." The Word is a dazzling, vulnerable good, with the promise, however, of becoming life giving. For the human word stands under the protection of the divine Word: "In the beginning was the Word, and the Word was with God, and the Word was God."

The Christmas horizon is illuminated only with this Word, the holy Word *God.* Therefore it is very much the task of the Evangelists to emphasize precisely this—the beginning with the Word, the beginning with God. As to that, one cannot be easily mistaken. The story of Christmas is, of course, clearly a human story. We may and must also speak of that in the exposition of our text. However, we remain faithful to the biblical perspective on Christmas only if we explain unmistakably: The beginning is in the hands of God. In their own way, Matthew and Luke say this when they speak of the Virgin Birth or when the angels join in the song of praise: "Glory to God in the highest." And now the same accent, especially clear in the prologue to John's gospel: "In the beginning was the Word, and the Word was with God, and the Word was God."

Begin with the beginning. This applies not merely to the Christmas story but rather—in its light—to the life of each and every one of us, to our words and the circumstances of our lives. We are exposed to many words in the course of our life. Helpful ones and hurtful ones. And we speak and write in our lifetime many words that are helpful and hurtful. Often in the thicket of words and life's circumstances we do not know our way around. Then it is good to hear and to recall that in the beginning was and remains the one Word, God. The original, inextinguishable light from above, set ablaze from that source, falls upon our life as in the Christmas story, in spite of all kinds of darkness.

One of the Swiss heraldic mottoes that spoke helpfully to me long before I came to Switzerland was the old motto of the Swiss: "Through human confusion and through the providence of God, the Swiss are governed"—a true key sentence for the meaning of our history. It would not be amiss if we would remind each other again and again of this motto. Make no mistake: The motto is not the exaltation of our complacency. In the course of history and in recent months we have received quite graphic instruction. We must consider it seriously. Yet it would be unfortunate to forget or to give up the second, the most important part of that sentence—the providence of God. Our country knows this, with other nations of this earth; or, better stated, the Christians of this country and all nations ought to know and recall this again and again. We believe, amid all kinds of confusion, in the gracious providence of God. At the beginning and at the end of our often crooked ways, the perpendicular Word. In the beginning and at the end of human history, God.

III.

Dear brothers and sisters, the Christmas story of John begins in the heights, in the incomparable heights of the creative Word of God. Yet the Word of God does not remain in the heavenly heights. As the Old Testament has attested on every page, it is of course the Word of movement and encounter. From the very beginning it aims down toward us, to us humans, to our creation. Verse by verse, step by step, this downward movement is described by John. It is the Word through which all things have come into being (1:3). "In him was life, and the life was the light of all people" (1:4)—the "true light, which enlightens everyone" (1:9). It was not and will not be universally received. It meets with denial (1:5), does not succeed in any way obviously, needs its witnesses. And then comes the truly central sentence, the heart of the Christmas story: "And the Word became flesh and lived among us" (1:14).

An unprecedented message, a shocking message then and now, and indeed irritating to many. Word and flesh, the enfleshed Word—that does not sound right. What has spirit to do with flesh?—so asked the greatest thinkers of antiquity, and the religious trends of the day were in accord. One should not speak about the Word and God in such primitive, materialistic terms!

Yet that is precisely the way John now speaks, and it is quite fitting for him to do so. For the good news of Christmas is at stake here. Like his colleagues Luke and Matthew, John can understand the Christmas event in no other way than as a story that is, in the fullest sense, none other than a human, unadorned, earthly story of a human being—one who appeared in the world amid pains of physical birth, was born into a family plagued with many troubles, and was soon exposed to the enmity of a bloodthirsty ruler. A *son of man*, an everyday human, born to an all-too-human lot.

John's concern is this unabridged humanity of the Christmas message, because with it the entire biblical understanding of God hangs together: no anonymous blind fate, no alien superpower, but rather one to whom nothing human is alien. The God turned toward us, passionately interested in our situation; the God *solidly joined* to us. In Isaiah and Matthew the name of the child brings this conclusively to expression: *Immanuel*, God with us!

This unconditional solidarity of God with us is now made concrete in two expressions: "The Word became flesh and lived among us." We have already suggested it. The expression *flesh* is an odd word connected with God. But when the message of Christmas has in view God's Son becoming a human being, then this definite word, *flesh,* has a special meaning. It signifies the biblically realistic view of the human condition. We are not only spirit and soul, but also body. Our created humanness also has this physical, sensuous side. We need not be ashamed of this, for the body also belongs in the focus of the Christmas message.

And the biblical word *flesh* adds yet another accent. Not only is it related to our natural condition, but it pointedly suggests our finite, estranged, guilt-ensnared humanity. With his "The Word became flesh," John also attests this: God enters into our guilt-ridden condition, steps not just into our "sun room," but also into the deepest cellar of our life; is with us just as we are, with heights and depths, in the hours of our power and weakness, even in our temptations and failures.

This "God with us" of "the Word become flesh" is still emphasized and illustrated, with a different accent: It *"lived among us."* Notice the verb *lived.* It indicates a definite duration. The Christmas story is no happening confined to one point in time, as enacted here and there in religious mythologies; no divine excursion to the mortals with quick return into the secure heavens. No! God *lived,* remained among us. God is concerned not only with the physical, but also with the historical, social condition of our life. "To live"—what an essential aspect of human existence! What good fortune to have a good place to live. All of us, of course, know that, whether we have such a place or are looking for one. What a danger is the need for housing! What a reduction of the prospects of living is homelessness!

Even this distress occupies a vast place in the Christmas story. In the center, a homeless family, a homeless child. Even to a problem like this, God in Jesus Christ is not a stranger. His involvement has to do even with our physical and social needs.

That hits us, dear brothers and sisters; that moves us. When the Salvation Army volunteers with their pots turn out on our streets during the days before Christmas, when for years in Basel the "customer Christmas" has been organized on Christmas Eve for the homeless and handicapped, when our newspapers are unusually preoccupied with the condition of the homeless, and when our collection on this day also turns out especially well—when all of that and still more happens, then "Christmasness" really happens among us, much more so than when we experience only the brightness and glitter in our streets and in our houses. These modest yet meaningful signs want to radiate into the everydayness of our lives. The involvement of God, in any event, calls and seeks after involved people.

IV.

Dear brothers and sisters, we want to celebrate Christmas in this spirit, in the light of our text. In the Christian world, and largely in the non-Christian world as well, we orient our reckoning of time around this Christmas event. We count our days and years "*post Jesum Christum natum*"—from the birth of Christ. For many, this is a banal custom. Yet for us who believe, it is an essential indicator: The story of our life is no longer to be separated from the story of the child in Bethlehem. We no longer merely count our days; we live our days "after the birth of Christ." After the birth of Christ— that changes the outlook and orientation of our lives. We may—we are supposed to—begin our calendar days with this beginning. In our earthly real flesh, we are no longer wordless, and therefore not worthless; we are no longer God-forsaken people eaten away by worries. Our temporal life has its eternal foundation.

Therefore, we praise God's friendliness toward humankind— even now, in the peaceful atmosphere of the Christmas service of worship, but also in the joys and cares of our human, all-too-human, everyday existence—as the very people to whom the liberating nearness of God is dedicated for all changes; indeed, for all possible captivities of life. For it *is* so, as we sing: "Our prison, where we sat, where grief beyond measure gnawed at our very heart, is broken open—and we are free." Amen.

14. The Darkness of Faith
Allen C. McSween, Jr.

Exodus 33:12–13, 17–23; John 12:27–40

John says, "Jesus departed and hid himself from them. Though he had done so many signs before them, yet they did not believe in him. . . ."

A strange word of hiddenness—a word of disbelief. Not exactly what we expect to hear in Scripture and sermon, but perhaps for that very reason a word we need to hear. We preachers are too often tempted to iron out all the wrinkles of life. Sometimes we give the impression that faith in God is the most obvious thing in the world. How could anyone not believe in God, surrounded by all the beauty of the world? On Sunday morning we sanitize the world of its darkness. We cross out its tragedy and terror, and offer a comic-book version of the gospel that sooner or later proves as useless as an umbrella in a hurricane. Faith that is real must find expression in a world of rough edges—a world that hides God every bit as much as it reveals God. To pretend otherwise would be to turn faith into a Sunday School pageant and rob it of its power. So we step into the darkness of faith.

To speak of the "darkness of faith" is a way of saying that whatever else God is, in a world like ours God is not obvious. God is deeply hidden—hidden by our human limitations, hidden by our

Allen C. McSween, Jr. received his M.Div. and M.Min. degrees from Union Theological Seminary in Richmond, Virginia (1968, 1976) and his S.T.M. from Yale University Divinity School (1969). He has served pastorates in Kentucky and North Carolina and is currently pastor of Fourth Presbyterian Church in Greenville, South Carolina. He has published two articles in *Journal for Preachers* (1978, 1979). He and his wife, Susan Higgins, have two children, Jean Louise and Michael Allen.

sin. God is no show-off. The God revealed to use in the pages of Scripture is a hidden God, who dwells in deep darkness. Isaiah exclaims, "Truly thou art a God who hidest thyself."

Time and time again I am struck by how intensely realistic the Bible is about the deep hiddenness of God in a world like ours. The religious propaganda of what sometimes passes for sermons might lead you to expect otherwise: You'd expect God to be as obvious as a billboard on the highway. But Scripture never shuts its eyes to the darkness that makes faith the most challenging of adventures. The Bible never pretends for a moment that God is easily known in a world like this. Job flings his cry into the darkness: "Oh, that I knew where I might find him. . . . Behold, I go forward, but he is not there; and backward, but I cannot perceive him; on the left hand I seek him, but I cannot behold him; I turn to the right hand, but I cannot see him . . . for I am hemmed in by darkness, and thick darkness covers my face" (Job 23:3, 8–9, 17, RSV).

Scripture itself demands that we acknowledge the darkness that hides God from us. Whatever else life is, it is not an open book in which we read clearly the ways and works of God. The novelist Father Andrew Greeley forces us to view the darkness head-on: "Life is filled with so many senseless events. Mindless tragedies fill our newspapers every day—airplane crashes, the murder of innocent children, insane terrorism, natural disasters. And much in our own lives seems without purpose or meaning—a rainstorm on a picnic day, a bad cold when we are having a party, a handicapped child, the early death of a parent or spouse, a broken marriage, a car that won't start in the morning, a wrong number in the middle of the night, the treason of friends and envy of neighbors."[1] Why do such things happen? Is there any point and purpose behind them? Or are we alone in a universe that cares not a bit for us?

That's how it seems at times. To some, dare we say it, it seems even worse. It seems that we are playthings of Fate or Chance, or even, God forbid, of God. Annie Dillard tells the horrible story of a neighbor, Julie Norwich, aged seven, who was playing in a field when a small airplane that had lost power hit a tree and crashed. Her father grabbed her and was carrying her to safety when the fuel tank exploded and she was hit in the face by a blob of flaming gasoline that burned her face almost beyond recognition. No one else was hurt. Confronted with such a tragedy, Annie Dillard, a woman of almost mystic faith, wants to scream out, "God despises everything apparently." God "treats us less well than we treat our lawns." In searing anger she writes: "Of faith I have nothing, only of truth; that this one God is a brute and traitor, abandoning us to time, to necessity, and the engines of matter unhinged. This is no leap [of faith]; this evidence of things seen; one Julie, one sorrow, one sensation bewildering the heart and enraging the mind, causing me to look at the world appalled . . ."[2]

How do you look at the world? How do I? If it is through rose-colored glasses, sooner or later the world will knock them off our faces. No use pretending otherwise: In a world like this faith does not come easy. It never has; it never will! Not *real faith* in a terribly real world! Real faith is not a matter of acknowledging an obvious God. It is a matter of clinging for dear life to a deeply hidden God in the midst of the darkness of a sometimes appalling world. The darkness that hides God is real.

And yet . . . there is something else that is real, too. In the midst of the darkness we catch glimpses of glory as we would fireflies on a summer evening. Surprises of grace come to us when we are least looking for them. These glimpses of grace can be easily overlooked. Some write them off as mere coincidences. But they happen. There is no denying that. You can't make them happen on cue. But they do happen!

The phone rings. A voice says softly, "I had you on my mind and just thought I would call and see how you are doing." "Oh, I'm fine," you say. You pause a moment. "No, I'm not doing fine at all. Look, I really need to talk to somebody. You couldn't have called at a better time." As the bumper sticker on the back of the beat-up Volkswagen said, "Grace happens."

Or I preach a sermon that the night before I have told my wife is so bad I am almost embarrassed to preach it. And on the way out of the sanctuary a man with tears in his eyes says, "I almost didn't come today. I'm glad I did. That was exactly what I needed to hear. I'll tell you about it someday." "Grace Happens."

Sometimes it even happens in committee meetings, of all places. I once took a young elder named Bill with me to a meeting of the Synod of Kentucky. Somehow he was put on the Bills and Overtures Committee—usually one of the dullest committees of all. On the way home from the meeting I apologized to Bill for such a waste of our time. Bill disagreed. Out of a conversation he just happened to have with a lawyer on the committee Bill was led to the person who helped him adopt the little girl that he and his wife had wanted for so long. Jennifer is now in college. "Grace happens."

You know how it is. It's happened in your life, too, hasn't it? Sometimes when things seem the darkest, suddenly it is as if a light has broken through—and with it a sense of peace you can't quite put into words. But somehow you know, *you know*, deep down that no matter what, life is good. You are loved.

In this life there is more than enough darkness to make us wonder how in heaven's name a good and loving God could be behind it all. And there is enough light to enable us to bet our lives on the goodness of God, come hell or high water. Always there is some of both, the light and the darkness. There is enough assurance to warrant the venture of faith, but not enough to take away the risk and adventure that are so much a part of the life of faith. Without what Lewis Thomas has called "the gift of ambiguity," human life would not be the real drama with high stakes we know it to be.

John sets before us "the gift of ambiguity" in the words of our text. In the Gospel of John there is no mystery as to who Jesus is. He is the Light that shines in the darkness. He is the Word of God made flesh. "He who has seen me has seen the Father," he declares. And yet even in the revelation of his glory, the ambiguity remains. Some see and some do not. Hearing the same voice from heaven, some say, "An angel has spoken to him." Others say it merely thundered. John says, "Though he had done so many signs before them, yet they did not believe in him." Even miracles are always ambiguous. They can be written off as mere coincidences. It is clear in Scripture that there is no proof that can ever take away the risk of faith. Now, there are clues all over the place. There are glimpses of grace that sparkle in the darkness. But still you must determine for yourself whether they are clues of a gracious Presence hidden in the shadows, or merely a deceptive will-o'-the-wisp. Sooner or later you must bet your life on which is the deepest reality of all—the darkness so real you can almost taste it, or the fireflies of grace, the glimpses of glory that give hint of a deeper joy and peace than anything you have yet known.

Always the mystery remains, and with it the risk of faith. And *that is how God intends it.* We might wish that it were otherwise. We might wish that God would light up the night sky with the words *I am* written in letters a thousand light-years high. But God will not. God will not take away the ambiguity of faith. God will not force our belief.

Moses, who has had about all the ambiguity he can take, finally comes right out and demands of God, "Show me thy glory." No more hints and clues. No more mystery. "Show me thy glory," face-to-face. But his demand is not granted, not as he asks it. In marvelous poetic imagery the Lord God hides Moses in a cleft of the rock and covers him with his hand as God's glory passes by. What Moses sees is not the blinding glory of God; it is the "back side of God," as it were. The Lord declares, "I will make all my *goodness* pass before you, and I will proclaim before you my name: Yahweh; and I will be gracious to whom I will be gracious and will show mercy on whom I will show mercy. But you cannot see my face, for no one shall see me and live." We are not given to see the full glory of God, not in this life. In this life we always see "through a glass darkly." What we see are glimpses of the "goodness of the Lord in the land of the living." And what we hear is the name that is the promise: "*I am* with you always." In every darkness, even to the close of the age, I am with you. Though you cannot know me in my full glory, I know you, and from my love nothing in life or death shall ever separate you. Trust that promise and cling to it for the dear life it is.

One of the best films of 1991 was *Grand Canyon*. It is one of the more powerful sermons I've ever seen. Most of the characters in the film live hopeless lives in a world that has lost its bearings—a world in which people are shot on the street every day and babies are abandoned in empty lots. One of the characters, Mack, speaks for many of us when he says, "The world doesn't make any sense . . . and we are getting used to it. I am beginning to wonder about the choices we have made."

As the film unfolds, terrible things happen. The harshness of life in the inner city is graphically portrayed. And yet in the midst of the terrible things that happen, acts of caring happen, too. Mack's life is saved by a black man who drives a tow truck, just as earlier in his life he had been saved by a woman wearing a Pittsburgh Pirates cap who pulled him out of the way of a bus. And Mack's wife, Claire, finds an abandoned baby while jogging and takes her home and bathes her and cares for her and eventually adopts her. In the midst of the harshness of life in Los Angeles, the "city of angels," friendship happens, caring happens, commitment happens, choices for life are made. Beauty is shared. And strangers that once had appeared threatening become bearers of messages of grace. That's what angels are, you know.

Claire says, "Everything seems so close together—all the good and bad things in the world." That's the way life is—always ambiguous, with good and bad woven closely together. So we are forced to decide what to make of it all. Is life merely a matter of chance and luck? Or is there a gracious Providence at work in the midst of even the worst that life can bring? Are the good things that happen merely coincidences? Or are they miracles that we have lost the language to name and experience as such? As Claire and Mack wonder about the strangeness of life, Claire suggests that maybe there is more to life than we in our secular society can see. She says, "Maybe we don't have enough experience with miracles, so we are slow to recognize them" when they happen. Maybe so!

At the end of the film, standing on the rim of the Grand Canyon, Mack's friend says, "What do you think?" Mack replies, "It's not all bad." No, by the grace of God, "it's not all bad," not by any means. For even in the darkness there are glimpses of glory. There are moments of joy that take our breath away and bring tears to our eyes. There is beauty all around us. We are called to help each other be more attentive to the surprises of grace that come our way. They do come, you know. To those with eyes of faith to see, they do come.

Always the ambiguity of life remains. But this much is clear: that faith does not shut its eyes to the darkness. It opens its eyes to see miracles of grace happening all around us. The promise of faith is that someday we shall "no longer see through a glass darkly, but face-to-face." Then we shall know in full, even as we are fully known and fully loved.

NOTES

1. Andrew Greeley, *The Great Mysteries* (New York: Seabury Press, 1967), 2–3.
2. Annie Dillard, *Holy the Firm* (New York: Harper & Row, 1977), 46.

15. And It Was Good
Richard Francis

Genesis 1:1–5; Romans 8:18–25; John 1:1–18

A famous scientist was giving a lecture on cosmology—that is, the study of the universe and how it works. In the lecture, he made the point that the earth is a sphere orbiting the sun, a not very important star located on one arm of a not very remarkable galaxy.

After the lecture an elderly woman approached the scientist. "I found your lecture very interesting," she said, "but it's all wrong, you know."

"What do you mean?" asked the scientist.

"That part about the earth being a ball going around the sun," she said. "The earth is really a flat dish resting on the back of a gigantic turtle."

"Very well," said the scientist. "What is the turtle standing on?"

"That's simple," she replied. "It's standing on the back of another, even larger turtle."

"I see," said the scientist, fascinated. "And what is *that* turtle standing on?"

"It's no use, young man," she said triumphantly. "It's turtles all the way down!"

Richard Francis, pastor of Westminster Presbyterian Church in Sioux City, Iowa, received his M.Div. from Fuller Theological Seminary. He has served pastorates in Missouri and Iowa and has published meditations in the *Upper Room* and the *Homily Service of the Liturgical Conference.* He and his wife, Kathy, have three sons, Peter, Matthew, and Jonathan. With the exception of three years when he was in seminary, he has lived his entire life within two hundred miles of his hometown in Iowa.

Stephen Hawking, perhaps the most brilliant scientist of our generation, tells that story at the beginning of his best-selling book, *A Brief History of Time.* He goes on from there to talk about how our understanding of the universe has changed from the classical model, which placed the earth at the center of the universe, to the present picture, which is far more complicated than most of us can understand.

Take black holes, for example. A black hole is not a hole at all, but a large star that has run out of gas. Normally, an ordinary star like our sun is constantly performing a kind of balancing act. It's essentially a gigantic nuclear reactor, and the reactions going on in the star produce so much energy that if it weren't for gravity it would all fly apart. On the other hand, the force of gravity is so strong in something as big as a star that if it weren't for the tremendous energy it produces, it would all collapse in on itself. But stars don't last forever. And what happens, according to the widely accepted theory, is that eventually a star that runs out of fuel actually does collapse in on itself, if it's big enough to begin with. No one has ever seen this happen, and no one ever will, but the scenario goes something like this: At the end of its life, a large star becomes unstable and explodes. The outermost layer of the star flies off into space, leaving the denser inner part of the star behind. Because there is no longer a fusion reaction going on, there's nothing to prevent the star from collapsing, the remaining outer layers being drawn toward the center by the incredible gravity. The matter becomes more and more tightly packed together, the way snow is packed in a snowball. The small it gets, the more dense it gets; the more dense it gets, the smaller it gets. Finally it becomes so dense that the very atoms are crushed. The gravity is now so strong that not even light can escape. That's why I said that no one will ever see this happen. There won't be anything to see. There won't be any light, and without light you can't see anything. What you have left is a black hole, which can be identified only by the tremendous gravitational attraction it has for everything in its vicinity.

Now, black holes, according to the theory, are not just oddities—things that happen once in a while. Black holes may be fundamental to the structure of the universe. For example, our galaxy, the Milky Way, is a gigantic dish of billions of stars slowly rotating around a more compact cluster of stars. But there aren't enough stars in the middle of the galaxy to produce enough gravity to hold the whole thing together. Suppose, say Stephen Hawking and others, there's a large black hole at the center of our galaxy, keeping it together. Suppose there is a black hole at the center of every galaxy!

This is not the picture of the universe you and I grew up with. We grew up in a stable, well-ordered universe where the earth orbits around the sun, the moon orbits around the earth, and everything is very settled and predictable. We didn't have to deal with black holes and neutron stars, gravitic lenses and cosmic superstrings.

We still don't, if we don't want to. But the fact remains that our understanding of the universe is changing in our lifetimes. We left the turtle theory behind a long time ago. We smile today to think that there was a time when people thought you could sail off the edge of the world. It would seem that the time is not far off when the view of the universe that we have will seem as naive and outmoded as the giant-turtle view seems to us now.

What does all this have to do with Christian faith? Quite a bit, it seems, because there is no way to study the universe without God intruding into the discussion. One prominent astrophysicist, contemplating the possibility that new evidence might challenge one of his cherished theories, remarked, "I wish there was a way for an atheist to say, 'God forbid!'" Stephen Hawking's book is filled with references to God, some lighthearted, but some serious. It's clear that, in pondering the mysteries of the universe, he has come up against the presence—or absence—of God again and again. He concludes *A Brief History of Time* by talking about the search for a Grand Unified Theory that will explain the physical universe and its workings, from the tiniest subatomic particle to the most massive galactic cluster. He writes:

> If we do discover a complete theory, it should in time be understandable in broad principle by everyone, not just a few scientists. Then we shall all, philosophers, scientists, and just ordinary people, be able to take part in the discussion of the question of why it is that we and the universe exist. If we find the answer to that, it would be the ultimate triumph of human reason—for then we would know the mind of God.[1]

Someone has said, talking of the new directions in science and the understanding of the universe, that it is as if scientists had spent their lives scaling an enormous mountain and, when they reached the summit, found a group of theologians who had been there for a long time. "Who has known the mind of the Lord," wrote the Apostle Paul, quoting Isaiah, "or who has been his advisor?" The answer, of course, is "no one." And I suggest—no, I predict—that if a Grand Unified Theory is developed, it will bring us no closer to the mind of God than the turtles did.

Now, I think that a Grand Unified Theory is worth working toward. The better we understand the universe, the better we will be able to deal with it—scientifically, intellectually, and emotionally. But the universe, after all, is speechless. It cannot, by itself, tell us who made it—or why. We say that "in the beginning, God created the heavens and the earth." Furthermore, we say that "the heavens are telling the glory of God; and the firmament proclaims God's handiwork." But those are statements of faith, made by and for people who have encountered the living God. They tell us who made the universe, but they don't tell us how. We are free to work that out for ourselves, and we have—many times. We left the turtles behind a long time ago, of course. But what about the view that Galileo challenged, the scientific view of the Middle Ages, which the philosophers and theologians of the time developed from Aristotle? Let's look at it for a moment:

Imagine yourself suspended in midheaven, the heaven of medieval thinkers. There, far below you, is the ball that is earth, a puny, insignificant thing compared with the beauty that surrounds you. For all around the earth is the sphere of the moon—perfect, transparent crystal. After that comes the sphere of the sun, the realm of fire, then the spheres of Venus, Mars, Mercury, Jupiter, each sphere higher and purer than the last. And you are bathed in light—pure, radiant, unquenchable light—from all the stars and planets. The only darkness is in the shadow of benighted earth; the fallen planet gives no light of its own. At its core is the dwelling of Satan; he is chained there, at the lowest place in the universe. For the highest place is all around you, beyond the sphere of the fixed stars: the very heaven of God.

Inaccurate? Of course. Unscientific? Not really, given the scientific knowledge of the time. Unchristian? Certainly not, for the imaginary heavens of the Middle Ages gave glory to God as much as do the more scientifically understood heavens of our own day. You can see how hard it must have been to give up that picture of the universe for the one presented by Copernicus, Galileo, and Kepler.

And the universe of Stephen Hawking, if we understand it, has wonders as well. Even black holes declare the glory of God in ways we can't comprehend. So we ought to pursue this as far as our interests and abilities will take us; as John Calvin reminds us, all truth is God's truth.

But let's not do it alone. As Calvin says elsewhere, "All knowledge without Christ is a vast abyss which immediately swallows up all our thoughts." A vast abyss—or a black hole? We cannot contemplate creation without reflecting on our place in creation; we cannot reflect on our place in creation without coming face-to-face with the Creator.

That Creator, whom we call "God," is known to us not in the creation, but in Jesus Christ. "In the beginning was the Word," John writes, "and the Word was with God, and the Word was God. . . . All things came into being through him, and without him not one thing came into being." We cannot divorce our understanding of the universe from our relationship to Jesus Christ. In our relationship to Christ, we understand our own purpose. In understanding our purpose, we have an inkling about God's purpose for the universe. Our destinies are bound together, "for the creation waits with eager longing for the revealing of the children of God."

As science comes to a clearer understanding of the universe and how it works, it will inevitably change the way we look at the world. But it won't change the way we look at God because that is based not on our understanding of the universe, but on what God has said and continues to say to us in Jesus Christ.

There's a wonderful poem I find myself turning to each year at Christmastime: "Wise Men and Shepherds," by Sidney Godolphin. It contrasts those two groups as they gathered at the manger, the wise men in their intellectual sophistication, and the shepherds in their simplicity:

> Wise men, in tracing Nature's laws,
> Ascend unto the highest cause;
> Shepherds with humble fearfulness
> Walk safely, though their light be less.

Though wise men better know the way,
It seems no honest heart can stray.

This is a vast universe, but we are not alone in it. We can walk day by day with God who set the stars in motion.

According to Genesis, God looked at each day's work of creation "and . . . saw that it was good." To believe in God is to keep looking, and to say, "Yes, Lord, it *is* good—very good!"

NOTE

1. Stephen W. Hawking, *A Brief History of Time* (New York: Bantam, 1990), 175.

16. What a Name!
William G. Carter

Matthew 1:18–25

A few years ago, I struck up a conversation in an airport with a man named Woody. We soon discovered two things we had in common: We were both Presbyterians, and we both loved baseball. Woody was from San Diego and a die-hard fan of the San Diego Padres. He told me about a "Presbyterian Day" at San Diego's Murphy Stadium, where the Padres play baseball. Local churches sold discount tickets for the game. In return, the Padres donated one dollar from every ticket to local Presbyterian mission projects. It was a fun event that promoted widespread interest in both mission and baseball.

As part of the festivities, the Padres invited a Presbyterian minister to throw out the first baseball. A natural choice was the stated clerk—the person who maintains the official records and denominational correspondence—of San Diego Presbytery. His name is Herb Christ. (That's C-H-R-I-S-T.) Herb went out to the mound to throw the ball. The Padres' catcher leaned to received the toss. Out in center field, the scoreboard flashed the message "HERB CHRIST WILL THROW OUT THE FIRST BALL."

William G. Carter, a graduate of Princeton Theological Seminary, is cofounder of the Homiletical Feast, an annual continuing-education group for preachers. He was pastor of Presbyterian Church in Catasauqua, Pennsylvania, for five years, and is currently serving a pastorate at First Presbyterian Church in Clarks Summit, Pennsylvania. He has published articles, sermons, and reviews in various periodicals including the *Journal for Preachers, Presbyterian Survey, Lectionary Homiletics,* and *Christian Ministry.*

Suddenly a voice rang out from the upper deck. "I thought his first name was Jesus!" When the laughter died down, someone next to Woody muttered, "Why shouldn't the first name of Christ be Herb?"

Well, why not? An angel told Joseph, "Call the baby Jesus." But why not call him Herb?

A lot of people think there's nothing special about the name Jesus. They casually toss that name around as if it is one more empty word. You hear "Jesus" on the golf tee as someone swings and slices. You hear the name out in the garage when the hammer hits the thumb. Some third-century monks said the word *Jesus* as a prayer, the simplest and holiest of prayers. Others, however, don't see it that way.

I came out of the shopping mall recently and followed someone to the parking lot. He was piled down with packages, his car keys in hand. He came to a Ford Escort and stopped abruptly. Someone had smashed his bumper. There, with all his packages, I heard him say, "Jesus!" I don't think he was praying. To him, at that moment, it was simply a word . . . even though the word *Jesus* is a proper name. In some cultures, it is a very common name. A member of our congregation worked with some migrant workers last summer. One night she stood outside the concrete-block bunkhouse, chatting with a man from Mexico. She asked, "What's your name?" "*Jesus*," he replied, pronouncing it *hey-SUSE*. "Really?" she said. "*Si, señora*," he said. "Three other men in the bunkhouse have the same name."

There is nothing special about the name Jesus. It has always been a human name, like John, or Jim, or Herb. Do you know anybody named Joshua? It is the same name. *Jesus* is the Greek version of *Joshua*. *Yeshua* is the way it sounds in Hebrew.

The Old Testament tells of seven different people named Yeshua, not least of which was the Joshua who led Israel after Moses and fought the battle of Jericho. In the New Testament, as many as five different people are named Jesus. One is the one we know. Another was a friend of Paul (Col. 4:11). A third Jesus was the father of an enemy of Paul (Acts 13:6). A fourth was an ancestor of Mary's husband, Joseph (Luke 3:29). And do you remember Barabbas, the criminal mentioned in the Gospels? An old tradition say that the first name of Barabbas was Jesus. "Which one should I release?" asked Pontius Pilate. "Jesus Barabbas or Jesus called

'Christ'?" (Matt. 27:17). All throughout the scriptures, in its various forms, Jesus was a common human name.[1]

So why did Joseph and Mary name their baby Jesus? Why not call him something else? Why not call him Herb?

Well, an angel said, "Joseph, I want you to name the baby Jesus." It's probably not a good idea to argue with an angel, even if the angel appears only in a dream. Angels are messengers from on high. They bring divine insight and significance. In today's story, this particular angel announces that this particular name is appropriate for this particular child.

That should not surprise us. When we bring children into the world, we want their names to fit. Someone asked the columnist Mike Royko, "What shall we call our first child? We don't want to name him after a relative. We want to name him something distinctive." Royko replied, "If it's a boy, call him Bronko or Bruno." The woman was shocked and said, "Why should I call him that?" "Because it's a tough world," said Royko. "With a name like Bronko, he won't grow up to be a wimp."[2]

Names carry significance and meaning. When a women gets pregnant, the prospective parents buy books that explain the meaning of names. *Brian* means "strength." *Nadine* means "hope." *David* means "beloved." *Laura* means "a crown of laurel leaves." And *Jodi,* like *Judith, Jane,* and *Joan,* means "God is gracious."

In the Old Testament, there was an old man, Abram, whose name meant "parent," even though his wife had never borne a child. Then God changed his name to Abraham, which meant "exalted parent of a multitude," and God said, "Abe, you and your wife, Sarah, are now parents of a multitude." Abraham laughed and said, "Lord, you are such a joker. We can't have kids. Look, I am a hundred years old. Sarah is pushing ninety. A baby for us? Lord, you have got to be kidding!" Nevertheless, God gave them a baby, right there in the old folks' home. They named the child Isaac, which literally means "laughter." Just think: Every night when those exalted parents called their child for supper, every time the syllables rolled from their tongues, they remembered the joke God had played on them in "laughter."

Every child's name stands for something. The name Jesus means "God saves." Technically speaking, the name is more than a prayer. It is a creed, a confession of faith. His name means "Trust in the Almighty; help is on the way." Not only was the name Jesus a Greek version of the name Joshua; the name announces the hope of the world, because it means "God saves."

And God knows we need saving. Not just me, not just you. All of us need saving. The angel said, "You shall call this child Jesus, for he shall save people from sins." Is it too much to say that all of us share a common need for saving?

While I was in seminary learning about the Bible, I spent my Saturdays working for a Yiddish tailor who taught me theology. One Saturday in December I arrived late, to see him gazing out the window. "Sorry I'm late," I said. "That's OK," he replied. "You're a schmuck."

"I couldn't find a parking place," I said. "I tried, but . . ." "Oh, that's OK," he said, looking at me with a smile, "but you're still a schmuck." Then he turned and looked out the window, and said, "You're a schmuck. I'm a schmuck. Everybody is a schmuck."

I said, "Are you having a bad day?" He said, "No, not really. My son just called from Chicago. I sent him money for a plane ticket to come home for the holidays. He never called the travel agent until yesterday. Now he has to fly standby. He'll get in late, if he gets in at all."

I said, "I'm sorry about that." He said, "That's OK. My son is a schmuck."

I said, "I hope your day gets better." He said, "Actually, it's not so bad. A woman just left the store with a purchase. She was looking for a Christmas gift for her boyfriend. I know him. He's the star of the university wrestling team. I found her thumbing through the sweaters. She picked out a pink one and brought it to the counter. I asked, 'Is this for your boyfriend?' She said, 'Yes.' I said, 'But he's a wrestler. He won't wear pink.' She said, 'I don't care if he wears it or not. I like it. That's what counts. If he doesn't like it, he can give it to me.' "

I said to the tailor, "Are you telling me she bought a pink sweater for a wrestler?" He said, "Yeah, but she's a schmuck." Then he added, "I'm a schmuck. You're a schmuck. Everybody is a schmuck."

In case you didn't know, in Yiddish, when you call somebody a schmuck, you are calling that person a fool. And when my friend called people by that name, he was not judging anybody in particular. Rather, he was describing everyone in general. According to him, we are all sad, helpless fools, walking the tightrope daily between comedy and tragedy. Is it too much to agree with him, to admit that there is a flaw in the fabric of our lives? Is it too much to say that all of us are sinners? I don't think so.

The theologian John Leith says the evidence is obvious in at least four ways.[3] First, we sin not only in our worst deeds but in our best deeds, which are flawed by our own self-interest. That is, we buy sweaters for other people in a color that we prefer. Second, we cannot guarantee the future even if we work to ensure it. In other words, even if you send cash for your child's airline ticket, that will not guarantee that your child will get in on time. Third, we cannot complete human life by our own efforts. Try as you might, there are days when you cannot find a parking spot. Fourth, we cannot escape daily frustrations, defeats, and tragedies. And so my tailor friend said, "I'm a schmuck. You're a schmuck. Everybody is a schmuck."

When we were born and given a name, our parents acknowledged us as somebody else's creatures. All our days we will remain captive to human limitations. Life does not always turn out the way we want. We are imperfect and incomplete. That is to say, sin is not merely a misdeed. It is also our condition.

And so the angel's message comes to us as news, as blessed good news. The angel said, "The one named Jesus shall save his people from their sins!" He is the hope of the world.

But wait a minute. Isn't that a tall order for such a little bitty child? Even before birth, the child born to Mary had expectations of the world's salvation loaded upon his shoulders. That is a tremendous burden for anyone. Maybe his parents should have let him off the hook and called him something else. Perhaps they should have called him Herb. After all, sometimes it is difficult to live up to your name.

Very early on I was told that my name, William, means "protector." Then my parents charged me, "Take care of your brother and sisters." Some days that was the last thing on my mind. I recall a few occasions when I put my little brother's life in mortal danger. He may still have the scars to prove it. Needless to say, I am still learning how to be William the Protector. My name is bigger than I am, like an oversize sweatshirt.

Just think: What would it mean to be told from your earliest days that your name, the name Jesus, means "savior"? It is not my name, so I really do not know. But I know the name "Savior" is an enormous name.

And by the grace of God, sometimes people grow into their names. I went to the high school prom with a classmate whose name summed up her life. She always seemed happy and upbeat, as enthusiastic as a cheerleader. Her name was Joy. A few years ago, I saw Joy at a class reunion with a toddler in each arm. Even while changing diapers, Joy was as effervescent as ever. I wondered: What was it like to grow up with everybody calling you Joy? It seems to have shaped her life. She has become what she has been called. As the years have passed, she has become Joy.

The angel said to Joseph, "Call the baby Jesus, that is, 'the Savior.' " By the grace of God, the baby grew up and became what he was called. Do you remember the story?

His name is Jesus, the Savior. According to the Gospel of Matthew, Jesus saved people by teaching them. Like a new Moses, he climbed a mountain and gave them a new law. He taught a higher righteousness beyond the keeping of religious rules. "God's kingdom has come near," he said, "and a new quality of life is possible." And he taught his people: "Love one another. Forgive your enemies. Cure the sick. Feed the hungry." You have to admit that his teachings sound very attractive, even if they are hard to keep. Jesus came to teach, but we cannot completely keep the new law of God's kingdom.

Nevertheless his name is Jesus—that is, the Savior. And so, Jesus not only taught people—he died for people. He died for us. In place of Jesus Barabbas, Jesus the Messiah was nailed to the cross by pettiness, jealousy, and sin. When he breathed his last, the sky turned black and the earth shook . . . and the veil of the temple ripped open, with the mercy of God spilling out everywhere. Even when people killed Jesus, God forgave us all. The Savior said as much: "My blood is poured out for the forgiveness of sins." God forgave us in the death of Jesus.

But don't forget: The name Jesus still means "savior." Death did not have the last word for him. On the third day, the Risen Christ climbed up the mountain again. With all authority, he sent out his forgiven people. He said, "Go and teach everybody what I have taught you before. Go and forgive one another as God has forgiven you. Go and baptize people in my name."

And by the grace of God, the entire creation is new and different because one little baby boy became what he was called.

Someone once asked Dale Carnegie, "How can I make it in this world?" "The first thing to do," replied Carnegie, "is to remember the name of everybody you meet." Generally speaking, that is good advice.

For you and me, there is one name to remember, and it is the name of the child born in Bethlehem. When that child was born, Joseph and Mary knew what to call him. They never considered calling him Abraham or Isaac, Bruno or Herb. Only one name could sum up his life. Only one name could sum up his death. Only one name captures all that he means to his people, in the power and authority of his resurrection. It is the name before whom every knee shall bow and every tongue confess.

When the child was born to Joseph and Mary, they called him Jesus, for he would save his people from their sins.

NOTES

1. See, for example, the articles "Jeshua" and "Jesus" in John D. David and Henry Snyder Gehman, *The Westminster Dictionary of the Bible* (Philadelphia: Westminster Press, 1944), 300–301.

2. *Chicago Tribune*, 4 June 1987.

3. John Leith, *The Reformed Imperative* (Philadelphia: Westminster Press, 1988), 58.

IV. ETHICAL

17. "Who Are My Mother and My Brothers?"

Scott Dalgarno

Mark 3:19b–35

> Survival is the second law of life. The first is that we are all one.
>
> —Joseph Campbell

I read several years ago of an incident where a police car was speeding across the Golden Gate Bridge in San Francisco, responding to a call about someone threatening suicide. The officers stopped suddenly beside a young man poised to jump from the bridge. In a moment the officer riding on the passenger side was upon him. The young man, in the act of jumping, was carrying the officer with him when the other officer grabbed his companion and, with the help of several passersby, pulled them both to safety.

"What in the world were you thinking, grabbing him like that?" said the officer to the other. "You were going over with him!"

"I wasn't thinking anything," said his partner. "I couldn't help myself."

Let me ask you, is there something extra special about that policeman that made him do what he did? Do you suppose that he was a heroic personality waiting for fate to expose him as such, or could there be something in each one of us that might lead us to imperil ourselves in order to save another—perhaps even to our own surprise?

Scott Dalgarno is pastor of Grace Presbyterian Church in Portland, Oregon. He was educated at Whitworth College, the University of Oregon, and San Francisco Theological Seminary. One of Dr. Dalgarno's sermons appeared in *Best Sermons 5*.

Just this week I saw a veteran of the recent war in Iraq on the television. This young lieutenant said that going into that war, he was plagued by two fears. First, there was the obvious fear of death. He knew that he could easily be killed in battle. Second, he said he was terrified that under fire he might let down the people under his command. Then he said something fascinating. He said that being part of the ground war taught him something about his fears. It taught him that fear of failing others was far greater than fear of his own possible demise.

Joseph Campbell, philosopher of religion, man of letters, great all-around human being, has said the following: "Survival is the second law of life. The first is that we are all one."[1]

And is this not what Jesus is talking about in the third chapter of Mark's Gospel? The crowds have gathered at his house. He has so attracted the multitudes that the house is full and there is not even room for them to eat together. Now word is going out that Jesus is endangering his own life. He is saying things that are getting him into deep trouble with the religious authorities. It is clear that his days are numbered and yet he continues to say things openly that incite some among the Pharisees. Therefore, people conclude that he must be mad. Oddly, even his family seems to believe this report. His mother and his brothers come looking for him.

"A crowd was sitting around him; and they said to him, 'Your mother and your brothers and sisters are outside, asking for you.' And he replied, 'Who are my mother and my brothers?' "[2]

I wonder if perhaps his family might have overheard those words. How painful they must have been.

"And looking at those who sat around him, he said, 'Here are my mother and my brothers! Whoever does the will of God is my brother and sister and mother.' "

Jesus had been breaking down one social barrier after another in his ministry: that between what was considered clean and un-clean, that between males and females, and now the ultimate bond, that of family—a bond that people in Middle Eastern societies hold as dearly as life, even more dearly than we who tout "family values." "Here are my mother and my brothers." Can you imagine his family cringing outside with their hands over their ears? Jesus, who was never iconoclastic for iconoclasm's sake, is here saying something about the value of the human family for those who might have ears to hear it.

In his splendid memoir, *Telling Secrets,* Frederick Buechner tells of a time years ago when he learned something about the crucial nature of relationships. One evening he was to have dinner with his mother. Just as the two of them were about to sit down to eat, the telephone rang. It was an old friend Buechner had taught with long before. The friend, grief stricken, was calling from the local airport. He had just learned that his father, mother, and pregnant sister had been in an automobile accident on the West Coast. It was uncertain whether any of them would live. He wondered if Buechner could come down to the airport and wait with him before his departure. Buechner's mother thought the idea of postponing their dinner was preposterous. The man was old enough to take care of himself. "For a moment I was horrified to find myself thinking that maybe she was right," said Buechner.

> Then the next moment I saw more clearly than I
> ever have before that it is on just such outwardly
> trivial decisions as this—should I go or should I
> stay—that human souls are saved or lost. I also saw
> for what was maybe the first time in my life that
> we are called to love our neighbors not just for
> our neighbors' sake but for our own sake, and that
> when John wrote, "He who does not love remains
> in death" (1 John 3:14) he was stating a fact of
> nature as incontrovertible as gravity.[3]

Doesn't the Apostle Paul say precisely this in the first chapter of his letter to the Colossians? Speaking of Christ, he says, "In him all things hold together" (1:17). In Christ is the glue of the universe. In Christ we find that gravitational power that can bind us to even the unlikeliest of people.

We've all had the experience of finding ourselves seated next to some stranger on an airplane or a Greyhound bus. We begin chatting and find a genuine connectedness with that person. Our lives have not touched before our chance meeting and yet we come to feel that we know each other profoundly. We know that we will likely never meet again, and yet because of the quality of the hour or two we have spent together we know that we have come closer to each other than we probably will ever come to certain relations of ours whom we see Christmas after Christmas.

There is a reputed saying of Jesus in what is known as the *Coptic Gospel of Thomas*. It is not found in our Bibles, but a number of scholars agree that it is very likely from Jesus himself. Whatever its source, I find it most compelling: "Love your neighbor like your soul; guard your neighbor like the pupil of your eye."[4]

I felt the spirit of that admonition very palpably at a meeting of Alcoholics Anonymous I attended years ago here in our city. The room was full of such a remarkable mix of people; some in overalls and others in thousand-dollar suits, but everyone oblivious to such superficial differences because of how important just being together there meant to them. I remember one woman speaking up who said simply, "I don't remember a thing I said here at my first meeting. I just went out of the door with a fist full of phone numbers. You people saved my life."

And so today I rejoice that within the walls of our own church meet groups like Cocaine Anonymous, Youth Club, and Parents Anonymous; groups where people of all ages can find "family" when their own families run out of ideas, run out of hope, run out of the resources needed to help their own. Thank heaven Jesus broke down those barriers of relationship once and for all. Thank heaven for the fact that "in him all things hold together"; he is the gravity in all our relationships; he is the glue in the universe.

Some of you may remember that when I first came to this church we hosted an English-language school of Hmong refugees. One morning, shortly after our school got under way, Lillian Sanders, who passed away last year, came to see me. She reminded me that for many years she had worked as a school secretary. She then shared a kind of secret with me. She said that though she had enjoyed her many years of work in school offices, what she had really wanted to do from young adulthood on was to teach. She had been so close to her dream all those years but had never done what she truly wanted to do. And now she wondered if we might be able to use her in the English program. "Of course," I said, and Lillian plunged into her work with enthusiasm and love. The next year, longing to be back in the public schools, she volunteered to be a classroom assistant; she would be called a "Foster Grandparent." She began working with "special" students, among them, one nine-year-old who was autistic and whose name was Danny. Like so many autistic children, Danny seemed to dwell in his own world. He seldom made eye contact with anyone; no one had ever heard him utter a single word. Lillian, ever patient, did what she could to draw him out. She spoke to him, touched him, and treated him like any other child in her care. One afternoon, months later, while shopping at the local grocery store Lillian happened to run into Danny, who was there with his parents. The little fellow brimmed over with surprise at seeing Lillian in a new place. Off he ran to her, arms open, shouting, "Gramma, Gramma." His parents dissolved in tears. It was the first time he had ever spoken.

"Gramma, Gramma." Who are my mother and my brothers? Who indeed? What was it Jesus said to his mother and the beloved disciple from his cross? "Woman, here is your son . . . , [Son,] here is your mother" (John 19:26–27).

In his letter to the Ephesians (1:17–18) the Apostle Paul prays that the Christians at Ephesus be given a spirit of "revelation"—not so as to see into the future, but rather "so that with the eyes of [their] hearts enlightened," they might be able to truly see one another and thus come to see how valuable is this, the fellowship of the Christian church. What might our vision be like if through the Holy Spirit the eyes of our hearts could become enlightened? What might the quality of our fellowship be like here in this church if we truly understood how precious is this thing we dare to call our "church family"?

The critical importance of such a vision is made clear in an engaging little story that was a favorite of the late Anthony de Mello. Let me conclude by telling a version of it for you now.

A certain spiritual teacher once asked his disciples, "How can you tell when the night has ended and the day has begun?"

One said, "When you can see an animal in the distance and tell if it is a cow or a horse."

"No," said the teacher.

A second disciple piped up, saying, "When you see an evergreen tree in the distance and can tell whether it is a pine or fir."

"No again," said the teacher.

"Well then, how can one tell?" asked the disciples.

"It is when you can look into the face of any man and recognize in him the face of your brother, or when you can look into the face of any woman and see in her the face of your sister. If you cannot do this, no matter what time it is by the sun, it is still night."[5]

May the eyes of all our hearts be so enlightened.

NOTES

1. *A Joseph Campbell Companion,* ed. Diane K. Osbon (New York: Harper Collins, 1991), 54.

2. All scriptural references are from the New Revised Standard Version, 1989.

3. Frederick Buechner, *Telling Secrets* (San Francisco: Harper San Francisco, 1991), 48–49.

4. John Dominic Crossan, *The Historical Jesus* (San Francisco: Harper San Francisco, 1991), xxi.

5. Anthony de Mello, S.J., *Taking Flight* (New York: Doubleday, 1988), 161.

18. The Power of Presence
Earl C. Davis

Acts 4:7–13, 16:25–28

I wonder if you police officers realize what a remarkable power of presence you have among us. There is power in your very presence! You do not have to do or say anything for most of us to be mightily impressed by your presence. I speak not so much of your presence here today as of your presence day and night on our streets and in our skies and on our waterways, serving and protecting us.

Watch Out—There's a Policeman!

Have you ever noticed how all the traffic—whether in front of you or beside you or behind you—slows down when there's a police car in the vicinity? I get whiplash and eyestrain switching from the rearview mirror to the speedometer when there's a police car behind me, even three cars back! The other day we were out at the police academy making some television spots announcing Police Appreciation Day at our church when a police car pulled up beside me. Even though I was there by permission, working with a motorcycle cop and the police helicopter and Mac the police robot, I still was uneasy for a moment when the police cruiser pulled up!

Earl C. Davis is pastor of the First Baptist Church in Memphis, Tennessee. He is a graduate of Stetson University and holds graduate degrees from Southeastern Baptist Theological Seminary and Southern Baptist Theological Seminary, where he received a doctorate. In addition to his published sermons, Dr. Davis is the author of *Life in the Spirit* and *Christ at the Door*. He delivered this sermon in honor of Police Appreciation Day.

A Behavior-Modifying Presence

As police officers you have such a powerful presence that you don't even really have to be there to influence us; it's enough for us just to *think* you are there—as the empty patrol cars parked out on the interstates of our nation prove. In fact, didn't I read somewhere that the British put pasteboard patrol cars along their roads? If we perceive you are there, that's usually enough to make us modify our behavior.

For instance, there's the story about Bull Jones. It really happened in East Tennessee, but it has also happened in every small town. This little town had only one policeman, which was appropriate since it had only one traffic light. Still, the city council decided something must be done about the speeders who came roaring through their little burg. The problem was, they didn't have enough money to purchase one of those newfangled radar units for the police car. Well, Bull Jones—isn't every county-seat police chief nicknamed "Bull" somebody?—well, Bull Jones allowed as maybe they did and maybe they didn't have enough money; he would look into it. A couple of mornings later, after the word had spread around town that maybe they were going to get a radar unit, lo and behold, old Bull was parked at the edge of town with a hand-held radar unit sticking out the cruiser window. He had simply taken his wife's hair dryer and was sitting there with it sticking out the window! And everybody hit the brakes when they saw him sitting over at the side of the road!

The power of a policeman's presence is a wonderful thing. You have the power, just by your presence, to shape folks' conduct and sharpen their conscience. As I mulled this remarkable power of presence, I began to ask some questions: Is the power totally in the trappings—in the uniform, the badge, the gun, the flashing light? Is there a power, an influence in your life whether or not you are in uniform? You shape other folks' conduct and sharpen other folks' consciences; *who shapes and sharpens your life?* Then I began to ask about all of us: Is there a power, a presence in our lives apart from the uniform, the company, the profession we are in? When we shed the role of doctor, lawyer, merchant chief—is there a power and a presence in our lives that influences others?

Whence This Presence?

As I reflected on that, in my mind the pages of my Bible began to turn, and I was standing in that crowd at the foot of the mountain as Moses came back down after meeting with God. As he walked through the crowd we could hear whisperings and sounds of excitement, and as he came closer I could see for myself: His face was glowing—a radiance that we all knew was there because he had been with God. *"And Moses wist not that his face shone"* (Deut. 34:29–30). Some folks' presence has a power that comes from fellowship with God. And the strange thing is, many of those folks don't know that their faces glow with the power and presence of God.

A few more pages and I watched the palace guard drag the prophet Daniel to the hole in the pavement that opened into the lions' den. We listened to the roaring of the beasts as the soldiers pushed the great stone from over the hole and lowered Daniel into the pit. I leaned over the edge and waited for the horrible screams that would signify that the beasts were tearing this man of God apart. After a nerve-racking silence I peered down into the shadowy pit. There stood Daniel, and there stood the lions—at a respectful distance. He was not harmed because of *the power of his presence*. There is a power that comes from a relationship of trust and prayer to Almighty God.

Then we turn to the Book of Acts, chapter 4, and read of the power of the presence of Peter and the other disciples when they were arrested. Verses 7 to 13 give Peter's explanation of the power in their very presence. And we read that the religious leaders finally got something right! They saw that these men were *agrammatoi* (ungrammared) and *idiotai* (idiots who didn't have great education), and they made the right assumption that their power was due to their having been with Jesus: *"They took knowledge of them, that they had been with Jesus"* (Acts 4:13). There is the power of the presence that comes from associating with Jesus and having *his very character*.

In the next chapter of Acts we read that Peter's very presence had such power that the sick folks in the villages of Judea were brought and laid in the streets through which he was to pass, so that his very shadow might fall on them and bring healing! The power of his presence extended even to his shadow. And consider our text story in Acts 16. Here are two men in jail. And I'll bet none of you policemen has ever arrested a man for the reason these men were in jail—preaching and witnessing to the power and presence of the Risen Christ! But such preaching and witnessing didn't set well with the populace in Philippi, and Paul and Silas were thrown in jail. The policeman on duty saw to it that these troublemakers were put into the darkest cell in the place. And even in prison they kept on talking about Jesus and singing. Along about midnight, there was a great earthquake that jarred all the doors off their hinges and set the prisoners free—but that's not the miracle, nor the point of the story. The point is that when the policeman in charge of the jail came running in to check on the prisoners and saw all the doors wide open, he figured the prisoners had fled and he would be executed for not being able to stop them. *"Don't harm yourself; we are all here!"* There's the miracle! Here's a man, Paul, in whose very presence there is such power and peace that even men penned up in prison don't want to leave that presence! *It is the power and presence of the gospel of Jesus in the life of a believer.*

Can Your Presence Have Power?

Let me raise an interesting question to those among us who are Christians: *Can your presence and my presence have such spiritual power?* Suppose there was an authentic spiritual power in our very presence—regardless of the uniform we wear during the week. A way of talking and acting that would be seen by those we deal with—whether we are giving out traffic tickets or teaching students or examining patients—as an expression of Christ within our lives. *A presence with power.*

Take a moment to recall the key to such a powerful presence in the lives of those biblical characters I have already mentioned. Moses' powerful presence is symbolized in the glowing face and reminds us that time spent in the presence of God makes a difference in our lives that others can see. The powerful scene of Daniel facing down the hungry lions underlines the presence of God that comes when we trust him with our very lives. Again, the disciples in the New Testament had a powerful presence explained by their enemies as due to the fact that they had been with Jesus. Are we with Jesus often enough to have a power in our presence?

The key to the healing power of Peter's shadow is seen not only in the faith of the sick person, but also in Peter's dedication and commitment to Jesus. And the sense of security and peace that the prisoners saw in the very presence of Paul and Silas spoke to the other prisoners.

The Power of a Presence

When I consider how all of us who are Christians are urged by biblical admonition to strive for the powerful presence of the Lord to be revealed in our daily life, I think of that grand old saint of South Africa, Andrew Murray. He served the Dutch Reformed Church in Wellington, South Africa—that strife-torn land so much needing the godliness and depth of a Murray today. Murray authored many books that still continue to bless the lives of Christians around the world. When he died some seventy-five years ago, his parishioners erected a statue of him in front of his church, facing the street. I am told that so great is the remembrance of his presence that for decades after his death, drunk people staggering home feared to pass that way, for, they said, "the old minister will see us." Even when drunk, they trembled to pass by so much as his likeness in stone, so holy was his life among them!

I say to you police officers again: *Do you realize the power of your presence in our society, on our streets, in our midst?* But the question comes not just to you; all of us can have an even more powerful presence if we let the Lord Jesus shine through our faces and lives. You say it is well and good to speak of such, and you do not doubt that the biblical folks had such a presence, and perhaps even a saintly preacher seventy-five years ago could influence people so— but is it possible today?

Let me tell you a true incident I remember from my childhood. When I was growing up, one of the finest Christians in our community was a schoolteacher, a high school principal named Simon Kinsey. One day Simon dropped by the barber shop to get a shave and a haircut. Now, back in those days you didn't make an appointment to get a haircut; you just went down to the shop with the barber pole out in front on the main street, and took your seat on the bench and waited your turn for the seventy-five-cent haircut. While you waited, the conversation covered everything from national scandals and scoundrels to local gossip. Dog-eared copies of the *Saturday Evening Post* and *Grit,* along with the local weekly newspaper, were strewn around. Over in the corner, the shoeshine boy was working away on "brought-in" shoes, but would stop to give you a shine for a dime. The place smelled like shoe polish and hot towels and after-shave lotion. The janitor was sweeping up the clippings from around the two barber chairs. Well, on this day as the conversation drifted into off-color jokes, a local wit began to hold forth. He was deep into a dirty story when the barber unwound the face of a man whose beard had been soaking and jacked the barber chair upright to shave him. The jokester turned to see this new audience, and when he realized it was Simon Kinsey, his face turned red and he sputtered out an apology: "Mr. Kinsey, if I had known it was you under that towel, I wouldn't have told that story." Folks, Simon Kinsey wasn't a preacher. He was just an ordinary schoolteacher who lived a life of Christian witness in such a fashion that there was power in his very presence among us.

Go thou and do likewise.

19. Discipleship, Unity, and Justice

A POSTINAUGURAL SERMON

Allan M. Parrent

Amos 3:1–8; 1 Corinthians 1:10–17; Matthew 4:12–23

Once again, this nation has survived a presidential campaign, election, and inauguration. No more political ads, no more simplistic political rhetoric, no more selling of the candidates like different brands of toothpaste, no more political posturing on what were loosely called "the issues," and no more Hollywood-style preinaugural excesses.

But perhaps we ought not engage too easily in the popular pastime of denigrating our politics, our politicians, and our political institutions. We have, through an orderly process, successfully elected a president as well as hundreds of other public officials. As our former parishioner Gerald Ford said at his installation, "Our Constitution works; our great republic is a government of laws and not of men." A peaceful, orderly, and legally prescribed process, open to all qualified citizens, has taken place. A corporate decision about the investiture of immense power has occurred by preestablished procedures without bloodshed, regicide, palace intrigue, civil war, or anarchy. The fact that we take that for granted should not diminish the fact that it has been historically, and still is, a rather infrequent occurrence among the nations of the earth. For that we can give thanks to God who is lord of all things, including the political realm.

Allan M. Parrent is Professor of Christian Ethics, Associate Dean for Academic Affairs, and Vice-President at the Episcopal Theological Seminary in Virginia. Dr. Parrent was educated at Georgetown College and Vanderbilt, Duke, and Durham (England) Universities. He contributes frequently to scholarly journals and speaks widely on ethical issues.

Although political authority can be and has been abused in history, although governments can become and have become demonic, there is nevertheless in Scripture and the Christian tradition a fundamental affirmation of the political realm, the political task, and political leadership that we cannot ignore. It is certainly dangerous for our soul's health to identify our faith with a particular political program, policy, or structure, though that at times is done on both the left and the right of the political spectrum. But it is equally dangerous to regard our faith as irrelevant to such programs, policies, and structures. Politics can at times be fairly criticized and ridiculed, but it cannot be legitimately dismissed by, or hermetically sealed off from, a vital Christian faith. We acknowledge this in fact every time we pray for "those who bear the authority of government in this and every land," or pray that God will "endue with the spirit of wisdom those to whom in Thy name we entrust the authority of government."

The question for Christians, then, is not *whether* but *in what way* God would have us understand the relation between our faith and our politics, not *whether* but *how* we are to live out faithfully our dual citizenship in what St. Augustine called the *civitas dei* and the *civitas terrena*—the City of God and the city of this world. Our three lessons today can perhaps help us in our search for an answer to that age-old dilemma. Each of the three is primarily a call to members of a religious community to act in a manner consistent with their religious commitments. But if we understand ourselves to be citizens of both a religious community and a political community, and accept that the two cannot legitimately be severed totally, the call in each case can also be understood to have implications for how we, as citizens of the Kingdom of God, are to live as citizens of one of the kingdoms of this world.

In the Gospel lesson Peter and Andrew and James and John are called to Christian *discipleship*. "Follow me and I will make you fishers of men." In the Epistle, the church at Corinth is called to *unity* in Christ. Paul's call to the Corinthians is "that all of you agree and that there be no dissensions among you, but that you be united in the same mind and the same judgment," for Christ is not divided. And in the Old Testament lesson Israel is threatened with punishment because of its previously cited transgressions that violated its call to *social justice*—selling the righteous for silver and trampling the head of the poor into the dust of the earth. Three themes: *discipleship, unity,* and *social justice.* Each is a call to us to shape our lives in certain ways within the Christian community. But each also has implications for how we are to shape our lives in the broader political community, and to shape that community itself.

Discipleship

Jesus' call to "follow me" does not mean and has never meant a call simply to a way of personal salvation for the individual. The call to discipleship does of course mean no *less* than that. But it does not mean that one accepts the lordship of Christ as governing personal and family life and the life of the Church while acknowledging another sovereign as governing the public life of society. That was precisely the point of the Barmen Declaration, issued by the Confessing Church in Germany in 1934, against the Nazi government's effort to curtail the church's effort to be the church, which included the freedom to exercise its discipleship by speaking truth to power.

No, the call to discipleship, to follow Christ, also includes a call to political responsibility. Christian discipleship includes the freedom of Christians, who have only one ultimate sovereign, both to support and to challenge the assumptions that govern those lesser sovereignties that shape the world of politics, economics, education, and culture. It includes the obligation to participate in trying to shape or reshape the moral ethos of the society of which we are a part. This certainly does not mean an effort to Christianize society, which is both impossible and disastrous when attempted, as history so clearly reveals. But it does mean an effort to make the social order a more humane and just order, one that is at least marginally more consistent with that love-inspired justice of which Scripture gives us glimpses.

There are those in our society who are wary of any mention of religion and politics in the same breath. For some this wariness is based on overt hostility to religion, a trait found especially among some of our cultural elites. It is said, for example, that today anti-Catholicism is the anti-Semitism of the intellectuals. For others it is based on a rather moot fear of an imminent theocracy somehow suddenly developing in our highly secularized society. For still others, including many Christians, the wariness comes out of an overly scrupulous desire not to be religiously intrusive, perhaps based on a misunderstanding of the religion clauses of the First Amendment.

Such sometimes well-meaning concerns, however, would in fact limit the exercise of our Christian discipleship to the private realm. It would create in our society's public life what has been called a "naked public square"—that is, a society from which is removed any trace of anything transcendent, any basis for an objective moral order to which a state can be held accountable, indeed any ultimate foundation for those inalienable rights proclaimed in the Declaration of Independence. The problem is that a naked public square won't remain naked. It is a vacuum that will be filled with other norms, other values, other concepts of what is just or true. And when there is a moral vacuum in a society, it is most likely to be filled by the moral descendents of Thrasymachus, Plato's antagonist in *The Republic*, who declared that in the public order "justice is the will of the stronger," or by those Isaiah had in mind when he said that where "truth has fallen in the public square, uprightness cannot enter" (Isa. 59:14–15).

At Harvard University a number of Christian groups sponsor the Harvard Veritas Forum. Their literature includes the official Harvard seal—a shield bearing the word *Veritas* ("Truth"). Originally, of course, the Harvard seal read: "Veritas Christo et Ecclesiae" ("Truth for Christ and Church"), followed by John 8:31–32: "And Jesus said, 'If you hold to my teaching, you will know the truth and the truth will make you free.'" In addition, the seal exhibited three books, two open and one turned face down, acknowledging the limits of human reason. Today the seal makes no reference to Christ, the Church, or John 8, and the third book is now open, suggesting perhaps that all is now known by human reason. "Veritas" now seems to be *veritas* for nothing, or perhaps *veritas* for anything, and as human history tells us, that can lead to the death of *veritas*. I believe it was Chesterton who said that when a people cease to believe in God they don't believe in nothing, they believe in anything.

If we as Christians believe that Jesus Christ is the way, the truth, and the life, then our discipleship in response to his call to "follow me" cannot exclude our discipleship as responsible citizens of one of the kingdoms of this world.

Unity

The second theme is the call to unity in Christ. To the Corinthian partisans of Apollos, or Cephas, or of Paul himself, Paul proclaims that Christ is not divided. This call to unity in Christ is *not* a call for an undeviating, unquestioning conformity to rigid dogma that is not to be questioned by our God-given reason. That, however, does not seem to be an imminent danger in a society increasingly called post-Christian, and in a Church where theological diversity and innovation are so widespread that Anglican theologians themselves find it difficult to define with much specificity what Anglican theology is. A friend of mine who once was director of a church-related peace institute said a few years ago, during the nuclear-freeze debate, that among his colleagues it would have been more acceptable for him to deny the Resurrection than to oppose the nuclear freeze. So much for where one finds rigid dogma today.

But unity in Christ *does* mean unity about the essentials. It does mean clarity about our ultimate commitments. It does mean knowing who was crucified for us—Christ, not Paul—and in whose name we were baptized—Christ's, not Paul's. It does mean knowing where we have our basic identity, by what community that identity is primarily shaped, and what that identity means in terms of character traits and virtues, both personal and civic, for those who are at one in Christ.

And that call to unity in the Christian community also has implications for the shape of the political community we seek to form here in the earthly city. If we are to maintain that balance of freedom and order necessary for a just civil community, we need clarity about our penultimate, this-worldly commitments as well as the ultimate ones. It is certainly desirable to celebrate our diversity as Americans, but diversity can lead to tribalism and social balkanization if a fundamental unity does not undergird it. Though it may seem paradoxical, it is only when we are rooted in the kind of unity that has a transcendent focus that we are really free to act with prudence in the public arenas of this world to promote the unity and common good of our broader society. That is to say, we are more likely to be effective in the public realm if we are grounded in a realm beyond politics, if we are rooted in a community whose transcendent allegiance not only calls us to promote human unity in this world, to the extent possible, but also liberates us from absolutizing the political agendas and projects of this world, which, while still very important, are only penultimately important.

History shows us that where factions, clans, and tribes are given ultimate allegiance, when they are absolutized, untempered by a more transcendent loyalty that relativizes them, they become idols. That was true of the Nazi idolatry of "blood and soil." That is also the issue today, for example, among the warring clans of the former Yugoslavia and the warring tribes of Somalia. As one writer put it, the basic unit in Bosnia has become "ethnos" rather than "demos" —the ethnic group, cleansed from the contamination of other ethnic groups, rather than a broader civil society based on law.

The war in Bosnia is seen by some as a "religious" war, though it is espoused by people with seemingly little notion of their religion and fought by people exercising none of the moral constraints imposed by their religion. The atrocities there are possible precisely because it is *not* a religious war, if by *religion* we mean a transcendent loyalty that relativizes our other loyalties in this world, and thereby allows for tolerance of, and civility toward, those with different this-world, penultimate loyalties. That understanding of religion is, for Christians, precisely one of the bases for advocating a political system that supports religious liberty. Religious liberty not only *allows* Christians to live out, in the public arena, the implications of their fundamental unity in Christ; it also *requires* that they do so, lest other, lesser gods become enshrined in the public pantheon, push Christian faith into the private sphere, and eventually become idols of destruction.

Social Justice

Finally, we are called as Christians to social justice. God's harsh words to his people, as reported by Amos, were: "You only have I known of all the families of the earth; therefore I will punish you for all your iniquities." Those words fall awkwardly on the ears of our rights-obsessed society, where, as one columnist put it, "the demand is for the right of anyone to do anything he or she pleases, and the right to be compensated for any unpleasant consequences." (Case in point: the young woman who sued Brown University for seven hundred thousand dollars because she hurt her arm on a broken soap dish while showering in a dormitory with her boy-friend.)

But those hard words of God to his people reported by Amos tell us that God is a God of justice, and that it is unjust to cheat in the marketplace or oppress the poor. We are called to hear the voice of God and to learn from him the difference between justice and injustice; it is not simply a matter of opinion or of cultural relativism. As Christians living in this world we are clearly not yet conformed to Christ, but we cannot claim that Christ has left us with no light on our path, no pole star to guide us. Indeed, we have some fairly clear ideas about the difference between justice and injustice, ideas that are conveyed to us through numerous stories and narratives in Scripture. And this call to social justice, found repeatedly in Amos and the prophets and throughout Scripture, is a call to translate this key biblical theme into concrete terms in the human community, thereby linking our citizenship in the City of God and our citizenship in the earthly city.

One of the values of our form of democracy, which we have seen work quite well this past week, is that it is based on a profound theological insight about human beings, who are mixtures of both altruism and selfishness, and who are trying to live together in community. That insight is expressed well in Reinhold Niebuhr's most often quoted sentence: "Man's capacity for justice makes democracy possible; man's inclination to injustice make democracy necessary." Christian faith, then, not only calls us to social justice; it also calls us to support political structures that make it possible for us to act on that call.

As Christians we are called to discipleship, we are called to unity, we are called to justice. Each of these is a call with implications both for the Christian community itself and also for how Christians are to relate to the political community of which they are a part. Each speaks to our dual citizenship in the City of God and in the earthly city. These interlocking themes are captured well in that profound prayer for our country in the Book of Common Prayer, and on this first Sunday after the inauguration, I would like to end with that prayer:

Almighty God, who hast given us this good land for our heritage: We humbly beseech thee that we may always prove ourselves a people mindful of thy favor and glad to do thy will. Bless our land with honorable industry, sound learning, and pure manners. Save us from violence, discord, and confusion; from pride and arrogance, and from every evil way. Defend our liberties, and fashion into one united people the multitudes brought hither out of many kindreds and tongues. Endue the authority of government, that there may be justice and peace at home, and that, through obedience to thy law, we may show forth thy praise among the nations of the earth. In the time of prosperity, fill our hearts with thankfulness, and in the day of trouble, suffer not our trust in thee to fail; all which we ask through Jesus Christ our Lord. Amen.

20. A New Commandment of Love

William Powell Tuck

John 13:34–35, 15:9–17

A pastor was talking with a group of young people in a discipleship class one day. He was teaching them lessons about the Ten Commandments, and had reached the point in the study where Moses came down from Mount Sinai with the commandments. The minister asked, "How many commandments are there?" One of the young girls in the class said, "There are eleven." The pastor looked puzzled and said, "Eleven? Oh, no, dear, there are only ten." "Oh, yes," she responded, "in our Sunday School lesson last week from John 13, we heard that Jesus said, 'A new commandment I give unto you that you love one another.' There are eleven."

Let us look at that little-known, and unfortunately not universally practiced, eleventh commandment from Jesus: "Love one another." Notice the context in which Jesus delivers this commandment. He and his disciples had gathered in the upper room to observe the Passover. The disciples had entered the room debating who was first in his kingdom. Jesus, seeing that none of them had washed their feet when they entered, assumed the form of a servant: Girding himself with a towel and taking a basin of water, he washed the feet of the disciples. Then they observed what you and I have come to call the Lord's Supper. Judas then leaves to betray Jesus. The atmosphere is charged with tenderness, love, affection, and sadness. Jesus, knowing this will be his last discourse with his disciples, seems to be searching to decide what his last words will be: "What do I tell my disciples in these last few moments?" He begins by telling them about a new commandment.

William Powell Tuck is pastor of First Baptist Church in Lumberton, North Carolina. Dr. Tuck is the author of several books, including *The Way for All Seasons*.

People often ask what the word *Maundy* means in the Maundy Thursday observance of Communion. *Maundy* comes from the Latin word *mandatum*, or "commandment." The word *Maundy* is used in recognition of the new commandment that Jesus gave his disciples at the Last Supper. "Little children," Jesus says, addressing them very tenderly, like orphan children. "Little children, soon I will leave you. And so I give you a new commandment."

The word *new* rings through the New Testament like a bell tolling a call for persons to respond to God's presence. Jesus said, "I give you a new commandment." He also spoke about "a new birth," "a new covenant," and "a new beginning." Paul wrote about "the new creation," "the new Israel," and "the new Adam." He also declared that Christ "will make all things new." John, on the Isle of Patmos, writes about the time when the Christians will experience "a new song" and a "new name," and when there will be "a new Jerusalem" and "a new heaven and earth."

"I give you a new commandment," Jesus said. What was the purpose of this new commandment? Jesus stated its purpose very clearly: His disciples are to love one another. But what is new about that? Wasn't love for other persons taught in the Old Testament? When Jesus summarized the law, he declared that the essence of the law was to love God with all of your heart, soul, mind, and strength, and that the second commandment was similar to the first: "Love your neighbor as yourself." Yes, there are powerful teachings about love in the Old Testament. This teaching did not deny or reject those teachings. Communities like the one in Qumran taught their followers to "love all the children."

So then, what is new about this command? Maybe this was the first time Jesus taught this view to his disciples. Maybe . . . but I think that is unlikely. Maybe the newness is realized in conjunction with the whole meaning of that night at the Last Supper. It is new as a part of the new covenant that was symbolized at that meal. This Last Supper depicted a new relationship that was being established with God. There was a freshness surrounding this commandment.

But how do you command love? Can you demand somebody to love you? Unfortunately for us, love is seen in our society mostly as an emotion, or a feeling. But the kind of love that Jesus is talking about here—*agape* love—is not a feeling. This kind of love is an act of the will. This kind of love is based on a decision. It is a choice—not a feeling. This love is something that you and I have to discipline ourselves to give in life. It is seen in the action of the good Samaritan who makes a conscious decision to help a person in need. Jesus is telling the disciples that the kind of love they must have comes about by an assertion of their will. This sort of love demands discipline to bring it into reality.

The extent of this love is depicted in the words *one another:* "You disciples are to love each other." This is a love that is different from your love for your neighbor or your enemy. The scope of this love is the love of Christian followers for each other. Here is a part of the newness. Jesus' disciples are to love each other in a way that is different from the world's understanding of love. This love is founded on the oneness that we have experienced within our relationship to Christ. When we stand at the foot of the cross, all barriers are down. All Christians are brothers and sisters in Christ. Paul would describe this relationship by saying: "In Christ there is neither male nor female, slave nor free, Jew nor Greek; all are one" (Gal. 3:28). Jesus Christ binds us into a new unity. All barriers are down. Christians are brothers and sisters in one family, whether we are Americans, Germans, French, black, white, men, or women. We are bound together in a fellowship of brotherhood and sisterhood by the blood of Christ. His sacrificial death has drawn us into a community built on love. Christ's death established a community of grace. We have first experienced love through Christ's love, and we love each other as we have been loved.

Christians need the love of other Christians. We need each other. Those of us who are Christians in our church need the love of other Christians in other churches so that we strengthen, support, and nurture each other. Every group of Christians formed into a church is like a small group of explorers who are establishing a new outpost on a frontier. As Christians, we carry the banner of Christ before us and attempt to plant it wherever we go in a hostile environment. We need each other. We are not strong enough as isolated Christians or as individual churches. We need all Christians. Paul describes the Christian church in Philippi as a "colony of heaven" (Phil. 4:1). The Philippians knew what it was like to be a Roman colony. That image was clear to them. Every Christian church should be a colony for Christ in the community where it exists. As the colony of Christ in the world, Christians are to be the salt, the light, and the leaven. Christians should make a difference in the world. To make a difference in the world, we have to love one another first. The love of Christ binds us together.

I have enjoyed reading Robert Fulghum's second book, *It Was on Fire When I Lay Down on It*. In that book he related an experience he had with a young woman in the Hong Kong airport. This young woman was sitting near him, and after a while, she burst into tears. He tried to comfort her and discovered that she had lost her plane ticket back to the United States. She had been sitting there for three hours. She did not know what to do. All her money had been spent for the ticket. She cried and cried. He listened to her story patiently and then he and an older couple, who had also befriended her, decided that they would take her to get something to eat, and then see if they could talk to the authorities and do something about her situation. The young woman slowly got up, and as she did so, she suddenly screamed. ("I thought somebody had shot her," Fulghum wrote.) "What is it?" he cried. "My ticket! My ticket! I have been sitting on it all the time! Here is my ticket!" As she left, running to catch her plane, Fulghum wondered to himself how many of us have the solution to our problem and don't know it because all the time we are sitting on our "ticket."[1]

Think of the divisiveness, disharmony, brokenness, confusion, and bitterness that exist in the churches of Christ today. And . . . here is the answer; it's like we have been sitting on the answer: Love one another. The answer is right before us. All barriers would come down if we really loved one another. If those of us in the church loved each other as Christ commanded us to do, our church—every church—would be radically different.

What is our guide for trying to accomplish this seemingly impossible kind of love? It is Jesus Christ. Jesus said, "Love one another as *I have loved you*." Here is the guide. Christ is the standard. He is the measurement for whether we have loved properly. He is the guide and example.

I am sure that you, like me, have walked through an art museum on some occasion and noticed an aspiring artist seated before a canvas, painting his or her own picture of some famous painting that is hanging on the wall. Have you ever stopped and looked at the one being painted and compared it with the one on the wall?

There is usually a lot of difference, isn't there? Yet this aspiring artist models himself/herself after the greater artist. So you and I seek to model ourselves after the Christ. He is the measurement of genuine love. He is our standard, goal, and guide for determining our love for each other. We seek to love as he has loved.

How do we measure the love of Christ? Look first at the breadth of his love. His love was inclusive and not exclusive. He opened his arms to any person who would come—the outcasts of society, the publicans, sinners, the lepers, and the sick. He invited all persons—men and women, rich and poor: "Whosoever will may come." He had come to call sinners to repentance, to be a physician to all who were ill. He reached out to all persons with the love of God. He did not exclude anyone who came. He opened his arms and welcomed any and all who would come to experience his Father's grace.

One of the great tragedies today is how many walls and barriers have been built in the church to exclude others. But this is not like our Lord. Black/white, male/female, rich/poor are all welcomed by Jesus Christ. A church in one of our mission fields found that it was able to buy a piece of property unexpectedly one day, because the owner had gone bankrupt. He had gone bankrupt building walls around his property. He never got around to building anything else on his property. All of his money went into walls to keep people out. There are times when I think some *churches* will go bankrupt as they attempt to erect walls to keep others out. Their church is designed to exclude. The gospel of Christ opens the door of God's love to all persons—from both sides of the track or around the world. As the hymn writer has reminded us, "There's a wideness in God's mercy like the wideness of the sea."

Look next at the length of Christ's love. His love seems to be endless. Jesus had unending patience. He taught his disciples for three years, but they never seemed to understand his message. But he repeated his teachings again and again. He was understanding and forgiving. To teach his kind of love, Jesus drew on images of Roman soldiers compelling persons to bear their packs. He told his disciples that if you are asked to go one mile, go two. If someone strikes you on one cheek, turn the other to him. Don't just forgive seven times, but seventy times seven. Your love is immeasurable. Jesus forgave Peter, listened to Thomas's questions, and encouraged the disciples to continue to watch even when they had just gone to sleep. There is no end to Christ's great capacity of love. There is no pit so deep that his love is not deeper still.

Next, look at the height of the love of Christ. The love of Christ reaches from earth to heaven. Paul reminds us that Christ did not count equality with God a thing to be grasped, but emptied himself and assumed the form of a servant (Phil. 2:7). The servant symbolized in the image of the towel and a basin where Jesus washes the disciples' feet is a foreshadowing of his sacrificial death. There was no limit to his sacrifice. Jesus knew that he could not save himself and others at the same time. He could not live for himself when living for others. He was not concerned about himself but laid down his life for his friends and his enemies. He gave his life that we might have life and experience God's great love.

No one can ever understand the greatness of Albert Schweitzer by seeing him only as a medical missionary. Something of the greatness of this man's heart was revealed when he came to the United States to receive an honorary doctor's degree from the University of Chicago. As he got off the train, he was met by some of the officials from the university. They shook hands with him and chatted for a bit, and then he disappeared. For a few moments they could not find him. Then they saw him carrying the suitcases of an old woman who had been on the train. Some wondered: "Why would he do such a thing?" Then they realized that this was who Schweitzer was. He was always reaching out to help others in need. It was a part of his Christian nature. Soon the university officials began to look around to see if they could find some elderly woman who had a suitcase they could carry.

How do we measure the depth of Jesus' love? He did not ask, "What can I get out of life?" Rather, he unselfishly gave his life for others. Jesus did not think about himself but about others. We raise the wrong questions when we ask, "What does this do for me? What can I get from life?" Our attitude needs to be: What can I give? What can I offer? What can I sacrifice? Jesus Christ is our model—our guide. This is frightening as well as reassuring when we recall the nature of his unselfish love and its high demands of us.

Leslie Weatherhead relates an awful experience that an Armenian woman and her family had when their home was broken into by Turkish soldiers during one of their raids. Her father, mother, and brothers were taken outside and shot by the soldiers. Her sisters were then handed over to the other soldiers to use at their will. The leader of the soldiers took this woman and used her for his lustful purposes. Several days later she was able to escape and fled to an Armenian refugee camp. There she, along with others, was taught nursing skills.

After a while, she, along with other nurses, had to care for some of the Turkish soldiers who had been captured. One night as she walked through the hospital ward, she glanced down and saw a face that she thought was familiar, and then she recognized him. She knew that it was the man who had killed her family and raped her. He was so ill that she really didn't have to do anything but neglect him and he would have died. But she could not. After she nursed him back to health, the doctor brought the nurse up to his bed and said to the young soldier, "But for this girl's devotion you would be dead." He glanced up at her and said, "I think we have met before." "Yes," she said, "we have met before." As she was walking away, the soldier hissed the words: "Why didn't you kill me?" She returned and said to him, "Because cruelty cannot be righted by cruelty, nor violence by violence. I am a follower of him who said, 'Love your enemies.' This is my religion." The soldier lay silent and then said, "I never knew there was such a religion. If that is your religion, tell me about it, for I want it." Each night she would come back to his bedside and share something of the gospel with him.[2]

This kind of love is not easy. Its claim on our lives and attitude is demanding. The love that Jesus Christ models for us goes beyond anything many of us have begun to imagine. This love demands the forgiveness of others, the unwillingness to cling to grudges or harbor hatreds, and the goal of being perfect like God. To be like Christ is to be unselfish, caring, patient, understanding, loving, and sacrificial.

What will the result of this kind of love be, if we have it? Jesus states the truth clearly: "If you have this kind of love, other people will recognize that you are my disciples." This kind of love begins as a sign within the church. The clearest test that we belong to Christ is whether we love each other. One of the ancient church fathers, Tertullian, said that the enemies of the Christian church used to say: "Behold, how the Christians love one another." But, brothers and sisters, unfortunately, that is not true today. Some of the saddest displays of disharmony, fragmentation, jealousy, fighting, and conflicts are evident within the community of faith. Bigotry, cruelty, self-interest, vilification, gossip, slander, and other worldly characteristics are reflected in the church. Christians seldom show much love for those who differ with them.

No one of us can say that my way of serving or my interpretation of the church is the only way! Since its beginning, the Christian church has had people from every walk of life—educated and uneducated, weak and strong, male and female, black and white, conservative and liberal, rich and poor, young and old—serving in the cause of Christ. Whosoever will may come. In recognition of this diversity, we affirm and support each other's gifts. The evidence within the church that we are Christ's followers is that we love one another.

The love Christians have for each other will be a testimony to the world for Christ. This love will be a witness to Christ's love. When the world sees the love Christians have for each other, it will want to belong to that kind of community. But the world is not going to want to belong to a church that is filled with criticism, disharmony, and disagreements and continuing fights between fundamentalists and liberals, Protestants and Catholics, modern and ancient thought. How will we win the world to Christ when we can't get along with each other? William Temple, the Anglican theologian, has written: "The Old Commandment stands as a universal, and universally neglected, requirement; the New Commandment *that ye love one another as I loved you* has a narrower range and a more intense quality. When the Church keeps the New Commandment, the world may keep the Old."[3] Friedrich Nietzche, the German philosopher, used to say, "I will become a Christian when I see one." I do not see much evidence in the life of many persons within the church today that models the kind of love that Jesus Christ has called us to exhibit.

Jesus has called his followers not to a philosophy but to a way of life. Our creeds are reflected in our deeds. Love is something you do not merely talk about. You cannot separate faith and works. James says, "I have faith and you have works. Show me your faith without your works, and I will show you my faith by my works" (James 2:17). The real evidence that we are Christians is demonstrated in our love for others, especially those within the fellowship of faith. This is the test. If we do not love one another, we are not Christians. Jesus is clear on the matter. Doctrines, creeds, laws, ideas are not the test. We pass or fail as his disciples in the way we love our fellow Christians. Love is the fulfilling of the law.

Let me conclude with a parable. Once day there was a man who was lonely and had no sense of meaning in life. But he heard that people in the Cube had love and life. So one day he entered the Cube, and he experienced ecstatic joy and love. His life was changed. For many years his life in the Cube was wonderful. But then one day he began to hear tones of disharmony, dissatisfaction, and criticism by those inside the Cube. Some didn't like the color of the Cube. Some didn't like the size of the Cube. Others didn't like the shape of the Cube. Still others began to say that the Cube was too hot or too cold. There were those who didn't like the music in the Cube. It was too loud, too soft, too familiar, or too unfamiliar. Others were critical of the Cube's leader. They didn't like some of the things he said or did.

Soon dissension began to break out in the group. Some declared, "There is only one way to understand the Cube. You have to believe in right angles to understand the meaning of the Cube." Others said, "Oh, no. It is the straight line that determines the correct understanding of the Cube." Still others declared, "Any angles are OK." Soon little cubes were built inside the big Cube. These little cubes were established with each little cube declaring that it had unique insights into what the Cube was really like: "My cube is more correct than your cube," each declared.

Then another, more vocal group arose. "The only way you can ever understand the Cube," they avowed, "is by knowing the square. Only those who follow the square book can be real members of the Cube. It is only those who read and interpret the square book squarely who are members of the Cube. These persons have to wear square hats, sit in square holes, follow square rules, and think squarely. They must listen to square talks by square, male preachers. Only male square preachers can really understand and explain the meaning of the Cube for the rest of us. Women are to serve the square men."

Unfortunately, this division continued for a long time. Then one day the One, who had founded the Cube, appeared in their midst, and he said to the people: "You have made me very sad. I built this Cube on a foundation of love. I laid down my life in love for you, and what I told you to do was to love one another. I told you that was all you needed to do." All of the smaller-cube builders were very ashamed. They began to dismantle their cubes, and harmony returned to the Cube again. Joy and love were once more experienced in the Cube. Then one day some of those outside of the Cube saw the love that those in the Cube had for each other, and they asked if they could come into the Cube and share in that love. They, too, wanted to be a part of such love. The members of the Cube pointed these persons to the founder of the Cube, who had taught them to love in this extraordinary way. This way of love surpasses all words and descriptions. He or she that hath ears to hear let him or her hear the meaning of this parable.

John, the elder, writing in his first Epistle, penned: "Dear friends, let us love one another, because love is from God. Every one who loves is a child of God and knows God, but the unloving knows nothing of God. For God is love, and his love was disclosed to us in this, that he sent his only Son into the world to bring us life. The love I speak of is not our love for God, but the love he showed to us in sending his Son as the remedy for the defilement of our sins. If God thus loved us, dear friends, we in turn are bound to love one another" (1 John 4:7–12, NEB). So let it be.

NOTES

1. Robert Fulghum, *It Was on Fire When I Lay Down on It* (New York: Villard Books, 1990), 191–93.

2. Leslie Weatherhead, *The Transforming Friendship* (Nashville, TN: Abingdon Press, 1977), 109–10.

3. William Temple, *Readings in St. John's Gospel* (London: Macmillan, 1963), 216.

21. Where You Stand Determines What You See
Judith Lynne Weidman

Jeremiah 48:11

Those of us who live in New York City know that a persistent question from friends who come to visit is whether you ever get used to seeing so many homeless people on the streets.

The answer, of course, is "No." And I usually add that I don't ever want to get used to it. This isn't a sight any person of religious convictions can dismiss. Of course it's not just our problem anymore. Homeless populations are increasing in communities across the country.

But as I walk the fourteen blocks down Broadway to my office in Midtown every morning, my own discomfort peaks at the point of realizing how little I really understand about how a person's life comes to this point—people either devoid of resources or alienated from the people or systems that could make a difference in their lives. There they stand, dirty, bent over, looking hollow, muttering to themselves.

There is for me a puzzle in all of this beyond the latest data on new housing starts and haggling over the adequacy of social programs for the poor, which have come to be known as "safety nets."

So I was struck recently when I came across a quote from the theologian Robert McAfee Brown: "Where you stand determines what you see."

I thought to myself, Perhaps my problem is where I stand. For better or worse, I am North American, white, middle class, Chris-

---

Judith Lynne Weidman holds degrees from DePauw University and Duke Divinity School. A Methodist, Dr. Weidman is Executive Editor of Religious News Service in New York City. She has edited three books and in 1987 was named United Methodist Communicator of the Year.

tian. Most of us in this congregation share these characteristics. They are, by and large, signs of privilege. But in fact, most of the world is not North American, white, middle class, or even Christian. I found myself in a form of isolation that didn't feel right.

So I decided to commit some vacation time this summer to hands-on work with the poor. Of course I could have done this in my own backyard, but as it happens I linked up with a group that went to Jamaica for ten days in mid-August. This had the advantage of casting these issues in a larger global context.

Once in Kingston, I discovered that the realities of caring for the daily needs of the poor get you down to basics fast. I was assigned to a center for the abandoned mentally retarded. Mopping up urine-soaked floors is how I started my day. Then there were mountains of laundry to be done for the sixty-seven residents—by hand, bent over a deep sink, outside in the August sun. Other members of our group of fourteen were across town giving baths to lepers.

"The poorest of the poor" they call these people—Roger, Maurice, Miss Lillian, Evette, Rosemary. "Nonproductive" persons—the old, the ill, the incapacitated—become an intolerable burden on poor families. They are left to die, abandoned on the streets of Kingston.

Modest programs by various church groups provide almost the only safety net in this poor country. And that's where the dividing line comes. The efforts of our volunteers at Christ Church, along with others across the city, in feeding and shelter programs supplement government efforts. In much of the third world, church work and other humanitarian efforts are often the first line of defense.

In Kingston I saw the Church in an absolute heroic mode. We rubbed elbows with the Missionaries of Charity, the order founded by Mother Teresa. Periodically they fan out across the city, checking the back alleys for abandoned people. Recently they had come across a man underneath a taxi who was covered with maggots. They brought him back to their center and cleaned him up. He died four days later, but I was touched by their sense of having touched this man with the hand of God before he died.

I worked at a center founded by Father Richard Ho Lung, a former Jesuit. He told about passing one of the worst slums in Kingston every morning on his way to the university. He said he did this for seven years, and suddenly he couldn't pass by on the other side anymore. He said with a twinkle in his eye, "Anyone can teach." He would spend the rest of his life rescuing the poor. He founded a new order, the Brotherhood of the Poor, starting with some of his former students.

Then there was Father Richard Albert, a priest from Brooklyn, who now works for the local diocese. He arranged for us to visit the city dump in Kingston, where more than five thousand people make their home. We were there for less than an hour, but during that time two different mothers approached us trying to convince us to take their babies. "You feed him," one said. I tried to imagine the despair that would cause a mother to want to give away her baby to strangers.

These experiences challenged my own sense of vocation. I didn't go to Jamaica with any illusions that a week of volunteer work would make a dent on the world's woes. The point for me was conversion—how I order my personal and professional life.

Without active intervention, my professional life stays locked in my white, Christian, middle-class notions of which events are worthy of making the news and who should be quoted. Journalists like myself, who are charged with interpreting the culture, can least afford this kind of isolation.

It's true: Where you stand determines what you see.

During times of study and worship with the group in Kingston, I found my condition addressed in the verse of Scripture that is our text this morning, Jeremiah 48:11: "Moab has been at ease from his youth and has settled on his lees; he has not been emptied from vessel to vessel, nor has he gone into exile; so his taste remains in him, and his scent is not changed" (RSV).

This passage is described as an oracle against Moab. The Moabites were a tribe of people with whom the Israelites had to do battle in their quest for the Promised Land. In this one verse, the writer personalizes Moab. A spoiled-teenager image emerges, or that of a yuppie who hasn't faced any of life's struggles yet.

The writer knew that the Moabites would understand this figure of speech from the local economy. In making wine, the juice was allowed to stand in large vats until the dregs settled to the bottom. Then it was emptied into another vessel and other impurities were allowed to settle. The process was repeated until the wine was clear and pure.

What I earlier called the need for intervention in my life, the writer of this oracle calls being emptied from vessel to vessel. Any way you say it, the image is that of an active God who calls us out of our comfort and our set ways.

It would play out differently in every profession, but I can't help wondering about the energy and creativity that would be released if organizations would free interested people one week a year for hands-on work with the poor. I think it would change not only what journalists write, but what teachers teach. What artists draw. What politicians legislate. What businesspeople sell.

We have come to this point: The gulf of injustice is so wide between the peoples of the earth that we don't even know who is on the other side. So we are left to say, each in our own way, that we will go to the other side. We will stand with the poor. And we will come home with our own vision enlarged.

22. On the Eve of the End of the World

Shelley E. Cochran

Jeremiah 32:1–15

I am what is affectionately known, at least among my family and friends, as a *tree hugger.* I have to admit, though, that I have never actually gone outside and physically hugged a tree. I've been tempted to, however, because I like trees. Trees are special to me, and I certainly hug them in my heart even if I haven't actually hugged them in person.

There are people who really are tree huggers, though. In fact, there is a whole big tree-hugging movement that got started a few years ago in Kenya, when some women there began to notice the alarming number of trees being cut down in their forests. Some of the trees were cut to clear the way to grow food for poor families. Some trees were cut to grow cash crops. Most of the trees these women saw, however—and unfortunately, that's an awfully big *most*—were cut so that the land could be used to raise beef cattle for North American hamburgers. That's right, North American hamburgers . . . that or cocaine, which was also grown for appetites here in the States.

Shelley E. Cochran is a workshop trainer and coordinator for the Judicial Process Commission, a faith-based, nonprofit organization in Rochester, New York. She is a trained interim pastor and has served churches in Kentucky, Indiana, Illinois, New Jersey, and New York. She has published several articles, including "Let the Children Come," in *Reformed Worship,* and "Passing the Peace," in the *Christian Ministry.* She is also a contributor to the homily section of a church school curriculum published by Resource Publications.

The Kenyan women, of course, were appalled. They were disgusted and horrified by what was happening to their trees, and in a fit of frustration they began wrapping their arms around endangered trees, sometimes even tying themselves to the trees, just daring the bulldozers to take them with them. Those women stood up to the bulldozers with the only weapon they had—their determination to save their precious forests.

At first there were only a few tree huggers. Soon more and more women in Kenya were also hugging trees and taking their stand against the axes, the bulldozers, and the buzz saws. Within a short time the movement spread to other countries, too. After a while women all over Africa were hugging and saving trees, and now even women here in the United States, and in countries all over the world, are hugging trees, or at least the next thing to it.

Some women, for instance—and now a lot of men, too—are planting trees as parts of city and rural beautification projects. Some of us are getting into recycling, source reduction, and using recycled paper products. Some of us are lobbying Congress. Some of us, like the women in Kenya, are even hugging real, for-sure trees.

I guess I come by my love of trees naturally, though. I caught it early on, I think, because as a child one of my best friends was a tree—a tall and graceful birch tree in our front yard. It was a beautiful tree, its gleaming white trunk glistening against the blue summer sky, its small green leaves rustling quietly in the warm Missouri breeze. I remember its delicate leaves in early spring and the funny wormlike seed pods it grew later on. I remember watching its leaves turn yellow and cascade down to the ground in the fall. I especially remember the many times my mother and I would watch anxiously as our beloved tree groaned under the weight of a winter ice storm. I loved that tree. I loved it so much I even cut the grass in the front yard, without even being asked, so my dad wouldn't be tempted to cut any of its branches to make room for a lawn mower.

It wasn't until my birch tree friend died of old age—the age I am now, in fact—that I really realized how much I cared for trees, and especially that tree. Until it died, my birch friend had always been there. It had always been a part of my life. The day the workers came to cut down its then barren frame, I waited inside.

I couldn't bear to watch. When the buzz saws started in, I actually felt pain. I literally cringed at the very sound, and soon I had to get away. I had to get in the car and drive away, leave it all behind, it was so awful.

In the years following, my appreciation for trees has increased. In my teens I made a pilgrimage of sorts to see the redwoods in California. Some years later I fell in love with the campus of the seminary I later attended because of the trees there. More recently I have even bought live Christmas trees so I can plant them later.

My present love of trees, though, came to real fruition during graduate school in New Jersey. Now that I think of it, I probably went to Drew University because of the trees there. In fact, Drew has, or at least did have, its own forest, a forest I often enjoyed walking in on my way home from work or classes. It was a beautiful, magnificent forest, so quiet, so peaceful, almost reverent.

Then the bulldozers came. One afternoon I set off on my usual woodsy path home from work and the trees along the path were gone, and in their place were mounds of dull brown New Jersey dirt . . . with a few scattered backhoes on top. The edge of that forest I loved so much—the edge that came right up to the house I had lived in when I first came to Drew, the edge to which I still went to meditate—was gone. There was nothing left of it but a big gaping hole of mud.

I stood there in shock. I stood there frozen by the horror of it all. I don't know how long I stood there. I don't even want to know. I finally was at least able to move, and as I at last turned away I heard in the background that dreaded sound from my childhood, that sound I knew I would never ever forget—the whirring of buzz saw and the unmistakable crack of falling trees.

I can't describe how terrible it was. I don't have the words. All I can say is that it felt evil, truly evil, and I usually don't say something like that lightly. It was that awful.

As the trees change colors each fall, I often ponder such things, and in many respects this year I am not encouraged. Every day several thousand acres of African rain forests still fall. Just about that much forest still falls in this country, too, especially in the Pacific Northwest. Each day several thousand pounds of lawn and agricultural pesticides still poison trees and other living things. We still don't know what to do with the waste paper we can't recycle, or how to reduce the amount of waste paper we use in the first place. And our national forests are still endangered, not by natural forces, but by the sheer number of people who want to visit them.

The recent Earth Days, of course, have made some progress. More and more counties like ours are recycling. I see more products made out of recycled paper being offered at the store. Fewer toxic wastes are being dumped illegally. People at church here are talking about bringing their own mugs to the coffee hour. I even see McDonald's making an attempt to recycle.

But still, I am not encouraged. For the more I think about it, the more uncertain I am that we're going to be able to do enough fast enough. Sometimes I'm not even sure we want to, that we even have the will to make the changes in our personal and national life-styles that are required to stem the tide of pollution and deforestation.

Some folks I know are so pessimistic that they are convinced we are truly at the edge of the end of the world, or at least the end of civilization as we know it. And the end won't come because of a nuclear holocaust, either, they say. It will come because of an ecological one, an environmental one in which the entire planet will be slowly, sometimes even imperceptibly, poisoned beyond our ability to inhabit it.

Jeremiah, I think, would have understood. Many people in his day didn't think they were going to last much longer, either. They, too, were facing possible slow extinction. In their case, of course, it was a war that threatened them, but the effect on their everyday lives was very similar. Most of the trees in the town had probably been cut for weapons. Water was either unfit to drink or being rationed because there was too little of it. Trash and garbage were piling up because no one dared go outside the city gates to dump it. It must have felt like the edge of the end of their world, too, the end of life as they knew it, the end of their civilization, the end of their nation, the end of their very lives for some of them.

Jeremiah particularly was not encouraged. "A horrible shocking thing is happening in the land," he said, "for we have defiled it. The ground is cracked and barren and pastures lie parched and withered. The whole land lies in ruins and the people groan because there is no bread. . . . Now even death itself is climbing into our windows and has entered our fortresses."

It was not a pretty picture. In fact, it was one of the most bleak pictures the people of Israel had ever faced. But fortunately, God apparently had other ideas. "Your cousin is going to come to you," God said to gloomy Jeremiah. "Your cousin is going to come and offer to sell you a field in Anathoth. Take it. When your cousin comes, I want you to buy that field. Pay him whatever he offers. Do whatever you need to do, but I want you to buy that field."

Now, Jeremiah probably thought it was a pretty stupid thing to do, especially considering the circumstances. At the time God came to Jeremiah with this strange request, the country was at war with the worst, most ruthless superpower of the ancient world, Babylon, and things were not going well. In fact, the capital city of Jerusalem itself was under siege and daily life was getting harder as blockades and economic sanctions began taking their toll. Everything was crumbling in around them. Their whole life, their whole society was falling apart.

And in the midst of it all was Jeremiah. He had already spoken out against the war—several times, in fact. He had already told the king what he thought about the situation. But no one had listened, and now there he was, sitting in the palace jail, arrested for having told the truth about how badly the war was going, and how badly the environment was suffering on account of it.

As he sat there in jail, reflecting on this latest and most out-rageous of God's requests, Jeremiah no doubt wondered what in the world buying that little field was going to accomplish. He probably thought to himself that it was dumb, that it was crazy. What good was buying a field going to do, especially a field that was currently in enemy hands? "What good is that?" Jeremiah probably thought. "People are starving. People are dying. Homes and fields all around us are being destroyed. Our whole world is being dev-astated and God wants me to buy a field? It's nuts!"

On the face of it, it does seem like a pretty foolish gesture. Buying that field does seem a bit insignificant, especially consid-ering the mess everything was in at the time.

Such a puny gesture, so inadequate, so futile, so utterly hope-less in comparison. And yet, God said, "I want you to buy that field. I don't care how crazy it looks, I want you to go and buy it."

And so he did. Jeremiah bought that field. As silly and foolish as it sounded, and no doubt feeling a bit stupid and all the rest,

Jeremiah bought that field in Anathoth. And not only that, he made a big production of it, too. He weighed out the silver. He publicly signed the deed. He even had the deed placed in a sealed jar for protection.

Jeremiah and his people were on the edge of extinction. They were on the edge of their world's total destruction. And yet Jeremiah went and bought that field. Even though he may have thought it was the dumbest thing he had ever done in his life, Jeremiah bought that field—in enemy territory, no less. He bought that field even when he was in prison, when he was himself confined by the palace guards.

And he bought it as a sign of hope. He bought that field, he said, as a symbol of hope, a symbol of the future, a future he himself was not sure he or his people would ever see. "God says fields and vineyards will once again grow in this land," Jeremiah told the people. "God says gardens and trees and bushes and flowers will once again flourish here. When the siege is ended, when the war is over, when we are taken into exile, and then are able to return here, this land will once again grow and bloom."

My friends, we may not be a prophet like Jeremiah, or have the wherewithal to buy a field as a sign of faith, but the Koran, the holy scripture of the Muslim faith, tells us something like that that we can do. "On the eve of the end of the world," the Koran says, "plant a tree." Even when everything looks hopeless, as it did for Jeremiah, when all seems lost, when nothing seems to work and the end looms in sight before us, even when we stand on the very eve of destruction, as we do in many respects today, the Koran says, plant a tree.

I don't know if we really are on the eve of the end of the world. Sometimes, when I see the beauty of the trees outside, when I hear of more and more people becoming concerned about the environment, I think, "Maybe there's a chance." Sometimes I get encouraged.

But mostly, I have to admit, I get discouraged, for signs of the end really are all around us: shrinking forests, dying wildlife, poisoned fish, increasing rates of cancer, hotter summers and long droughts, water many are afraid to drink, and air people, especially elderly people, are advised not to go out in. Sometimes when I see things like that I wonder. Sometimes I even get a bit scared.

My biggest consolation, though, is the same hope Jeremiah had. My consolation is the same hope that made him go and buy that field—the hope that somehow or another God has something other than the end in mind for us. That is my hope—that in the midst of all the signs of destruction, God has something else in mind, something more hopeful, something more healthful, something more beautiful. That's what keeps me going. That's what keeps me hugging trees in spite of how puny my action seems compared with the power of the buzz saws. It is the hope that God is indeed not finished with us yet. It is the hope that indeed fields and vineyards will once again flourish where now only the forces of destruction seem to prevail.

"On the eve of the end of the world, plant a tree." Maybe it is silly. Maybe it is crazy. But, God help us, it may be the only hope we have.

23. Ministry of Response
Bob Dorr

Acts 3:1–16

Peter and John were on their way to church. They were going to the temple to pray at the scheduled time—to do the things they had always done, in the ways in which they had always done them. But they were interrupted—interrupted by human need. They responded and they found themselves involved in ministry, involved in a way that they had not planned and could not have predicted. Their lives were never the same. They had been given a new agenda.

Some members of the Seventh Baptist Church, about twenty-five years ago, were busy being church.[1] We were worshiping, studying, and caring for each other. We were doing the same things we had always done in the ways in which we had always done them. But we were interrupted by human need. We responded as best we could, and we found ourselves involved in ministry, in ways in which we had not planned and could never have predicted. The life of the church was never the same again. Our lives were never the same. We had a new agenda.

As we looked at all the need, we wrestled with the question, What does it mean to be a middle-class church in an inner-city neighborhood? We had no future in traditional ways in which

Robert W. Dorr served as a pastor for thirty-six years before retiring in 1989. For almost twenty-six years of his pastoral ministry, he was pastor of one congregation, the Seventh Baptist Church in Baltimore, Maryland, an inner-city church with active ministry, worship, and education programs. He received his B.A. and M.A. degrees from the University of Maryland (1947, 1949), his B.Div. from Duke Divinity School (1953), and his D.Min. from Southeastern Theological Seminary (1979).

churches measure success. It became clear that we were to follow the example of our Lord—we were to serve. But how? Whom? So much need, so much pain, and our resources were so few.

Learning from the example of other churches and our own experiences, and being supported by biblical principles, we came to the realization that ministry is the result of two things coming together—need and gifts. It was a formula: need plus gifts equals ministry (or mission, if you prefer).

If we have the gifts to touch a need, we have a call to ministry. Let us look at these two elements.

I.

The first part of the formula is *need*.

In the story from Acts, we see Peter and John moving toward the temple at the regular time for prayer. As they moved along, a man approached them and asked for alms. Peter and John looked at him—"fastened their eyes upon him" is the way the King James Version puts it; they really saw him. They saw a man who had been lame from birth, who was carried by others to a strategic place to beg—a man who had lost his ability to work, and therefore his dignity, his sense of worth as a man. Peter and John saw him and they responded.

In Baltimore, some members of the Seventh Baptist Church began to open their eyes; we saw people not as interruptions, but as persons with needs.

We saw children being raised in the city in poverty, without playmates, without stimulation—"I didn't know he was supposed to talk until he started to school," said the young mother, who was only a child herself. We saw the houses with five families crowded into a building that was meant for one; the front yards were concrete stretching out to the busy street, and the backyards were filled with trash and glass and an occasional rat.

We saw elderly people, too—the isolated ones, without families, many trapped in the city (somehow never able to get back to North Carolina or Virginia). Georgia lay on the floor for twenty-four hours before she was found; Irene was helped only after the Meals-on-Wheels volunteer saw her food collecting mold and roaches. We saw men and women facing the enemies of the elderly in the city—malnutrition, fear, and loneliness.

We saw persons leaving psychiatric hospitals before they were ready. Without families, many did not have the resources, financial or emotional, to live by themselves. They, too, lived in fear, overwhelmed by the city.

We saw young adults in transition, a Vietnamese refugee family, people without shelter and food, and more.

We saw, too, persons who needed God and the church, who looked at our intimidating buildings and our well-dressed congregations. They deeply needed what the church stood for, but never guessed that somehow it was for them.

And seeing the needs, people responded—day care and nursery school, a psychiatric halfway house, apartments for the elderly with many support systems, a boutique to offer clothing with dignity, a young-adult residential community, and more. The particular things that we did are not important in themselves, because each congregation will see different needs and make different responses, but the principles are the same for all.

And when we grew discouraged, knowing that all we did could only scratch the surface of the city's needs, we were helped by the kind of thinking enunciated by Mother Teresa in this poem:

> I never look at the masses as my
>   responsibility.
> I look at the individual. I can only love one
>   person at a time. I can only feed one person
>   at a time.
> Just one, one, one . . .
> So you begin . . . I begin.
> I picked up one person—
> maybe if I didn't pick up that one person I
>   wouldn't have picked up 42,000.
> The whole work is only a drop in the ocean.
>   But if I didn't put the drop in, the ocean
>   would be one drop less.[2]

Mother Teresa saw need in India, people dying on the streets of Calcutta, and she responded. In Baltimore, we saw different kinds of need, and there was response. And all over the world other Christians are seeing a variety of needs and are making their own responses. Yet there are many Christians sitting on their hands; many churches are still content to do the same things in the same old ways, while their cities lie in pain around them. Let us then open our eyes to see—really see—the needs around us, and let us then respond.

II.

The second part of the formula is *gifts*.

Peter and John were asked for alms—for money—and Peter gave the classic reply: "I have no silver and gold, but I give you what I have." He could offer no money, but he offered something better, something quite practical—healing. And with the healing of his lameness, the man was given back his ability to work, his manhood, his dignity. This was social ministry—no strings attached; it was done in the name of Jesus, but there was no sermon to listen to, no requirement of religion, no pressure to join the church. Later, the opportunity arose when they would use other gifts—preaching and exhortation—but initially, it was just an act of love; Peter and John simply saw a need and they responded with their gift of healing.

This became our working principle: We are to meet whatever needs we can with whatever gifts we have. For us the definition of *gift* was quite simple: A gift is anything we have received that we can give back to God by using it in service to others.

Many gifts were called forth and used in ministry. For the nursery school, compassion sent two young housewives back to school to study early-childhood education; some men built cubbies and painted rooms; a CPA set up the books; a lawyer wrote the charter for a nonprofit corporation; many people helped with fund-raising.

After-school programs developed for children. Several people tutored; some taught Bible studies, others taught sewing and cooking, and still others did recreation.

A camp for inner-city teenagers developed. Dora was the camp nurse and Lynette was the cook; a businessman spent his vacation teaching leather work.

Jean led a mothers' group for single women to help them with their parenting skills and to help them break the cycle of violence and abuse.

Frank was a quiet, unassuming man, retired, a recovering alcoholic, who liked ceramics and people. Karen met him at a crucial time in her life. She was a woman in her middle twenties who had left home when she was thirteen to become a go-go girl. She had three failed marriages behind her, her two children were in foster homes, and she was living a pretty wild life. She would have nothing to do with the church, but she was fascinated with ceramics. And that was the first step for her. Then she went to Jean's mothers' group, and later she went to Sunday School with Jean. She made a profession of faith, joined the church, got her GED, got her children back, and married a stable man. And it all started with Frank's love for people and ceramics.

All kinds of gifts were called forth—gifts of many ordinary people doing simple, ordinary things. But when those gifts were channeled to meet human need in the name of Christ, ministry emerged, mission was accomplished.

James Wright helped me with this concept of gifts. He was eighty years old, arthritic, and confined to his apartment. I saw him fairly often, and one day he said to me, "I write letters, you know." Since I didn't know, I asked him to explain. He was a man who listened to the radio, watched television, and read the papers. He knew what was going on in the world, and he had strong Christian convictions. He wrote letters to the mayor, the governor, congressmen, editors, even the president. And after he had told me that, without further introduction, he said,

> I am only one, but I am one,
> I cannot do everything, but I can do something.
> What I can do, I ought to do,
> And what I ought to do, by the grace of God,
> I will do.[3]

His gift was letter writing, and he expressed a principle that I repeated many times: Everyone can do something, everyone has a gift; and if the gift can be used to touch human need, there is a call to ministry.

Gifts plus need equals ministry. I am convinced that ministries will develop, needs will be met, and lives will be changed—the lives of those who receive and the lives of those who give.

Perhaps in conclusion there is only one more thing to be said, and to say it, I'll quote again from Mother Teresa's poem. "So I began," she wrote, "I picked up one person, / just one." And then she says to all of us:

Same thing with you,
same thing in your family,
same thing in the church where you go,
just begin . . . one, one, one.

NOTES

1. The Seventh Baptist Church is in Baltimore, Maryland. I was pastor there for almost twenty-six years, until my retirement. I preached this sermon at the Second and Fourth Baptist Church in Baltimore on July 12, 1992.

2. Mother Teresa, *Words to Love By* (Notre Dame, IN: Ave Maria Press, 1983), 79.

3. I wrote the poem down as soon as I left his apartment that day. Later, I learned that it was written by Edward Everett Hale.

24. The Eleventh Commandment

C. Michael Caldwell

Exodus 20:1–6; Luke 9:46–48

About ten years ago near the beginning of my part-time ministry with a small rural church in western Maine, I invited the congregation to request sermons on specific topics or scripture passages.

A woman by the name of Sylvia requested Exodus 20, verse 5—part of the text of the Ten Commandments we just heard. Almost in desperation—I think because of some consternation in her extended family life—she said to me, "I just don't understand this: 'The sins of the parents shall be visited on the children to the third and fourth generations of those who reject me.' Why should innocent children pay the price for the sins of their parents? How can God say such a thing? My God is a loving God, not a punishing God!"

I could tell that Sylvia had thought a lot about the passage. She took her faith very seriously. She took her Sunday School teaching very seriously. She had a high degree of integrity, and she expected it from others and from God. She knew she could not accept what she was hearing, as she understood it. It was a profound test of

C. Michael Caldwell is pastor of the Second Congregational Church in Hyde Park, Vermont. He is also Pastoral-Counselor-in-Training with the American Association of Pastoral Counselors. He received his B.A. from Dartmouth College (1975) and his M.Div. and D.Min. degrees from Andover Newton Theological School (1982, 1993). He has served as pastor of churches in Maine and Vermont, and as interim pastor of churches in Massachusetts and New Hampshire.

faith, because the question arose where it did—smack dab in the middle of the Ten Commandments, a central underpinning of our entire Judeo-Christian tradition.

I can't remember exactly what I said in the moment in response to her question. I wondered the same thing she was wondering. This God seemed different from the God of Jesus. I think I said something consoling and something to the effect that this may be God's way of explaining why people in a lot of families don't seem to change from one generation to another—why fathers and sons and grandsons, and mothers and daughters and granddaughters, seem to get stuck in the same old ruts and can't find a way out as the generations turn and the years go by.

And the sermon I preached a few weeks later developed that interpretation. This sermon develops it more, because I had to wrestle with it a long time before it made any sense. Even biblical commentaries are loudly silent about the meaning.

Ten years later, after a lot of wrestling, I don't pretend to have a full answer. What I can give is a personal witness to what I now believe, based on a long period of sitting with the text in light of the Holy Spirit, and in light of my personal experience. In sharing that with you, I pray it may contribute to your own struggle with this and other difficult passages of Scripture, as a way of respecting the authority of Scripture rather than denying our serious questions about what some of Scripture says.

What I found I needed to do in this case was imagine another commandment within the Ten Commandments—a commandment not stated but implied, which I am calling "the eleventh commandment." And it is this:

Honor thy children.

The media have given a lot of moral witness to the need for such a commandment to be a foundational part of our society. Child abuse is as widespread as an epidemic—physical, sexual, and emotional abuse that undermines a child's basic sense of self and trust so profoundly that most children carry the wounding for life and pass it on to the next generation, like passing on the family coat of arms. Most abuse is from parents, coming mostly from fathers. Healing is difficult and rare.

The implications for global social change, social justice, and peacemaking are also profound. In this regard I simply ask a rhetorical question: What if Saddam Hussein had dealt with his abuse as a child? What if Adolf Hitler had done so? They were both children of abusive parents.

The implications for the church's mission are also profound. Dayl Hufford of Andover Newton Theological School says, "The unaware church is a barrier instead of a bridge. When the church and its people are unaware, uninformed, and unresponsive, children anguish in silence."

But it's not only in abusing that we fail to honor our children. Neglect, absence, distance, belittling, and what Matthew Fox calls "adultist condescension" all contribute to the problem.

So, an abusive parent begets an abusive child.

A controlling parent begets a controlling child.

A father with a hot temper will often produce a son full of rage.

A mother who is an obsessive worrier will often have a daughter with obsessive-compulsive disorder.

And people who take various kinds of often very subtle debilitating psychological issues into their adult lives—without examining themselves and changing their behavior patterns—will inevitably pass along these same patterns to their offspring. For example: discomfort about expressing feelings, emotional unavailability, the inability to listen well, difficulty in sustaining emotional intimacy, denial of normal grief, and, on the part of men, the basic macho male patterns of dominating women.

All these patterns, and more, prevent us from keeping the first commandment, elaborated on in Deuteronomy 6 and expanded upon by Jesus in Luke 9 and 10. In other words, if we are

- to actually have no other gods before the one true God;
- to actually love the Lord our God with all our heart, soul, mind, and strength;
- to actually love our neighbors as ourselves;
- to actually love our children as the divine father or mother loves the divine son or daughter;

then we need to deal with the unconscious or conscious demons that demonize and demean our children in the way we parent them.

It requires more of a profound commitment to giving ourselves to God and honoring God than we may ever have realized.

Honoring God means doing whatever personal work we need to do to honor our children—whether they're our own biological children, our adopted children, our foster children, the children around us in our church and community (if we don't have our own), or the children of the world who hunger and starve due to our distant but direct neglect.

In this sense, the eleventh commandment is the flip side of the first and the second—in the sense that one of the most profound ways we can honor God is to honor our children.

Jesus knew this. It was a central part of his message:

- "Unless we become as children, we shall not enter the Kingdom of God."
- "Let the children come to me, for to such belongs the Kingdom of God."
- "And placing a child in the midst of his disciples, he interrupted their argument about which one was the greatest by saying, 'Whoever welcomes this child in my name welcomes me . . . for the least among you is the greatest.' "

There are so many examples I could share to demonstrate how honoring our children is like honoring God. I'm choosing one amazing story I recently heard from Carey Kinder's dedication ceremony up at Podunk Ridge Farm a year or so ago.

As I heard the story (and I think I've got the basics right), Tom and Dorian had invited people to share a blessing to honor Carey. One friend of theirs shared that when her second child was born, her three-year-old wanted time alone with the infant. She and her husband were a bit taken aback and concerned about what the three-year-old would do, given sibling rivalry and the natural resentment of a young child to a new baby. But after some consultation, they made a plan. They rigged a way to see into the room where their three-year-old would be allowed to be with their new baby, so they could monitor the situation. And what they heard astonished them. The three-year-old said to the baby, "Tell me what God is like. I'm beginning to forget."

To honor our children is literally to honor God, as that three-year-old knew, and as Robert Coles's stirring book, *The Spiritual Life of Children,* has emphasized.[1]

How can we really do this well? For myself, parenting is the hardest work I've ever done, which is why I'm so concerned about it. I'm comforted by the fact that it's difficult for anyone at times, regardless of his or her family history. To do it well seems akin to applying ourselves with the discipline and the commitment of a devoted artist. Parenting is a difficult art; yet we need to believe we may become masters of this art, taking our children as our teachers.

To really honor the children around us, to really love them proactively, takes the same kind of active love as does any fervent act of faith.

Can we honor our children with the same zeal with which we honor our fathers and mothers, as in the fifth commandment?

Can we honor our children with the same zeal with which we carry out any of the other commandments?

And can we find simple ways to do it well in the moment? Ways such as:

- taking a minute to validate a child's hurt feelings even when we think the child is overreacting;
- just hanging up a child's artwork on the refrigerator with a word of praise;
- loving a child with great patience for who the child is, even when his or her behavior irritates us to no end;
- making a daily renewed commitment to "discipline, yes; violence, no."

In these simple ways in the complex moments of emotionally difficult days, and in countless other ways we can each name for ourselves, can we love, honor, and cherish our children better than we have, perhaps with the seriousness of a marriage vow?

If we can, Matthew Fox says, there is the very source of the second coming of Christ.

If we can, Alice Miller says, the full potential of each child will naturally unfold rather than get stuck.

If we can, John Bradshaw says, we will avoid the damaging and wounding and shaming that demeans and debilitates many of our children for life.

If we can, Jesus Christ says, we will know the joy of the Kingdom of God in the very midst of us.

In honoring the child, we honor God, where the blessings of the fathers shall be visited upon the sons, and the compassion of the mothers shall be visited upon the daughters from generation to generation.

This commandment can give a unity to all of us, conservative and liberal, young and old. May we seek to carry it out by doing the personal work we need to do, and believing that the church community can be a place for the kind of sharing and consultation that can help us move through the real difficulties to the real blessings.

Honor thy children.

I pray this for all of us here this morning and for the mission of Christ's church throughout the whole world. Amen.

NOTE

1. Robert Coles, *The Spiritual Life of Children* (Boston: Houghton Mifflin, 1990).

V. PASTORAL

25. The Key Is Missing
Dianne Bertolino-Green

2 Samuel 18:24–33; Psalm 102:1–12; Ephesians 5:15–20;
John 6:51–58.

Easter Day has come and gone again. And the victory is ours
through Jesus, the Risen Christ. The Church proclaims the witness.
But for many this day in the midst of their suffering, the victory
is hard to discern. This shouldn't surprise us, for even the Gospels
record incredulity. Matthew tells us (28:17) that some were doubt-
ful, and Luke records (24:11) that the victory story proclaimed by
the women appeared at first, *even to the disciples,* to be nonsense,
and they refused to believe. I expect that their personal pain made
the victory hard to feel. Despairing, they were probably lost in
their thoughts of sorrow.

Paul Simon, of Simon and Garfunkel fame, wrote these sad
lines to despair in one of his recent songs: "A good day . . . ain't got
no rain; a bad day's when I lie in bed and think of things that
might have been . . . slip sliding away." In the scripture readings
that I've chosen for today it was that kind of day for David. "It's a
good day" the first messenger, Ahimaaz, said. "No rain. All is well.
Good news from the battle front." And I guess Ahimaaz had a
right to expect a reward. After all, he got there first with news of
victory. "Blessed be the Lord, your God, who has delivered up the
men who raised their hand against my lord the king." But David
doesn't cheer, and there's no reward. He expected to win; it was no
surprise. In preparation for his victory, he told the commanders,
"Deal gently for my sake with the young man Absalom. Protect
him. I know he's a traitor, but he's my son." David was sure to win.

Dianne Bertolino-Green is Associate Professor in Pastoral Theology
and Director of Spiritual Formation at Western Theological Seminary
in Holland, Michigan. Until this year she was a lecturer in pastoral
theology and Director of Field Education at Perth Theological Hall
of the Uniting Church in Western Australia.

He made positive assessments about the message before the runner even got there. Wishful thinking? Confidence? Perhaps even arrogance that Yahweh would stop the plans of the rebels and vindicate his chosen king. David was an experienced military strategist; he was not without important friends. His army may have been smaller, but he was better equipped. David dismissed the good news, seeking, almost obsessed with, the fate of his son: "Is it well with the young man, Absalom?" Ahimaaz stuttered, "I saw a lot of commotion, but I really couldn't say what happened. Now, about the good news." The good news had little power because the *key* news David was looking for was missing.

The first messenger, Ahimaaz, was told to stand aside, sans reward. In came the second messenger, the Cushite, the foreigner. As a slave, he had little to lose. He brought the whole truth—couched in the language of the court, of course. "It's a good day," he said. "For the Lord has vindicated you, delivering you from the power of all who rose up against you. You're safe now, you've won." Again David skirts the victory celebration. "What I really want to know," he said, "is how's my boy? Is he OK?" The Cushite answered, "May the enemies of my lord the king, and all who rise up to do you harm, be like that young man."

David must have been torn in half with mixed emotions. He was confident of his victory, and no doubt glad of it. He set it up that way. His military prowess proved, all right, that he was king and he'd stay king. But the cost, the cost. Such a loss; could he bear it? "Oh my son, Absalom, my son, my son Absalom! Would that I had died instead of you, O Absalom, my son, my son!" "A good day . . . ain't got no rain; a bad day's when I lie in bed and think of things that might have been . . . slip sliding away."

I can imagine that when David retired to his chamber he lay awake and thought of things that might have been. Absalom might not have rebelled. He might have been captured and then repented. David might even have been big enough to forgive him. And, of course, there was the reminder of his own sins, reenacted through his sons, and all of that was slip sliding away. Absalom was dead. It may have ultimately been a good day for Israel, but it didn't feel like that to David. Emotively, he wished that he himself had died instead. It would have been easier than bearing this intolerable pain. Like most of us, in the face of crisis David was shattered. I imagine, by his lament, that David was asking why,

trying to make sense of it all. He was looking for the key to meaning, but it wasn't to be found. Hear a story by Idries Shah from *The
Exploits of the Incomparable Mulla Nasrudin:*

> A man saw Nasrudin searching for something on
> the ground. "What have you lost, Mulla?" he
> asked. "My key," said the Mulla. So the man went
> down on his knees too, and they both looked for
> it. After a time the other man asked: "Where
> exactly did you drop it?" "In my own house."
> "Then why are you looking for it here?"
> "There is more light here than inside my own
> house."

I imagine that there was more light anywhere than in David's
house that night—no key, no light. Like David, you and I have had
days like that, when we felt so low we had to look up to look down,
as the saying goes—days so bad that the only good thing you could
say about them was trivial and powerless: Well, at least it's not
raining. "A good day . . . ain't got no rain; a bad day's when I lie
in bed and think of things that might have been . . . slip sliding
away."

The text that I chose for our Old Testament reading today was
hard enough. The Psalm that is usually paired as a response to 2
Samuel 18 was even worse. I wasn't ready for the Psalm. Verse 3
was difficult for me to read, let alone to preach about: "For my
days pass away like smoke, and my bones burn like in a furnace."
That's not an Easter portrait. No celebration here! God may be
enthroned forever, as the Psalmist declares, but even the affirmation is surrounded by lamentations. Sorrow is repeatedly mingled
with our earthly joy. We are constantly surrounded by the hard
realities of life, *even of Easter.* Let me share with you why this Psalm
was especially hard for me. Five years ago this Eastertime my
mother-in-law, whom I loved deeply, had an accident. She had
gone ahead to the old home place in Louisiana, where she was
born. Dad remained in Texas for church responsibilities. She was
preparing a nest where they were to retire. On Monday morning
early, she lit the stove and it exploded. She caught on fire and
somehow managed to get outside, screaming for help. A neighbor
heard her and thought she was being attacked. He rushed out, gun
in hand, to aid her and saw her burning. He rolled her on the
ground and with the help of family was able to get her to the

hospital. The only part of her that was not burned was the bottoms of her feet. That was the only part of her that we could touch, to convey our love. She struggled, fully conscious, for ten days and then died. It was a living nightmare that wouldn't go away. They were some of the worst days of my life. I remember lying in bed and thinking of things that might have been. She might have not gone that weekend. She might have smelled the leak and escaped. God might somehow have intervened. But there were no miracles that day and it was all over, slip sliding away.

Like David, we search for the key to meaning. Like the mulla, we often look for the key in the wrong place. Mom was not afraid of death. Her relationship with God was deep and ongoing. She lived her faith out as a missionary in Brazil, a wife, a mother, a preschool teacher, and a specialist. She wanted us to have the Hallelujah Chorus sung by a full choir at her funeral. It was her way of reminding us that God would ultimately overcome evil, in God's own time. We grieved for ourselves. Sometimes, we still do. Like David, even fully conscious of the victory, we had experienced a deep emotional loss.

Sometimes people respond to this kind of loss with intense anger at God. A young man was killed in military combat, just like Absalom. The chaplain went to see the father. In inconsolable rage the father challenged the chaplain: "Where was God when they killed my boy?" Thoughtfully, the chaplain responded, "He was probably where he was when they killed his boy." Where do we find the key to meaning? The clue is in today's Psalm, verse 12. The answer is not in our finitude but in God's eternal reign. The key to meaning and to hope is in Christ Jesus. God cared enough about our condition that God planned the Christ event, God's self-disclosure in human form, Emmanuel, God with us. And Jesus came that we might have life, more abundant life, even in the tragic world of which we are a part. Through the incarnation, he identified with our brokenness, our pain, our sin, and even our death. And through his death and resurrection he overcame death. He offered us a relationship with himself that would be without end. He said, "I am the bread who came down from heaven; whoever eats of this bread will live forever." And in Communion we experience Easter again and again.

This doesn't mean that we won't have days when we feel like David did, overcome with loss. And it doesn't mean that we won't have days when we feel like the psalmist, overcome with a sense of affliction beyond our ability to endure. What it does mean is that on those days we may need to look for the key in the right place.

26. Christ Alone Gives the Fullness of Divine Life
Pope John Paul II

The celebration proper of World Youth Day began on Saturday evening, August 14, 1993, with a prayer vigil in Cherry Creek State Park in Denver, Colorado. The service was marked by scripture readings, prayers, hymns, and testimonies by young people from various nations. At three different moments of the celebration the pope addressed the young people on themes suggested by the Scripture, focusing his remarks on Christ's words "I came that they might have life, and have it abundantly." The pope spoke mainly in English, with occasional passages in Spanish, French, and Italian.

Part One

Dear Young People, Young Pilgrims on the path of Life:
"I came that they might have life, and have it abundantly" (John 10:10).

This evening these words of Christ are addressed to you young people gathered for the World Youth Day.

Jesus speaks these words in the parable of the Good Shepherd. The Good Shepherd: what a beautiful image of God! It transmits something deep and personal about the way God cares for all that he has made. In the modern metropolis it is not likely that you will see a shepherd guarding his flock. But we can go back to the tra-

---

Pope John Paul II was born Karol Wojtyla in Wadowice (near Krakow), Poland. He was ordained to the priesthood in 1946; appointed bishop in 1958; became archbishop of Krakow in 1964; was proclaimed cardinal in 1967; was elected pope on October 16, 1978, and installed on October 22, 1978. As Karol Wojtyla, he wrote plays and poetry; as John Paul II, he has written numerous books, including *The Redeemer of Man* (1979), *Christian Meaning of Human Suffering* (1984), and *Virgin Mary* (1987). Among his leisure interests are skiing and rowing. The text of the pope's homily was taken from *L'osservatore romano* (English edition).

ditions of the Old Testament, in which the parable is deeply rooted, in order to understand the loving care of the Shepherd for his sheep.

The Psalm says: "The Lord is my shepherd, I shall not want" (Ps. 23:1). The Lord, the Shepherd, is God-Yahweh. The One who freed his people from oppression in the land of their exile. The One who revealed himself on Mount Sinai as the God of the covenant: "If you will obey my voice and keep my covenant, you shall be my own possession among all peoples; for all the earth is mine" (Exod. 19:5).

God is the Creator of all that exists. On the earth which he created he placed man and woman: "Male and female he created them" (Gen. 1:27). "And God blessed them, and God said to them, 'Be fruitful and multiply, and fill the earth and subdue it; and have dominion over . . . every living thing that moves upon the earth'" (Gen. 1:28).

The special place of human beings in all that God made lies in their being given a share in God's own concern and providence for the whole of creation. The Creator has entrusted the world to us, as a gift of responsibility. He who is eternal Providence, the One who guides the entire universe towards its final destiny, made us in his image and likeness, so that we too should become "providence"—a wise and intelligent providence, guiding human development and the development of the world along the path of harmony with the Creator's will, for the well-being of the human family and the fulfillment of each individual's transcendent calling.

Yet, millions of men and women live without giving a thought to what they do or to what will come later. Here, this evening in Denver's Cherry Creek State Park, you represent the young people of the world, with all the questions which young people at the end of the twentieth century need to ask themselves, and rightly so.

Our theme is life, and life is full of mystery. Science and technology have made great progress in discovering the secrets of our natural life; however, even a superficial look at our personal experience shows that there are many other dimensions to individual and collective life on this planet. Our restless hearts seek beyond our limits, challenging our capacity to think and love: to think and love the immeasurable, the infinite, the absolute and supreme form of Being. Our inner eye looks upon the unlimited horizons of our hopes and aspirations. And in the midst of all life's contradictions, we seek the true meaning of life. We wonder and we ask ourselves, "Why?"

Why am I here?

Why do I exist?

What must I do?

We all ask ourselves these questions. Humanity in its entirety feels the pressing need to give meaning and purpose to a world in which being happy is increasingly difficult and complex. The bishops of the whole world gathered at the Second Vatican Council expressed it as follows: "In the face of modern developments there is a growing body of people who are asking the most fundamental of all questions or are glimpsing them with a keener insight: What is man? What is the meaning of suffering, evil, death, which have not been eliminated by all this progress? . . . What can man contribute to society? What can he expect from it? What happens after this earthly life is ended?"[1]

Failure to ask these basic questions means renouncing the great adventure of seeking the truth about life.

You know how easy it is to avoid the fundamental questions. But your presence here shows that you will not hide from reality and from responsibility!

You care about the gift of life that God has given you. You have confidence in Christ when he says: "I came that they might have life, and have it abundantly" (John 10:10).

Our vigil begins with an act of trust in the words of the Good Shepherd. In Jesus Christ, the Father expresses the whole truth concerning creation. We believe that in the life, death, and resurrection of Jesus, the Father reveals all his love for humanity. That is why Christ calls himself "the sheepgate" (John 10:7). As the gate, he stands guard over the creatures entrusted to him. He leads them to the good pastures: "I am the gate. Whoever enters through me will be safe. He will go in and out, and find pasture" (John 10:9).

Jesus Christ is truly the world's Shepherd. Our hearts must be open to his words. For this we have come to this World Meeting of Youth, from every state and diocese in the United States, from all over the Americas, from every continent: all represented here by the flags which your delegates have set up to show that no one here this evening is a stranger. We are all one in Christ. The Lord has led us as he leads the flock:

> The Lord is our Shepherd; we shall not want.
> In green pastures he makes us find rest.
> Beside restful waters he leads us:
> He refreshes our souls.
> Even though we walk in a dark valley we fear no
>   evil; for he is at our side.
> He gives us courage.
> (cf. Psalm 23)

As we reflect together on the Life which Jesus gives, I ask you to have the courage to commit yourselves to the truth. Have the courage to believe the Good News about Life which Jesus teaches in the Gospel. Open your minds and hearts to the beauty of all that God has made and to his special, personal love for each one of you.

Young people of the world, hear his voice!

Hear his voice and follow him!

Only the Good Shepherd will lead you to the full truth about Life.

Part Two

I.

At this point the young people gathered in Denver may ask: What is the Pope going to say about Life?

My words will be a profession of the faith of Peter, the first Pope. My message can be none other than what has been handed on from the beginning, because it is not mine but the Good News of Jesus Christ himself.

The New Testament presents Simon—whom Jesus called Peter, the Rock—as a vigorous, passionate disciple of Christ. But he also doubted and, at a decisive moment, he even denied that he was a follower of Jesus. Yet, despite these human weaknesses, Peter was the first disciple to make a full public profession of faith in the

Master. One day Jesus asked: "Who do you say that I am?" And Peter answered: "You are the Christ, the Son of the Living God" (Matt. 16:16).

Beginning with Peter, the first apostolic witness, multitudes of witnesses, men and women, young and old, of every nation on earth, have proclaimed their faith in Jesus Christ, true God and true man, the Redeemer of man, the Lord of history, the Prince of Peace. Like Peter, they asked: "To whom shall we go? You have the words of eternal life" (John 6:68).

This evening we profess the same faith as Peter. We believe that Jesus Christ has the words of Life, and that he speaks those words to the Church, to all who open their minds and hearts to him with faith and trust.

"I am the Good Shepherd. The Good Shepherd lays down his life for the sheep" (John 10:11). Our first reflection is inspired by these words of Jesus in the Gospel of Saint John.

The Good Shepherd lays down his life. Death assails Life.

At the level of our human experience, death is the enemy of life. It is an intruder who frustrates our natural desire to live. This is especially obvious in the case of untimely or violent death, and most of all in the case of the killing of the innocent.

It is not surprising then that among the Ten Commandments the Lord of Life, the God of the Covenant, should have said on Mount Sinai, "You shall not kill" (Exod. 20:13; cf. Matt. 5:21).

The words "you shall not kill" were engraved on the tablets of the covenant—on the stone tablets of the law. But even before that this law was engraved on the human heart, in the sanctuary of every individual's conscience. In the Bible, the first to experience the force of this law was Cain, who murdered his brother Abel. Immediately after his terrible crime, he felt the whole weight of having broken the commandment not to kill. Even though he tried to escape from the truth, saying, "Am I my brother's keeper?" (Gen. 4:9), the inner voice repeated over and over: "You are a murderer." The voice was his conscience, and it could not be silenced.

With time the threats against life have not grown weaker. They are taking on vast proportions. They are not only threats coming from the outside, from the forces of nature or the "Cains" who kill the "Abels"; no, they are scientifically and systematically programmed threats. The twentieth century will have been an era of massive attacks on life, an endless series of wars and a continual taking of innocent human life. False prophets and false teachers have had the greatest success.

In the same way, false models of progress have led to a threat against the earth's ecological balance. Man—made in the image and likeness of the Creator—is called to be the good shepherd of the environment, the context of his existence and life. This is the task he was given long ago and which the human family has assumed not without success throughout its history, until recently when man himself has become the destroyer of his natural environment. This has already occurred in some places, where it is still going on.

However, there is still more. We are also witnessing the spread of a mentality that militates against life—an attitude of hostility towards life in the mother's womb and life in its last phases. At the very time that science and medicine are increasingly able to safeguard health and life, threats against life are becoming more insidious. Abortion and euthanasia—the actual taking of a real human life—are claimed as "rights" and solutions to "problems," problems of individuals or those of society. The killing of the innocent is no less sinful an act or less destructive because it is done in a legal and scientific manner. In modern metropolises, life—God's first gift and a fundamental right of each individual, the basis of all other rights—is often treated more or less as a commodity to be controlled, marketed, and manipulated at will.

All this takes place although Christ, the Good Shepherd, wants us to have life. He knows what threatens life; he knows how to recognize the wolf who comes to snatch and scatter the sheep. He can identify those who try to enter the sheepfold but who are really thieves and hirelings (cf. John 10:1, 13). He knows how many young people are wasting their lives, shirking their responsibility and living in falsehood. Drugs, the abuse of alcohol, pornography and sexual disorder, violence: these are some of the grave problems which need to be seriously addressed by the whole of society, in every nation and at the international level. However, they are also personal tragedies, which must be faced with concrete interpersonal acts of love and solidarity through a great renewal of one's personal responsibility before God, before others, and before one's own conscience. We are our brother's keepers! (cf. Gen. 4:9).

II.

Why do the consciences of young people not rebel against this situation, especially against the moral evil which flows from personal choices? Why do so many acquiesce in attitudes and behavior which offend human dignity and disfigure the image of God in us? The normal thing would be for conscience to point out the mortal danger to the individual and to humanity contained in the easy acceptance of evil and sin. And yet, it is not always so. Is it because conscience itself is losing the ability to distinguish good from evil?

In a technological culture in which people are used to dominating matter, discovering its laws and mechanisms in order to transform it according to their wishes, the danger arises of also wanting to manipulate conscience and its demands. In a culture which holds that no universally valid truths are possible, nothing is absolute. Therefore, in the end—they say—objective goodness and evil no longer really matter. Good comes to mean what is pleasing or useful at a particular moment. Evil means what contradicts our subjective wishes. Each person can build a private system of values.

Young people, do not give in to this widespread false morality. Do not stifle your conscience! Conscience is the most secret core and sanctuary of a person, where we are alone with God.[2] "In the depths of his conscience man detects a law which he does not impose upon himself, but which holds him to obedience."[3] That law is not an external human law, but the voice of God, calling us to free ourselves from the grip of evil desires and sin, and stimulating us to seek what is good and true. Only by listening to the voice of God in your most intimate being and by acting in accordance with its directions will you reach the freedom you yearn for. As Jesus said, only the truth will make you free (cf. John 8:32). And the truth is not the fruit of each individual's imagination. God gave you intelligence to know the truth, and your will to achieve what is morally good. He has given you the light of conscience to guide your moral decisions, to love good and avoid evil. Moral truth is objective, and a properly formed conscience can perceive it.

But if conscience itself has been corrupted, how can it be restored? If conscience—which is light—no longer enlightens, how can we overcome the moral darkness? Jesus says: "The eye is the body's lamp. If your eyes are good, your body will be filled with light; if your eyes are bad, your body will be in darkness. And if your light is darkness, how deep will the darkness be!" (Matt. 6:22–23).

But Jesus also says: "I am the light of the world. No follower of mine shall ever walk in darkness; no, he shall possess the light of life" (John 8:12). If you follow Christ you will restore conscience to its rightful place and proper role, and you will be the light of the world, the salt of the earth (cf. Matt. 5:13).

A rebirth of conscience must come from two sources: first, the effort to know objective truth with certainty, including the truth about God; and second, the light of faith in Jesus Christ, who alone has the words of Life.

Against the splendid setting of the mountains of Colorado, with its pure air which gives peace and serenity to nature, the soul spontaneously is lifted up to sing the Creator's praise: "O Lord, our Lord, how glorious is your name over all the earth!" (Ps. 8:2).

Young pilgrims, the visible world is like a map pointing to heaven, the eternal dwelling of the living God. We learn to see the Creator by contemplating the beauty of his creatures. In this world the goodness, wisdom, and almighty power of God shine forth. And the human intellect, after original sin, too—in what has not been darkened by error or passion—can discover the Artist's hand in the wonderful works which he has made. Reason can know God through the book of nature: a personal God who is infinitely good, wise, powerful and eternal, who transcends the world and, at the same time, is present in the depths of his creatures. St. Paul writes: "Ever since the creation of the world, his invisible attributes of eternal power and divinity have been able to be understood and perceived in what he has made" (Rom. 1:20).

Jesus teaches us to see the Father's hand in the beauty of the lilies of the field, the birds of the air, the starry night, fields ripe for the harvest, the faces of children, and the needs of the poor and humble. If you look at the world with a pure heart, you too will see the face of God (cf. Matt. 5:8), because it reveals the mystery of the Father's provident love.

Young people are especially sensitive to the beauty of nature, and contemplating it inspires them spiritually. However, it must be a genuine contemplation: A contemplation which fails to reveal the face of a personal, intelligent, free, and loving Father, but which discerns merely the dim figure of an impersonal divinity or some cosmic force, does not suffice. We must not confuse the Creator with his creation.

The creature does not have life of himself, but from God. In discovering God's greatness, man discovers the unique position he holds in the visible world: "You have made him little less than the angels, and crowned him with glory and honor. You have given him rule over the works of your hands, putting all things under his feet" (Ps. 8:6–7). Yes, the contemplation of nature reveals not only the Creator, but also the human being's role in the world which he created. With faith it reveals the greatness of our dignity as creatures created in his image.

In order to have life and have it abundantly, in order to reestablish the original harmony of creation, we must respect this divine image in all of creation, especially in human life itself.

When the light of faith penetrates this natural consciousness we reach a new certainty. The words of Christ ring out with utter truth: "I came that they might have life, and have it abundantly."

Against all the forces of death, in spite of all the false teachers, Jesus Christ continues to offer humanity the only true and realistic hope. He is the world's true Shepherd. This is because he and the Father are one (cf. John 17:22). In his divinity he is one with the Father; in his humanity he is one with us.

Because he took upon himself our human condition, Jesus Christ is able to communicate to all those who are united with him in Baptism the Life that he has in himself. And because in the Trinity, Life is Love, the very love of God has been poured out into our hearts through the Holy Spirit who has been given to us (cf. Rom. 5:5). Life and love are inseparable: the love of God for us, and the love we give in return—love of God and love of every brother and sister. This will be the theme of the last part of our reflection later this evening.

Part Three

Dear young pilgrims:

The Spirit has led you to Denver to fill you with new Life: to give you a stronger faith and hope and love. Everything in you— your mind and heart, will and freedom, gifts and talents—

everything is being taken up by the Holy Spirit in order to make you "living stones" of the "spiritual house" which is the Church (cf. 1 Pet. 2:5). This Church is inseparable from Jesus; he loves her as the Bridegroom loves the Bride. This Church today, in the United States and in all the other countries from which you come, needs the affection and cooperation of her young people, the hope of her future. In the Church each one has a role to play, and all together we build up the one Body of Christ, the one People of God.

As the third millennium approaches, the Church knows that the Good Shepherd continues, as always, to be the sure hope of humanity. Jesus Christ never ceases to be the "sheepgate." And despite the history of humanity's sins against life, he never ceases to repeat with the same vigor and love: "I came that they may have life, and have it abundantly" (John 10:10).

How is this possible? How can Christ give us Life if death forms part of our earthly existence? How is it possible if "it is appointed that human beings die once, and after this the judgement" (Hab. 9:27)?

Jesus himself provides the answer—and the answer is a supreme declaration of divine Love, a high point of the Gospel revelation concerning God the Father's love for all of creation. The answer is already present in the parable of the Good Shepherd. Christ says: "The Good Shepherd lays down his life for the sheep" (John 10:11).

Christ—the Good Shepherd—is present among us, among the peoples, nations, generations, and races, as the One who "lays down his life for the sheep." What is this but the greatest love? It was the death of the innocent One: "The Son of Man is departing, as Scripture says of him, but woe to that man by whom the Son of Man is betrayed" (Matt. 26:24). Christ on the Cross stands as a sign of contradiction to every crime against the commandment not to kill. He offered his own life in sacrifice for the salvation of the world. No one takes that human life from him, but he lays it down of his own accord. He has the power to lay it down and the power to take it up again (cf. John 10:18). It was a true self-giving. It was a sublime act of freedom.

Yes, the Good Shepherd lays down his life. But only to take it up again (cf. John 10:17). And in the new life of the resurrection, he has become—in the words of St. Paul—"a life-giving spirit" (1

Cor. 15:45), who can now bestow the gift of Life on all who believe in him.

Life laid down—Life taken up again—Life given. In him we have that Life which he has in the unity of the Father and of the Holy Spirit. If we believe in him. If we are one with him through love, remembering that "whoever loves God must also love his brother" (1 John 4:21).

Good Shepherd:

The Father loves you because you lay down your life. The Father loves you as the crucified Son because you go to your death giving your life for us. And the Father loves you when you conquer death by your resurrection, revealing an indestructible life. You are the Life and, therefore, the Way and the Truth of our life (cf. John 14:6).

You said: "I am the Good Shepherd, and I know mine and mine know me, just as the Father knows me and I know the Father" (John 10:14–15). You who know the Father (cf. John 10:15) —the only Father of all—know why the Father loves you (cf. John 10:17). He loves you because you give your life for each one. When you say: "I lay down my life for my sheep," you are excluding no one. You came into the world to embrace all people and to gather as one all the children of the whole human family who were scattered (cf. John 11:52). Nonetheless, there are many who do not know you. "However, I have other sheep that do not belong to this fold. These also I must lead" (John 10:16).

Good Shepherd:

Teach the young people gathered here, teach the young people of the world, the meaning of "laying down" their lives through vocation and missions. Just as you sent the Apostles to preach the Gospel to the ends of the earth, so now challenge the youth of the Church to carry on the vast mission of making you known to all those who have not yet heard of you! Give these young people the courage and generosity of the great missionaries of the past so that, through the witness of their faith and their solidarity with every brother and sister in need, the world may discover the Truth, the Goodness, and the Beauty of the Life you alone can give.

Teach the young people gathered in Denver to take your message of life and truth, of love and solidarity, to the heart of the modern metropolis—to the heart of all the problems which afflict the human family at the end of the twentieth century.

Teach these young people the proper use of their freedom. Teach them that the greatest freedom is the fullest giving of themselves. Teach them the meaning of the Gospel words: "He who loses his life for my sake will find it" (Matt. 10:39).

For all of this, Good Shepherd, we love you.

The young people gathered in Denver love you because they love life, the gift of the Creator. They love their human life as the path through this created world. They love life as a task and a vocation.

And they love that other Life which, through you, the Eternal Father has given us: the Life of God in us, your greatest gift to us.

You are the Good Shepherd!

And there is none other.

You have come that we may have Life—and that we may have it abundantly. Life, not only on the human level, but in the measure of the Son—the Son in whom the Father is eternally pleased.

Lord Jesus Christ, we thank you for having said: "I came that they may have life, and have it abundantly" (John 10:10). The young people of the Eighth World Youth Day thank you from their hearts.

Maranatha!

Here, from Cherry Creek State Park in Denver, from this gathering of young people from all over the world, we cry out:

Maranatha! "Come, Lord Jesus" (Rev. 22:20).

NOTES

1. *Gaudium et spes,* n. 10.
2. Cf. *Gaudium et spes,* n. 16.
3. *Gaudium et spes,* n. 16.

27. Stones and Bones
Eugene L. Lowry

Acts 6:1–14, 7:51–60

This is the story of a man who didn't know when to keep his mouth
shut. I mean, he is in big trouble—
brought before the authorities on a charge of undermining
the community.
And he must now answer for himself.

I wish he had come to me; I could have helped him.
My business is helping people address listeners.
I could have told him to keep it short.
People will get irritated if you go on and on—
particularly if you continue to tell them what
they already know.
Always know the mind-set of the listeners,
appeal to their values,
show congruity and affinity between your concerns
and theirs.
One must achieve a commonality with listeners you want to
influence.

But here he is rambling on and on—first about Abraham,
mentioning Isaac and Jacob,
and then moving toward a long section about Joseph.
Pretty soon it becomes clear that this is going to be a very
long speech.
He moves on to Moses while they start looking at their
watches.
He doesn't miss a lick—detailing Moses' birth,

Eugene L. Lowry is Professor of Preaching at St. Paul School
of Theology in Kansas City, Missouri. He is the author of *The
Homiletical Plot* and *Doing Time in the Pulpit*.

his killing the Egyptian,
the Ten Commandments,
the forty years in the wilderness—
the whole ninety-nine yards.
I'm surprised they didn't kill him sooner.

Who does he think he is, anyway? Some of them had probably
forgotten more about Hebrew history than he'd ever know.
Besides, the high priest had demanded to know if the charges
were true.
But Stephen just doesn't bother to defend himself.

Well, it's not enough for him to go on and on.
Finally, he attacks them personally—"You stiff-necked
people, uncircumcised in heart and ears."
For good measure he adds an attack upon their
ancestors: "Which of the prophets did your fathers not
persecute?" he asks rhetorically.
Then he calls them "betrayers and murderers."
Well, enough is enough.
They are enraged—the text says they "ground their teeth."
So they take him out and stone him to death.

But there is something peculiar about this stoning of Stephen.
Who is it, anyway, who becomes the first martyr of the
Christian movement?
Well, not one of the chief leaders of the movement.
Not one of the disciples, prominent and visible.

This is Stephen the table waiter.
Remember, the twelve disciples had decided that their roles
were too important to be wasted on waiting tables—
so they consecrated seven to serve food while the
disciples served up the Word.
Well, for a waiter, he apparently had a lot to say—even before
this long speech.
The text notes that "Stephen, full of grace and power, did
great wonders and signs among the people."
Not only that, but his opponents couldn't win any arguments with
him either. But note that it was a servant who did the dying.

You know, there was another servant on the scene that day,
too—checking coats—whose name was Saul.
Tradition has it that he, today's servant and
tomorrow's Paul, also became a martyr for the faith.
In the papers this very week are the accounts
of the five nuns in Liberia who were killed.

Servants so often seem to do the dying.
But there's another fact worth noting as we celebrate
All Saints' Day.

At this very hour,
while we note with gratitude the price that has been paid
regularly for our heritage,
making possible our being engrafted into the faith
and our privilege of worship—
at this very hour we could be home watching some
televangelist promise that if we cozy up to Jesus we
are going to find material abundance and peace of mind.
But that is not good news;
that is a phony promise—
false to the gospel.
The good news that Stephen and Paul experienced
and that the five nuns in Liberia knew—
and all the saints and martyrs in between have embraced—
is that there is something in this world worth dying for.
To recall the saints of all the ages
and the price exacted for their faithfulness
is a tribute not only to personal courage
but to the ground of that courage—
the hope that undergirds us all.
Thank God for the hope that is worth everything—
even life itself.

A number of years ago I was preaching in Bellefontaine Neighbors, Missouri—once a small village,
but now surrounded by the city of St. Louis.
Preparing to take my usual walk to center my thoughts before
preaching, I opened the back door of the church.

There behind the building was the church cemetery.
So I walked paths around and in between the tombstones.
I noted several family names; Huffman was one.

No stone there had the inscription "Saint . . . ,"
but I know they were there—
devoted Christians of other generations
whose sacrificial ministry was known to
at least a few.
Saints.

But then I noticed that the center path wound back through the cemetery
and ended at the front door of a house—
obviously the parsonage.
The minister of that congregation lived there.
I check it out after the service.
"Yes," he said, "that's the parsonage."
Turns out that there used to be a parsonage off to the
side of the church building.
But they needed to enlarge the parking lot—
so they tore down the old parsonage for the sake
of asphalt.
Since they owned the land behind the cemetery
they decided it could be used to locate the
new parsonage.

"You mean," I asked, "that every Sunday morning when you get
ready to head to the church to preach the Word, you have to
go through the cemetery?"
"Every Sunday," he replied.
"That's the only way to get there."

Think of it: On the way to preach the Word, the pastor is
surrounded—
literally surrounded by the saints.
One wonders if the pastor ever hears any whispers
in the ear, on the way.
I'll bet the parsonage family doesn't have many trick-or-

treaters on Halloween—on All Hallows' Eve.
They would have to walk through a graveyard to get
there.
The whole thing is so awesome,
we turn it spooky in order to manage.
So, one walks for a pastoral counseling session—
through the company of the saints.
One heads to a board meeting—
through the company of the saints.

I mused momentarily—a reflection broken by the pastor's voice.

"There is something else you should know about the building
of that parsonage.
When the contractors began digging for the foundation
of the house they discovered human bones there.
It seems that the cemetery didn't end where they
thought.
Behind the burial plots of the church members was
the final resting place for the slaves of the
community."
No grave markers, of course,
no tombstones,
no names.
The forgotten ones.

Other saints, no
doubt, but not
honored even by a
name.
(One wonders if anybody considered halting construction.)

I got to thinking.
How could you serve that church as pastor—
knowing that the house in which you live is sitting
literally on the bones of the servants?
Can you imagine?
You finish up on Saturday night—
having gone over your sermon notes for the next day.

And you lie down for a good night's sleep—
to be ready for tomorrow.
But what would it be like to sleep there—
knowing that the bed on which you lie
is resting on a floor
that is sitting on a foundation
that in turn is being held up by the bones
of a previous generation?
How could you do it?
How could anybody even get to sleep, there?

I don't know—

but we all do.

28. Opening Day
Robert G. Trache

It was Mark Twain who probably spoke for a lot of us when he said, "I have never seen what to me seemed an atom of proof that there is a future life. And yet—I am strongly inclined to expect one." Easter Day meets our reason, our scientific minds, and our skeptical modern selves with a bold proclamation that there is more to creation than we can know, more to our lives than we suspect, and more to the mystery of God incarnate, wrapped around every fiber of life, than we are willing to believe.

I hope you will indulge me this Easter. I have been thinking about preaching a sermon like this for some years. I don't know why this year I have the courage; perhaps it's just longevity. Actually, I think it has more to do with my oldest son leaving home to go to college. And Easter is, after all, about a father/son relationship.

Most of you know that I have a not-so-secret love of baseball, and baseball has formed a bond between me and both of my boys, Dylan and Brendan, over the years that goes far beyond a game. It is out of that bond that I want to preach the sermon. Baseball has been for us a context for a relationship, a way of expressing friendship, trust, and our feelings. Much as religion is the context for our relationship with God, and is a way of expressing our faith, hope, and feelings about life.

Already you are probably wondering what baseball has to do with Easter. Aside from the fact that Easter usually occurs close to baseball's Opening Day, it is a question that appears to have no likely answer. But before you decide that your rector has lost all his marbles, hear me out. There is a certain way of understanding baseball as a myth. There are untold numbers of books that have been written about how baseball recapitulates life. And so it does, for those who want to see its metaphorical possibilities.

Robert G. Trache is rector of Immanuel Church-on-the-Hill in Alexandria, Virginia. He has degrees from George Washington University and Harvard University.

At any rate, this all started to formulate one day as I was riding to Fredericksburg for yet another diocesan meeting. I was listening to one of those new sports talk shows. One caller kept insisting that baseball was an anachronism: As a sport it was simply too slow to be enjoyed. He said that it took hours to play and sometimes you can go for a very long time without any significant actions, except the subtle nuances of the game, appreciated only by those who play it. I was astonished that the talk-show host agreed with him, saying they should have a time limit to baseball, like football or basketball.

Most of you know enough about baseball to know it is played by a team. And yet it is a game of individual performance and challenge. There is not, for instance, the same kind of teamwork as in football or basketball, where everybody moves at once. Baseball requires more personal challenge in the midst of reliance on others. This is one reason it feels like life. When a batter faces a pitcher, for instance, it is one against the other.

Baseball has sometimes been described as a ballet. There are moments of beauty in baseball—a runner chasing down a fly ball, the tension of the perfectly executed squeeze play, the skill of a curve ball that actually breaks. To those who understand baseball it is a dance of life, of tears, and of beauty, of loss and of hope, of winning and of starting over.

The caller on that talk show who asked for a clock to speed up the game didn't understand baseball. Baseball is a game of stories, of people, and of uncertainty. It can be incredibly boring, or intensely exciting; its paces change from inning to inning. One inning might take only ten minutes; another could take almost an hour. You can never be certain that the game is over. Thomas Boswell, the *Washington Post* columnist, once said, "In baseball, you see, no one ever believes he's really lost it." The caller wanted more action, artificially stimulated excitement and pleasure. He missed the need for patience, and the waiting necessary to catch the beauty of baseball. Time to smell the grass, the night air, the rawhide—time to go into a slump and break out of it, time for indecision. This caller wanted all that to change, to speed up.

The caller reminded me of a lot of people I see in my office. People searching for the meaning in religion, looking for the answer, as if it could be read in a textbook. People who want religion to work for them when they are eager to have it work. I am afraid that we are a lot like the caller when it comes to our faith. We want it artificially stimulated—there when we need it—but are unwilling to invest the time and patience necessary to see the connections in the mystery. And we get frustrated when we need it and it isn't there.

On Easter Sunday, it is that which connects baseball to Easter— never losing, never having it be too late. We come here today to speak about the Resurrection, not a ball game. But like baseball, faith requires patience. It is subtle, and you have to wait upon it if you would understand it. There is no immediate gratification in religion, no way to artificially stimulate your deepest hopes and fears toward God; one has to go and watch for the Resurrection, which might come at any time in the middle of the game.

Donald Hall, in an article entitled "Fathers Playing Catch with Sons," writes:

> Baseball is fathers and sons. Football is brothers
> beating each other up in the backyard, violent and
> superficial. Baseball is the generations, looping
> backward forever with a million apparitions of
> sticks and balls, cricket and rounders, and the
> games the Iroquois played in Connecticut before
> the English came. Baseball is fathers and sons
> playing catch, lazy and murderous, wild and
> controlled, the profound archaic song of birth,
> growth, age, and death. This diamond encloses
> what we are.[1]

Baseball works as an Easter metaphor because it is one of those timeless things in which generations make connections. The Resurrection is the story about God saving those connections between fathers and sons, mothers and daughters. Those oblique, uncertain feelings with mystical quality about being connected to another, to your past and to your future, are not idle imaginings. They are true apprehensions of the connectedness between you and those you love. Resurrection faith is faith in tomorrow and in God's forgiveness. The game for Christians is never over. The season is never lost. Tomorrow is another Opening Day. No matter how poorly life has been played, the Resurrection offers hope in God's tomorrow for each of us. The tombs that control and bury us, the clock that governs our success and failures, is done away with in

Christ Jesus. No stone is too heavy to be removed, no grave too deep to be delivered from.

The clock never runs out on our faith or God's love for us. This Jesus will stay with us, wait with us, and raise us together with bonds formed in God's love. The Resurrection is God's grace, God's forgiveness, and God's hope in our tomorrows connected to each other in Christ Jesus.

Roger Kahn, the noted baseball writer, wrote:

> My years with the Dodgers were 1952 and 1953,
> two seasons in which they lost the World Series to
> the Yankees. You may glory in a team triumphant,
> but you fall in love with a team in defeat. Losing
> after great striving is the story of man, who was
> born to sorrow, whose sweetest songs tell of
> saddest thought, and who, if he is a hero, does
> nothing in life as becomingly as leaving it. A whole
> country was stirred by the high deeds and
> thwarted longings of The Duke, Preacher, Pee
> Wee, Skoonj and the rest. The team was
> awesomely good and yet defeated. Their skills
> lifted everyman's spirit and their defeat joined
> them with everyman's existence, a national team,
> with a country in thrall, irresistible and unable to
> beat the Yankees.[2]

This is Easter, too—God's way of connecting with our losses and our failures. We can't fix them, rebuild them, make them right, beat the Yankees; but God can do it. I have never found all those Eastery hymns about victory very appealing. I mean, a victory implies that there are losers, and though through life we all know what it is to lose, at Easter there are no losers anymore. Pilate is not a loser, Judas is not a loser, Caiaphas is not a loser, the crowd is not filled with losers. Jesus opens the tomb, and in doing so opens the tomb of our hearts and redeems all those losing experiences at his expense, not ours.

The pathos of living, of playing our games, of our winnings and losings, echoes in eternity, but the connection between the care, the affection, and the love is saved by the Resurrection. To know love and to be loved is the first clue to the Resurrection. The warmth of a friend, the giving of yourself in honestly meeting another, the caring for someone without expecting anything in return; to know the peace and the pleasure that come from sharing life, when one reveals his or her true being and another life accepts and embraces that revelation; to be trusted and to trust, to care and be cared for, to forgive and be forgiven—these are the richest, deepest moments of our lives and point toward a glimpse of life's true meaning and endless depth, and of life's infinite potential.

These connections are glimpses of God's presence. They never capture or exhaust it. Life is always bigger than we know or imagine. The more deeply we live, the more recklessly we can invest ourselves, the greater is the hope and meaning in life, or so Jesus taught us. And just as we know what it feels like to be loved, we also know what it feels like to be hurt, to be misunderstood, to be alone, to be outside the forgiveness of a friend. We know the ache and harshness of life as well. Separation from love is an unbearable reality, for it is a denial of life. The separated and lonely inevitably turn inward, trying to meet their own needs, and this exhausts their reserves—until we learn that we are not alone in this world. Easter overcomes our separations. Easter is the promise that all will be healed, cared for, loved, and forgiven.

Easter allows us a new Opening Day, which is today. Roger Angell, the author of the book *The Summer Game*, writes:

> Baseball's time is seamless and invisible, a bubble
> within which players move at exactly the same pace
> and rhythms as all their predecessors. This is the
> way the game was played in our youth and in our
> fathers' youth, and even back then—back in the
> country days—there must have been the same
> feeling that time stopped. Since baseball time is
> measured only in outs, all you have to do is
> succeed utterly; keep hitting, keep the rally alive,
> and you have defeated time. You remain young
> forever.[3]

Let me substitute some words for you: Faith is seamless and invisible, a bubble within which Christians move at exactly the same pace and rhythms as all their predecessors. This is the way faith happens in our youth and in our fathers' youth, and even back then—back in the country days—there must have been the same feeling that time could be stopped. Since faith time is measured only in Christ, all you have to do is succeed utterly; keep trying, keep the rally alive in your heart, and you have defeated time. You remain young forever.

Jim Bouton, the former Yankee pitcher, wrote in his book *Ball Four:* "You spend a good piece of your life gripping a baseball and in the end it turns out that it was the other way around all the time."[4] We spend a good deal of our lives trying to grip God, to get handles on the mystery of resurrection, and finally one day we sense that it is the other way around: God has a grip on us, and we are part of the mystery.

One of the bonds that baseball developed between me and my boys was trust. They had to learn to trust me. They had to learn that the ball could hurt, but to face it anyway. They had to learn where to throw, and when to take a lead. Most of all they had to learn to trust in themselves. And I had to learn to trust them, not overcoach them. I had to learn that no matter what the book said, there was always an individual way of doing things. I taught my sons how to play baseball. They taught me how to be a coach. It took patience. It took love and it took trust. It was a long way from T-ball to Little League to high school. We learned how to trust each other and root for each other.

This may seem way too simplistic, but this resurrection story is about trust too. Jesus had to trust God and trust himself. He had to be able to walk into what looked like total failure and trust that his connection with God was real. And God had to trust Jesus not to run away. The Resurrection is always based on trust. Trust in God, and trust in yourself, who you are, and what you believe. The Resurrection cannot be proved, as Mark Twain reminded us. It is a faith relationship between God and us. Baseball works as metaphor because it is made up of human stories told within a game. Christian stories work because they are faith stories told within the religion about human struggles, trials, defeats, and victories. This Easter moment will pass away soon and Easter Monday will begin another week for you and me, and if Easter is to make a difference, it is for us to realize inside that the connections we make between God and ourselves, and between each other, are holy bonds, out-lasting time and space. They do live in God, and Jesus has been raised from the dead. I cannot offer you proof, but as surely as the first star that shines after sundown, we who live in hope will be renewed in this life and in the life to come. Play ball!

Let us pray:

O Lord Jesus, who lives within us and among us, lift us to live in accordance with your spirit. Give us an eye for beauty, the will to play out our lives on your team, the sure and certain knowledge that when we stumble we are not lost, so that we may be risen to live with hope and a resurrected life in you, raised from the dead, abiding in us and with us forever. Amen.

NOTES

1. Donald Hall, "Fathers Playing Catch with Sons," in *Diamonds Are Forever,* ed. Peter Gordon (San Francisco: Chronicle Books, 1987), 143.

2. Roger Kahn in *Diamonds Are Forever,* ed. Peter Gordon (San Francisco: Chronicle Books, 1987), 83.

3. Roger Angell, *The Summer Game* (New York: Viking Penguin, 1990), 156.

4. Jim Bouton, ed., *Ball Four* (New York: Macmillan, 1990).

29. Dear Harold
REMARKS AT THE MEMORIAL FOR HAROLD HALE

Ralph V. Norman

The first words I have for this gathering today will take the form of a plea, or of urgent counsel and advice. In any case, these first remarks are in the imperative.

If there is someone you love very much, or someone you feel especially grateful to, or someone who has been an immensely important part of your life, at some point in your life, tell him so. Tell her so.

Do it now. And again next week. And again next month. Don't wait. Not always necessarily in words, or even most often in words. More often, preferably with your presence—with a visit, or a gesture, or a gift, or a call, or some other special token of affection. But *sometimes* in words. Do it now. Don't neglect it.

Two weeks ago Sunday, we had been getting word that the prognosis for Harold was not good at all and that we might lose him soon. In the silly confidence we always have that we can pretty

Ralph V. Norman is a professor at the University of Tennessee, where he founded the Department of Religious Studies in 1966. Since 1973 he has been Associate Vice Chancellor and Vice Provost. He is the editor of *Soundings: An Interdisciplinary Journal* and the author, with Charles Reynolds, of *Community in America*. He holds one undergraduate and two graduate degrees from Yale University (B.D., Ph.D., M.A.) and a B.A. and M.A. from the University of Tennessee. He has presented lectures and scholarly papers in Germany, the Netherlands, Scotland, Hungary, and Taiwan. A layman in the Episcopal Church, he and his wife, Cornelia Shirley Norman, have two children and two grandchildren. Benjamin Harold Hale—the subject of this message—was born in Jackson, Tennessee, on October 31, 1927, and died in Lancaster, Pennsylvania, on March 14, 1993. He was married to Sara Jane Norman for forty-five years. At the time of his death he was president of High Steel Service Center in Lancaster. These remarks were given at Rose Memorial Chapel in Knoxville, Tennessee, on March 19, 1993.

well gauge the Lord's timetable, I said to Connie, "This week I am going to sit down and write a letter to Harold to tell him all the things he has meant to me and to us, to our family, my whole life long, because I've never done that. I've never said such things to him, and he needs to know in some concrete, focused way before he leaves us that I love him very much." We agreed that I should write that letter on Monday. That was a week ago Sunday. Monday came and went—you know the story, don't you?—and Tuesday, and appointments and a long day at the office and I can't quite get my thoughts together, and Wednesday, and Thursday and Friday, and the Lord moved in His good time, not in ours, and on Sunday morning the letter had never been written and was of course never received.

Here, too little and too late, is the letter I wanted to send. It is not unlike the letter I wish I had had time to send to my father and my mother, and to my dear grandparents, and to my beautiful, wonderful uncles and aunts who have since passed on—to all those beloved members of my first and abiding, enduring world. Here is what I wanted to write to my brother Harold.

Dear Harold,

I know the recent news about your health has not been good. But like everyone else I only half believe the doctors, and in a part of my brain I believe in miracles and impressive cures. I do believe that for reasons of his own Jesus made the lame to walk and the blind to see and made Lazarus to rise from the dead. And I know that in ordinary life things turn out exactly opposite what we often predict or anticipate. You and I both know many friends and relatives of whom it was said that they would not live so many weeks or months and we have seen them outlive their brothers and sisters and husbands and wives and even children and grandchildren. By the time you read this letter I may be dead, or someone else who is close to you and me, or some great world figure who strides the stage today.

But the chances, the odds, they say, are that you will go into that good night before most of the rest of us. We will in all likelihood, my good and gentle brother, follow just a little farther behind. Not far behind, as the decades go—hardly any time at all in God's reckoning—but a little later. And although I desperately do not accept your going, it just may be time for me to say what I have always felt, what I feel now, what I will always feel about you.

You came into our lives in 1945, just at the war's end. I was almost thirteen and you were eighteen. There were many things about you that I fell in love with as much as Sara did, or more. I was in love with your know-how, your intelligence, your worldliness, your irreverence, you ability to put things together and make things happen. Your Windsor knots, your spread collars, your cuff links, your special spiffiness and polish as to shirts and shoes and suits that you have never lost. I fell in love with your knowledge of big cities and mixed drinks and Harold Lloyd movies and Satchel Paige and the mysterious ways of beautiful women. I loved the raciness of your nickname, one of the all-time great, jaunty, mud-in-your-eye nicknames. Goda you were first, Goda you have remained to this day to many of your old friends, the Sweet Melody Boys and the Kappa Sigs and your old Knoxville High classmates. If you became Harold when Janet and Mark and Matthew came along, it was not because you ever lost any of that jauntiness, that handsomeness of temper and mind and gentility you seemed so inexplicably to have had at the slender age of eighteen.

Granted, thirteen is an impressionable age, and fifteen not much less so—my age the year you and Sara were married in Central Church. What you always managed to convey then, and still do, is that there is something grander, and better, and more worth loving and admiring out there in the big world than most of the people we know ever acknowledge. Most people are ready to settle for so much less than you are. So when at age nineteen and twenty you sent postcards from business trips to Buffalo and Philadelphia and New York, and pictures of yourself in a homburg hat, well before Eisenhower popularized the homburg in 1952, you gave me a sense that the world, if it is to be large, must be large inside of oneself. It is a matter of one's own temper and soul. You taught me that. I have known very few people who lived it as well as you always have.

It was indescribably thrilling in the late 1940s to come home from high school, from the tedium of algebra and civics and study hall, and find in the mail a letter with a picture of you and Sara driving across the country from Chicago to New York in what looked to me like the largest and sleekest Oldsmobile convertible in the Western world. And it is still hard to believe you were later to allow me to do some serious dating in that same convertible.

You were only twenty-one when you and Sara took me from Philadelphia to see New York for the first time in my life. The Holland Tunnel, the Empire State Building, the Statue of Liberty, Wall Street, Central Park—we saw them all on that hot, deserted New York summer afternoon. You, of course, knew them all. Knew about them all. Knew what to do in and with the city. Knew what a sixteen-year-old would want to do.

This love of introducing people you know and love to things you think they will enjoy and admire has remained with you to this day. You make it such a pleasure to see anything—a barn near Lititz or an old church in Baltimore or a harbor in Annapolis. That was why I cherish so much our last trip together, you and Sara and Connie and me, to New York City once again, and again you wanted to do something special for us, a new way of approaching the city. Had we ever come to Manhattan from Staten Island? No? Then we must do it. Did I mention an obscure branch of the Metropolitan up on the north end of the island? No problem. We would get there if we had to drive through detours in Harlem and various parkways and thruways and crossways in the Bronx and Westchester County. At that very moment you were already sick and uncomfortable, but you wanted us to see not so much just what *you* liked, but what you thought *we* would enjoy.

That's the way your life has always been. You have showered us all with the benefit of your great admiration of the world. As your children grew up, you showered them with toys, with clothes, with good things of every kind and description. You were prodigal in what you wanted your family to drink in of the world and its wonders. You showered them with places, with trips, with new things to see and do. I know as well as I am sitting here that if you get a chance you will go again to Buffalo and Grand Isle and relish the showering Matthew and Lisa will try their best to lay upon you.

It will not be easy for them, because you will already know so much about any place you go. Before you ever left Tampa, you had all the books on Lancaster. You had not been in Lancaster six months before you knew more about the country from Harrisburg to Baltimore than any ten other steel executives.

But how did you know so much about the world that first year I knew you, when you were only eighteen? You had worked since you were twelve. You have never stopped working.

You were right for the time in which you have lived. Your marriage began in the great age of postwar reconstruction, and you raised your family in that heyday. It was Howdy Doody and automobile fins and Sid Caesar and Levittown. It was finding one's thrill on Mockingbird Hill and it was the Tennessee Waltz and it was Nature Boy and the naughty lady of Shady Lane. It was something new called interstate highways. America was creating a new infrastructure, and you knew where the steel was to do it with. More important, you knew *why* the steel was, where it came from, what it was to be used for. You built companies the way you built personal relationships—by asking yourself what people needed and would want and then by moving heaven and earth to get it for them.

I think you were honestly puzzled and hurt by the way the takeover accountants who bought out the first business you built failed to understand this simple truth about actually serving people. You were impatient with the guys who know how to make balance sheets look good but who don't know one piece of steel from another. It may be proof of a providence in our lives, but probably just proof of your own extraordinary intelligence and ingenuity, that you found in High Industries the kind of people who understood immediately what you were talking about when you talked about service.

But another thing you tried to teach me was not to be afraid of the future. You became adept at management and business techniques that had not even been dreamed of when you began work at Glazer Steel in the 1940s. You took to them, you mastered them, you made them work for you and for the real people whose real work you knew and understood and respected.

Harold, dear gentle Harold, I must bring this to a conclusion, though it is hard to see how I can. There is so much more to say. I have loved you most for your always thoughtful, selfless, painstaking care for Sara and your family, and for taking the rest of us into those very firm, very self-assured arms. The pleasure has been entirely mine.

Your admiring, and very proud brother,
Ralph

Now that, or something like that, is what I should have written and
didn't. Each of you today could say a thousand much more important things about the good man we have lost. We could talk
about his life in the church, in the choir at Central Methodist and
in Lititz, on the vestry, in the National Association of Steel Service
Centers. Or we could talk about his sense of humor, his wonderful
sense of humor. Today he would have noticed, for instance, who
was wearing what, whose dresses were getting a little tighter, whose
coat or perhaps necklace was especially beautiful, and he would
have commented on most of them.

Henry James, in *The Golden Bowl*, created an unforgettable
character, Mrs. Assingham, of whom it was said that she was a
person on whom nothing was lost. Harold Hale was a man on
whom nothing was lost. Did you have a favorite ice cream? He
remembered it. Did you wonder in what year Myrna Loy made her
first big motion picture? He could tell you. Were you especially
happy about something you had accomplished? He noticed it. Was
there something you had been neglecting to do for yourself or
others? He noticed.

Now, you cannot be a person on whom nothing is lost and
remain sane and not be a person who has a sense of humor. Matthew and Hayley and Sara have told us a few things he said in
those last confused hours before he left us.

We have said he liked to minister unto rather than *be* minis-
tered unto. At one point Hayley bent over to see whether he was
conscious. "Are you hearing me, Boopah?" she asked. "That," he
answered, this gentle grandfather who had nurtured her for so
long but now had something else to face, "is the least of my problems."

"Big tip," he said to his beloved son as Matthew helped him
struggle to the toilet, and he winked or smiled as he said it.

During one especially trying set of ministrations, he said something like this: "I'm not sure what we are learning from all this."
That we should be learning something from whatever is happening to us, even while we are moving on, as Eliot says, into yet

another intensity, into another dimension—that is what our good friend Harold will continue to teach us.

This day we praise God for his servant Harold Hale, and we yield back, oh so reluctantly but so gratefully, the gift of his remarkable life.

30. Caught?
A STORY AND SOME QUESTIONS
Mary Zimmer

John 7:53–8:11

Once upon a time, there was a group of very religious men. For all of their lives, from boyhood for as long as they could remember, they had been taught and had learned to carry the responsibility for their fathers' religion. The sacred books and collections of rules for daily living had been handed down for centuries. These books told the story of their people from the beginning of remembered time.

These rules kept the social order for their people. They told about the right way for food to be prepared, the right way for government and religious bodies to operate, and the right way for men and women to relate to one another.

These religious men were people who followed all the rules. For them, following the rules was the only imaginable way to live. All the stories of their people pointed to the survival of the people when they followed the rules. The stories also told of the near-extinction of their people when the rules were not followed.

But for this particular group of men, life had become much more complicated. The people now lived under the rule of a foreign emperor whose rules and soldiers determined their political and economic lives. So the religious life and laws about rituals, sacrifices, and morality were the only arena of power left to them.

Into this place and time, even into their very temple, there came a stranger. He was a poor man from a poor town. The story about him was that he had actually rejected his own mother and

Mary Zimmer is an instructor in the School of Christian Education and Assistant to the Dean of Christian Education at Southern Baptist Theological Seminary in Louisville, Kentucky. She conducts workshops and retreats on personal spirituality and biblical women, and is the author of *Sister Images*.

brothers and collected a ragtag group of both men and women who followed him through the countryside.

Other stories about him were fantastic. It was said that he healed the blind and the lame and even violated laws about the holy days to do his healing. The people said he taught about a beloved kingdom that would soon come and change all of life.

But worst of all, this man was drawing crowds when he stopped in towns to teach. Since he claimed to have power from God and performed miracles, the crowds gathered to hear him. The religious men began to fear that the people were no longer controlled by the traditional rules. What if the crowds brought trouble from the emperor's soldiers? Certainly this man was from an insignificant part of the country, but it seemed he was threatening the whole fabric of their society because he did not follow the rules. Some people even whispered the word *Messiah* about him.

Something had to be done. The religious men began to share their fears with one another about this strange man who seemed to be beyond any of their rules. They resolved to confront the man with a moral dilemma that would condemn him in the eyes of the people no matter what he answered.

The choice of the dilemma was easy—a woman accused of adultery. Everyone knew that a woman unfaithful to her husband had committed an unpardonable sin. Such women denied their place in life as a husband's property. For some of the oldest laws said that a man who committed adultery with another man's wife was to be stoned to death for stealing the husband's property. The woman was, of course, also to be stoned to death, her sinful body mangled by the rocks. Such a painful and humiliating death would enforce physical penance for moral violation.

If this teacher judged the woman to be guilty, he would have her blood on his hands. If he set her free, he would clearly be in violation of their laws.

And so the scene was set, and we all know the rest of the story. For centuries this story has been debated in commentaries. There is confusion abut exactly which Gospel it belongs to. There is much speculation about what, if anything, Jesus was actually writing in the dirt. Such an enigmatic detail has provoked interpreters to distraction.

St. Augustine argued that the story was left out of early manuscripts over a fear that Jesus' absolution would grant sexual license to married women.[1] Certainly the early church's condemnation of women's embodiment and the silence of contemporary churches about sexual and physical violence against women have provided adequate repression.

Whatever the validity of such speculation might be, a close look reveals that there is someone missing in this story, someone whose part in the story is central to the Pharisees' plot, but whose absence reveals the truth of their motivation. A hermeneutic of silence and absence requires that we ask: "Where is the man who would necessarily be part of the act of adultery?" For Levitical law required that both parties to the sin of adultery be brought to public justice and stoned to death.

Some commentators assert that one explanation is part of a darker plot.[2] That is, that the Pharisees knew of a dissatisfied husband who hoped to have his wife put aside, which he could legally do only if she were unfaithful to him. So, if he could manipulate her adultery, even by a rape, he would have a case for divorce. The law required two witnesses, so if he was rich and desperate, he could also just bribe two men to testify against her. The woman in either instance would have no recourse.

The law also required not only that the witnesses testify but that they be willing to throw the first stones to prove the validity of their testimony.[3] If there are truly any witnesses in this story, they leave quietly with the rest of the crowd.

Whatever the unknown truth about the adultery is, the Pharisees have violated their own law by bringing only the woman to judgment. Out of their fear that the power of Jesus' teaching might be beyond their own law, they have violated their own tradition, after dedicating their whole lives to teaching the law. Thus they have violated their own integrity also, because they have compromised the primary commitment of their whole lives. Finally, of course, they have violated a daughter of Abraham by their plot. A rock musician, Bruce Springsteen, has a phrase to describe the Pharisees: they are "waist deep in the Big Muddy."

As part of the deep irony behind the story, the man Jesus has a peculiar relationship to women accused of sexual immorality. The relationship begins, astonishingly, early in the genealogy in Matthew. For there are four women listed in the genealogy, and each of them has acted in some way outside the traditional morality of Hebrew law. Tamar dressed as a prostitute in order to persuade

Judah to live up to his requirements as a tribal patriarch. Ruth is a Moabite, a descendant of the people who came from Lot's incest committed upon his daughters. The wife of Uriah committed adultery with King David. And finally, there is Mary, his mother, pregnant before her marriage.

As one teaching and preaching the gospel given to him by God, Jesus gives to women a number of healings that are related to their status as legally unclean or sexually aberrant. There is the woman with the issue of blood, the Samaritan woman married five times and living with a man not her husband, the woman who humbles herself in public and touches Jesus in order to bathe his feet with oil and wipe them with her hair. And, of course, there is Mary Magdalen, cured of seven demons; commentators have assumed that at least one of the seven must have created sexual havoc and consider her a former prostitute.

So in this dramatic scene, confronted with the self-righteous Pharisees and the angry crowd carrying rocks in their hands, Jesus is not repulsed by this woman accused of adultery. He does not recoil or turn away, fearful of her publicly proclaimed sexuality. Instead, he apparently ignores everyone and kneels to write with his finger on the ground.

This is a stop-action sequence and the scene is frozen, but the Pharisees insist on a judgment.

And they get one: "Let anyone among you who is without sin be the first to throw a stone at her."

It is a sermon in a sentence: a judgment laid on the accusers instead of the accused. And the compromised rule-followers slink away. The misuse of their power has drained them of humanity; they are hollow men who have no argument against Jesus. They have only enough integrity left to drop their stones and walk away.

Some people have mistakenly concluded that the message here is that we are to try to live without judging others at all. But not only is that impossible; it is not a valid conclusion. Jesus does make a judgment. But it is a judgment that cuts through the shadowy manipulation of the Pharisees. It is a judgment that levels the power relationships of the accusers and the accused. Those who have misused their power have no victory against Jesus and his message. For the real intended victim here is Jesus. The woman is just a tool for the Pharisees.

The next scene is quiet and solemn as Jesus turns to write on the ground again. The woman has stayed, most likely in a state of shock that one sentence from this stranger could save her from a humiliating and horrible death. Jesus speaks to her: "Where are they? Has no one condemned you?" She has been accused, but there is no basis for condemnation. So Jesus makes clear what his judgment of the situation is: "Neither do I condemn you. Go your way, and from now on do not sin again."

This woman has been through the deep waters of near death by stoning, but Jesus promises that she will not be overwhelmed. She has experienced a fiery trial, but her dross, whatever it is, will be consumed and refined. In three short sentences, Jesus has sanctified her public and private distress.

Was she guilty? is the wrong question. What is important is the mirror of judgment that Jesus holds up to all accusers and the movement of mercy toward this strange, anonymous woman.

The words of Jesus to the woman are analogous to the theme of Hosea: "I desire mercy, not sacrifice." They are part and parcel of life's witness to women and to those who would violate them. The response of Jesus is not in any way an excuse for sexual infidelity; it is an example of the wise mercy we are to offer those used in plots by people hollowed out by fear or hollowed out by the misuse of power.

And what about the witness of the story to us as we live out our lives in a society polarized by fear. A world in which religious fanaticism results in armed cults, and moral fanaticism results in murder outside a clinic. We are all in this story. At one time or another, we all fill all the roles.

We are most at risk to act as the Pharisees did when we are afraid of moral chaos, when we feel personally responsible for the social order, when we believe that our own inner circle is responsible for the moral fabric of our community. We pick up stones to punish designated scapegoats because we have abandoned the providence of God. At that point, we no longer have faith in the working of the Spirit, but only in the work of human argument and influence.

That kind of faith denies the communion of community. For just like each of us as individuals, a community must sometimes work out its salvation in the environment of fear. Sometimes a rock is placed in our hands by another and we are swept along with the crowd by the energy of righteous indignation. Courage is required to stop in the middle of the mob, to stand and say, "What is really going on here? Who stands to gain power by the judgment that is being demanded?"

And chances are, as ministers of the gospel, we will all, at one point or another, be dragged into the public arena by people who are terrified of change. We will be accused of unfaithfulness to a law—most likely unwritten—that is held by our accusers. It may be that we will be accused by those who do not honor the principle they pretend to uphold.

Following Jesus requires that we risk faithfulness including, and gracefully beyond, a legal or moral formula. It may require taking the chance of being accused of unfaithfulness by the purist and the compulsive hunter of motes in others' eyes. And it requires growing in faith until we can say, with all the saints, that we fear no one but God, even though that is unimaginable to those who rely on human power.

But finally, more than anything, being a minister today requires trust. Trust that Jesus will once again draw in the dust and confound our accusers until they have dropped their stones and walked away in shame. And trust that somehow, sometime, those who accuse us falsely will be confronted by God with their own sin. Can we trust that there in the temple, humiliated by the dishonorable behavior of others, we will look up into the loving eyes of a Savior who says, "There is no one left to accuse you. Go in peace and the forgiveness of sin"?

And though we might resist the idea, there will be days when we are just sitting somewhere teaching and preaching and someone will be brought to us for judgment. Out of the darkness created by fear, the morally self-righteous at either end of a polarized spectrum will demand our decision. We may find ourselves in a situation where none of our traditional rules seem to apply.

In this story, Jesus gives us two strategies as a basis for judgment. First, determine what is really going on. Who has power? How are they using their power? What is the balance of power that is required by the commandments of Jesus? Perhaps most important, who is carrying rocks and who inspired them, by whispers in the shadow, to pick up those rocks?

Second, Jesus teaches us to seek mercy, not sacrifice. In times of critical judgment, what is the needed act of mercy? Who are the victims in a given situation? Who needs our mercy? How and when do we pour out mercy?

Perhaps we should do more writing in the dirt, deflecting attention while we ponder the leading of the Spirit. Prior to passing important judgment, we need to pray for the discernment of truth about any situation and for the wisdom to search beneath accusations for the complex motivations and true intentions. Most of all, in a world torn by hatred and fear, we pray for a spirit of Christ's mercy in our hearts.

Dear God,

Open our hearts to the light of your mercy here in Lent as we bring our honest confession to you. Open us to the grace and love of a Savior who walked up a hill and paid the whole cost for our words and deeds of darkness. And send us out now, today, and every day, to offer mercy and love to a fearful and hate-filled world. In the name of Jesus, the Christ, who is the memory, hope, and authority of the future. Amen.

NOTES

1. George Beasley-Murray, *John,* Word Biblical Commentary, vol. 35 (Waco, TX: Word Books, 1987), 143–44.

2. Ibid., 146.

3. Ibid.

31. No Flowers by Request
Don Affleck

John 12:1–8 (the anointing at Bethany); Philippians 3:7–14

You must have been as surprised as I was when you read that recent advertisement in the "Funeral" column of our local newspaper, which said:

> RELATIVES AND FRIENDS OF LAZARUS ARE
> RESPECTFULLY INVITED TO ATTEND HIS FUNERAL.
>
> NO FLOWERS BY REQUEST.
>
> DONATIONS TO THE LAZARUS FOUNDATION
> MAY BE LEFT AT THE CHURCH.

This was followed by the regular, paid advertisement from the Lazarus Foundation:

> RESEARCH PARTNERS
>
> What would they have
> wanted—a floral tribute or
> funds to help others fight on?
> Knowing them, you know
> the answer to that.

Donald A. Affleck is parish minister for the Tumut-Gundagai Parish of the Uniting Church in New South Wales, Australia. He has received diplomas in divinity and religious studies from Methodist Theological College in Sydney and a B.A. from Australian National University in Canberra. For eight years he was senior lecturer in religious studies at Riverina College of Advanced Education, Australia, and in 1992 he returned to parish ministry after an absence of twenty-five years. He and his wife, Marie, have three daughters.

Donate to the LAZARUS FOUNDATION
and become a partner in our
life-giving research programmes.

All donations are tax deductible.

I'm allowed to speak in this tongue-in-cheek manner because, five years ago, my life was given back to me by means of heart surgery involving a triple bypass, and I remain indebted, as long as I live, to the research programs of the National Heart Foundation.

Nevertheless, I really do like flowers. I like to give flowers and I like to receive flowers—on both sad and joyous occasions.

And I really do hate being told not to send flowers but instead to only send money to a specific foundation.

I am aware that this liking of mine for sending flowers puts me at odds with much of contemporary funeral practice. However, I am totally unrepentant, and in this sermon you will learn why.

I.

There is an abundance of New Testament assessment and assertion surrounding this particular Gospel incident in John 12. The same story, or something very similar to it, is reported in all four Gospels. Not all locate it at the same time and place in the Jesus story.

I am going to deal with it as it stands in John's Gospel—between the raising of Lazarus from death, in Bethany, and Jesus' entry into Jerusalem.

Brendan Byrne, in his amazing little book, *Lazarus,* includes this incident of the anointing as part of what he calls "the aftermath" of the raising of Lazarus.[1] The raising Byrne sees as the most powerful of six major "signs" done by Jesus, all pointing to the advent of God's kingly rule, and around which John structured his unique presentation of the Jesus story.

"Lazarus," says Byrne, "becomes a type, a representative of a world-wide company of believers.

"It is to underline this 'typical' role of Lazarus that the evangelist has Lazarus' story continue somewhat beyond the actual raising."[2]

In our text, Lazarus is present in the house when Jesus' feet are anointed with the expensive ointment. Indeed, the anointing is done by one of his sisters.

Is it just me, or have you noticed, too, how silent Lazarus is? He never speaks; he doesn't even say, "Thank you." But then, perhaps a person who has experienced resurrection would, by definition, never know that he had been dead.

Byrne refers, briefly, to what he terms "the somewhat passive role" played by Lazarus.[3] That has to be the understatement of the aeon! Lazarus is about as active as a tombstone! The gratitude that we expect to come from Lazarus's lips comes instead from someone else.

Byrne again: "In the context of Jesus' own movement towards his death, Mary's loving service is totally appropriate. Jesus has given life to her brother—but has done so at the cost of his own life, a cost soon to be required. By anointing his feet with costly ointment (so costly that its aroma fills the whole room), Mary shows both that she appreciates the cost and that she is ready offer something costly in return."[4]

II.

Two important things stand out in this story:

First, the nature of love is that it just has to be extravagant . . . wasteful . . . over the top.

Paul Tillich once preached about Mary anointing Jesus' feet with the costly ointment. He said that she represents the ecstatic, impulsive, reckless element in our relation to God. The disciples, on that day, represent the reasonable element in our relation to God.[5]

In well-to-do circles in Palestine, anointing the body with olive or vegetable oils was quite customary, as a means of refreshment (or in connection with a meal).

But in the circles in which Jesus usually moved it was a practice too expensive to be common.

So, the action of Mary anointing Jesus' feet with the costly ointment would have come as a complete surprise to Jesus, to his disciples, and to any other guests. And who could blame the disciples for being angry about the immense waste Mary had created?

Certainly not a church elder who visits unemployed parishioners . . . certainly not a social worker who knows so many financially needy persons but hasn't got the funds to assist them . . . certainly not someone who, through well-researched treatment, has survived the threat of cancer . . . certainly not the mother of one of those starving children in Somalia who stare at us, through the TV set, as, each night, we sit eating our dinner.

The disciples could not be blamed by any sane, well-balanced person who has his/her emotional life under control and who sees the woman's act, in this needy world, as being almost criminal.

But . . . Jesus accepted Mary's deed done to him, and he rebuked his very practical disciples!

Jesus did not raise the question of how much human passion and how much considered reasoning made up Mary's motivation. He saw a deed of abundant affection and devotion, and he accepted it.

A calculating love is no love at all! Religion that always acts within the safe bounds of reasonableness is a mutilated religion!

One of my treasured stories concerns the hungry tramp who knocked on the door of a house occupied by a woman known for her Christian devotion and asked her for something to eat. The woman went to her kitchen, cut two very thick slices of bread, put them in a paper bag, and gave them to the tramp with the words, "Remember, my man, that I am not doing this for your sake but for Christ's sake." The tramp looked at the bread and replied, "Then for Christ's sake, put some butter on it."

That's not just a good story; it is also good theology. It reminds us that the new world of the Kingdom of God—which stands before us in the ministry of Jesus, and which is signified in the restoration of Lazarus to his family—can never be entered into by the cautious and calculating souls of this world.

It is accessible, as St. Paul says in today's Epistle, only to those who are prepared to be completely *disengaged* from their past (with all its goodness, its safety, its correctness, its reasonableness) and then recklessly *reengaged* with the *new* creation that God discloses only moment by moment, situation by situation.

The broken bread and the poured-out wine are the symbols of the most complete and most holy *waste* . . . done out of the overflowing love of God.

Second, with Jesus as our model, we who have been graced, called, and gifted to lovingly serve others must also make it possible for others to serve us extravagantly and recklessly.

Many persons find this extremely hard to do. We are good at giving but not very good at all at receiving.

Why are so many of us hiding behind a wall of activity?

Why can't we invite others to share tasks with us, and so minister *to us?*

What are we afraid of?

Could it be that we know we would have to become vulnerable to others if we did this?

Perhaps the model of Jesus as a vulnerable person—here shown as vulnerable to Mary and her reckless act of gratitude—frightens us far more than it fascinates us and compels us.

But if we are to allow our love and service to be defined and directed by Jesus, then we must risk living with openness and vulnerability to the love of others—as he himself lived.

This is especially true in those situations where pain and anguish are intensified by the cosmic silence that meets our questions: Why? . . . Why me?

William F. May is the author of *The Patient's Ordeal.* Writing from the patient's point of view, he pleads for all care givers to recognize and accept his observation that "suffering does not pose a question; rather, suffering demands a response."[6] He goes on to claim that suffering is not a puzzle but a mystery; it demands not a solution but a ritual.

A short time ago a beautiful and very expensive arrangement of flowers was delivered to me. It was a complete surprise.

It came from the family of an eighty-four-year-old man whose funeral I had conducted some weeks before. The flowers were accompanied by a lovely letter thanking me for the service and for the pastoral care I had given to the wife and family.

Surely a letter would have been enough thanks on its own. The money spent on the flowers (which soon died and were thrown away) could, instead, have been given to the Forrest Centre at Calvary Hospital, where the old man was cared for, for over two years.

If we would truly minister to others, in Christ's name, then we must learn how to back off and allow others to minister to us.

I love flowers, and the family knew that. I'm grateful that they decided to waste their money on me and not send it to the Forrest Centre. They did a beautiful thing for me. It was a deed of *loving waste.*

It felt good to be loved like that, and at this Communion table, it always feels good to be loved with the reckless, over-the-top generosity of the God and Father of our Lord Jesus Christ, and our God.

III.

So, when I die, do us both a favor and, for Christ's sake, send flowers—by request!

Now to him who by means of his power working in us is able to do so much more than we can ever ask for, or even think of: to God be glory in the Church and in Christ Jesus for all time, for ever and ever!

NOTES

1. Brendan Byrne, *Lazarus* (Collegeville, MN: Liturgical Press, 1991), 66.

2. Ibid., 67.

3. Ibid., 67–68.

4. Ibid., 83.

5. Paul Tillich, "Holy Waste," in *The New Being* (New York: Charles Scribner's Sons, 1955), 46–47.

6. William F. May, *The Patient's Ordeal* (Bloomington, IN: Indiana University Press, 1992).

32. The Most Misunderstood Emotion

George B. Wirth

Psalm 145; James 1:19–21

Be angry, but do not let the sun go down on your anger.

—Ephesians 4:26

Introduction

The idea for this sermon was literally "ignited" one evening several years ago in the kitchen of our home up in Pittsburgh. A family disagreement after dinner turned into an argument, and I lost my temper. It was not one of my better moments, and as the volume of my voice escalated to a high pitch, I looked out the kitchen window and saw through the curtains the figures of two people standing on our back porch.

Instantly, I remembered that I had invited a young couple to come over and talk about how they were doing in their marriage, and there they were, overhearing this major blowup at the manse.

Seconds later, they were gone, and as I stood in the kitchen trying to calm down, the front doorbell rang. I went to the door

---

George B. Wirth, pastor of First Presbyterian Church, Atlanta, Georgia, is a graduate of the University of North Carolina at Chapel Hill and of Princeton Theological Seminary. In 1986 he received an honorary D.Div. from Waynesburg College in Pennsylvania, and he completed his D.Min. program through Pittsburgh Theological Seminary in 1990. He is a trustee of Princeton Theological Seminary, Warren Wilson College (Swannanoa, North Carolina), and the Westminster Schools (Atlanta, Georgia).

and found the young couple there, looking at me with anxious eyes and what must have been mixed emotions, wondering, perhaps, if I knew that they knew what had gone on in the kitchen, and wondering to themselves, perhaps, if it might not be better to try another night, when the pastor who had invited them over for counseling had gotten hold of himself.

I walked out the door with them and we went around the corner to the church study. As we sat down, I looked them both straight in the eye and said, "I know that you heard what went on in the kitchen, and I am sorry that you had to hear it. But now at least you know that I'm not perfect." They said, "We already knew that." I said, "Well, now you know that your pastor has a temper." They replied, "We didn't know that." I took a deep breath and went on to say, "Let's talk about how you are doing in your home, and after a while, I'll go back and take care of things in my own home."

Which is exactly what we did. And that night, after I had asked my wife, Barbara, and our children, Alyson and Matthew, for their forgiveness, I sat down alone and began to write the introduction to this sermon. Please listen:

Anger is the most misunderstood emotion. Most people aren't exactly sure where it comes from, and Christians in particular have a hard time handling it, because we're supposed to be loving, kind, peaceful, and able to control ourselves. But it happens anyway, and when it does, when anger erupts, some of us attempt to avoid it, others seek to suppress it, still others try to deny it, and many more of us are simply overwhelmed by it. It is time for me to dig deep down inside and decide what I am going to do about it.

That's what I wrote several years ago. I'm still working on it, and I suspect that many of you are still working on it, too. So let me share with you this morning a book that I have found helpful in my own struggle with this most misunderstood emotion, and then point toward a passage from the Bible that gives us some guidance as we all seek to deal with anger we feel and need to face.

I.

Back in 1981, Dr. Richard Walters, a Presbyterian pastor and psychologist from Boulder, Colorado, wrote a book entitled *Anger:*

Yours and Mine and What to Do About It. Toward the beginning of the book, Dr. Walters offers some assumptions about anger that come from his own counseling experience and from his reading of Scripture. Listen:

> First, anger is an emotion and a feeling, not a behavior. Feelings generally are neither right nor wrong, but they can lead either to right and constructive behavior, or to wrong and destructive behavior.
>
> Second, anger is a universal emotional response, and, therefore, Christians are not immune to becoming angry.
>
> Third, anger is an emotion which is most often tied to other emotions, such as hurt, envy, fear, loneliness or frustration.
>
> Fourth, although the emotion of anger often comes quickly, we do have a choice about how we behave and we are responsible for that behavior.
>
> And, fifth, living a disciplined Christian life can reduce the number of occasions on which we inappropriately and unnecessarily let our anger loose.[1]

Now, this book has been helpful to me, not only in exploring where anger comes from and what to do about it, but also in reminding us that in the Bible, God, and many people of faith expressed anger—"righteous indignation"—in the face of injustice and oppression.

When Jesus saw the money changers in the temple making a desecration of God's house and taking a profit from the people who had come to worship there, Jesus was angry and threw them out! And suddenly, in my mind's eye, that meek and mild picture of Jesus on the Sunday School wall changes. His eyes flash, his face turns red, he grabs a whip from one of the bystanders and chases those money changers from the temple, turning over their tables and shouting out loud: "My house shall be called a house of prayer. But you have made it a den of robbers!"

II.

But for most of us, the kind of anger that haunts us and taunts us and causes us to explode like volcanoes or turn cold with resentment and bitterness—that kind of anger, which is also found in the Bible and in our own hearts and minds and homes and churches, has the potential to overwhelm us and to hurt us if we fail or refuse to get a handle on it.

My hunch is, that's what James was dealing with in the first-century church in Jerusalem. Biblical scholars tell us that this letter was probably first delivered as a sermon, and it could be that James, the leader of the church in Jerusalem, was trying to tell those Christians, as he is trying to tell us today, how to deal with anger, how to live together in peace, how to love and forgive one another through the grace and mercy of the Lord Jesus Christ.

So, in the first chapter of this letter, James says: "Let everyone be quick to hear, slow to speak and slow to anger, for our anger does not work the righteousness of God. Therefore, put away all . . . wickedness and receive with meekness the implanted word [of God] which is able to save your souls" (James 1:19–21).

James is telling us, first of all, to open our ears and hearts and minds before we open our mouths. "Be quick to hear" he says, and when anger begins to well up inside us, that is where we can begin to deal with what we are feeling.

We need to listen—not only to what others are saying, but also to what our own inner voice is saying and sometimes screaming out from the depths of our souls. Dr. Harriet Lerner, a therapist from the Menninger Clinic in Topeka, Kansas, wrote in the introduction to her book *The Dance of Anger:* "Our anger may be a message that we are being hurt, that our rights are being violated, that our needs are not being adequately met, or simply that something is not right. . . . Anger is something we feel . . . and it always deserves our attentions."[2]

To be sure, that is not easy to do. When anger erupts, in the heat of the moment it is hard to hear what is going on outside or inside of us. Some people try counting to ten, while others find it helpful to pray. Sometimes it is best to get away from the situation, to take a walk or go for a run. One man I know has a punching bag in the basement, and when he gets angry, that's where he goes!

However we try to handle it, James is telling us that when anger erupts, we need to hear—to listen to what others are saying and what our own inner voice is saying. And as we try to clarify where our anger is coming from and why, that will open the doors of our hearts and minds to the Spirit of God, whose voice seeks to say to us: "Peace. Be still."

III.

First says James, "Be quick to hear." And then "Be slow to speak." I can't remember who wrote these lines, but they speak to me:

> Angry words, like arrows from a bow,
> Once set in motion, to the target go.

You see, once words are spoken, they cannot be taken back. And when they are spoken in anger, our words not only sting; they can break a heart or ruin a relationship. James is telling us that as Christians, we need to learn how to control our tongues before they get us into a lot of trouble.

A little girl got into trouble with her mother one day. She came home from school with mud caked all over her new clothing, and her mother hit the ceiling: "Young lady, that's a brand-new outfit. Just look at you! Now, you go right down to the basement, put those dirty clothes into the washer and dryer, and make sure they're clean before you come upstairs."

With tears in her eyes, the daughter descended into the basement, did as she was told, and then went up to her room. Minutes later, the mother, who was still furious, shouted down the stairs at the top of her lungs, "Are you still down there, running around with your clothes off?" And a big voice boomed back from the basement, "No ma'am, I'm down here reading the gas meter."

"Be slow to speak," said James, lest our tongues, in a fit of fury, in the heat of hostility, get us into a lot of trouble. We can't take those words back, once they have been let loose. So let the Lord help you to tame your tongue, and with some practice, over time, we can all learn to be "slow to speak."

IV.

Finally, James says, "Be slow to anger." The Psalmist once wrote that "God is slow to anger, and abounding in steadfast love," and ultimately, that is our goal as well. Anger, as we have said throughout this sermon, is not only a misunderstood emotion; it is also a natural reaction to all kinds of fears and frustrations, to stress and strain, to oppression and injustice, to abuse and pain; anger is part and parcel of who we are and the way God made us.

And if we can learn during our lifetime to be slow to anger, to deal with what we feel, to try to clarify where the anger is coming from and why, then James puts before us a promise: that the "implanted word of God," which is the very presence and peace of the Lord Jesus Christ, will help us handle our anger and channel it, yes even change it, from destructive behavior to a more constructive way of living and loving. James said, "The implanted word of God is able to save your soul."

That promise leads us to the text of this sermon, which is my hope and prayer for everyone in this sanctuary today and all those within the sound of my voice: From the fourth chapter of Ephesians, the twenty-sixth verse, listen to these words: *"Do not let the sun go down on your anger."*

If you are struggling with anger in your own life right now; if you have harbored hatred in your heart; if you have hurt someone else or been hurt yourself by bitter words; if you feel like you're about to explode, or have allowed your anger to turn into cold resentment—then don't let another day go by without deciding to do something about it. Don't let the sun go down on your anger.

Because life is too short, people are too precious, and your own emotional health is too important to let anger destroy you or ruin your relationships.

You may need to talk about it with family members or friends. You might need to seek professional counseling. And you will surely need the help of God, who can heal your heart, forgive your sins, and bring you back into reconciliation with him and with those you love.

Don't let the sun go down on your anger. And may the peace and grace and love and forgiveness of the Lord Jesus Christ be with you, now and forevermore.

NOTES

1. Richard Walters, *Anger: Yours and Mine and What to Do About It* (Grand Rapids, MI: Zondervan, 1981).

2. Harriet Lerner, *The Dance of Anger* (New York: Harper Collins, 1985).

33. The Grasshopper Complex
THE FEAR OF INADEQUACY
Robert E. Buchanan, Jr.

Numbers 13:25–33

According to Dr. Harold Levinson, approximately 30 million Americans live in fear.[1] In another survey of 3,000 people about their worst fears, 41% responded that public speaking was their worst fear, 32% said they were afraid of heights, 22% were afraid of insects and bugs, 22% feared financial problems, 22% feared deep water, 19% were afraid of serious diseases (such as AIDS and cancer), 19% were afraid of death, 18% were afraid to fly, and 14% feared being alone or abandoned.

A couple of years ago I saw a cartoon that described a fear that is unique to ministers. The "medical" terminology for this fear is *transcontinental congrephobia*—"the feeling, even when you're 1,800 miles from home, that one of your church members is eavesdropping in the next booth."[2]

What are you most afraid of in life? Maybe you're afraid of rejection? Maybe you're afraid of failure or even success? Maybe you're afraid of death or even God? The Duke of Wellington once

Robert E. Buchanan, Jr. is pastor of Parkway Baptist Church in Duluth, Georgia, and has served churches in Florida, Indiana, and Georgia. He attended Southern Baptist Theological Seminary, from which he received his M.Div. and D.Min. degrees. He has served on numerous associational, denominational, and community service committees and received several honors, including the Clyde T. Francisco Preaching Award (SBTS, 1981). This sermon is the first in a series of sermons entitled "Taming Monsters, Slaying Dragons: Facing Your Fears with Courage!"

said, "The only thing I am afraid of is fear." Henry David Thoreau wrote in his journal on September 7, 1851: "Nothing is so much to be feared as fear." Franklin D. Roosevelt said in his inaugural address on March 4, 1933: "The only thing we have to fear is fear itself."[3]

Whatever your fear is, it can paralyze you and keep you from experiencing all that God wants for you.

Maybe the one fear that keeps you from reaching your fullest potential in life is your own feeling of inadequacy. The legendary Knute Rockne knew how to psyche out his opponents by making them feel inadequate. One day Notre Dame was facing a critical game against a vastly superior University of Southern California team. Coach Rockne recruited every brawny student he could find on the Notre Dame campus and suited up about a hundred "hulks" in school uniforms. On the day of the game the USC team ran out on the field first and awaited the visiting Fighting Irish. Finally, out of the locker room came an army of green giants who kept on coming and coming. The USC team panicked. Their coach reminded them that Rockne could play only eleven men at a time, but the damage was done. USC lost. USC did not lose to one hundred men, but instead they were beaten by their own fear of inadequacy.

In Numbers 13, verses 25 to 33, the children of Israel felt inadequate to the task that was before them. Let's back up for a moment and review what had taken place in Israel's history up until this point.

After the people had experienced years of oppression and slavery, Moses beckoned Pharaoh to let his people go free. Before Pharaoh yielded to this unknown shepherd, Moses turned the Nile into blood and brought a rash of deadly plagues upon the Egyptian people. Pharaoh's hardened heart finally broke as he listened to the cries of sorrow resonating from every home where the firstborn children had died.

When Pharaoh and his men realized that they had lost a cheap source of labor, Pharaoh changed his mind and pursued the Israelites. An enormous sea lay in front of the Israelites and an angry army was approaching fast from the rear. Some of the people cried out, "It would have been better for us to serve the Egyptians than to die in the desert!" Moses encouraged them to stand strong and believe that God would deliver them again.

Moses raised his wooden staff, stretched out his hand over the sea, and divided the waters so that his people could walk into the Promised Land on dry land. Just as the last Israelites stepped up on the bank of the other side, the waters rushed back into the valley and drowned all of Pharaoh's army.

Three months after the Exodus, as Israel sat camped in the Desert of Sinai, Moses ascended to the top of Mount Sinai, where God carved out his covenant with his people. As Israel continued to roam around in the desert, God provided manna and quail for her to eat.

According to Numbers 12, soon thereafter Moses moved the Israelites farther up the Sinai Peninsula and set up camp in the Desert of Paran. In chapter 13, verse 1, Moses chose one leader from each of the twelve tribes and commissioned them to explore Canaan, the Promised Land. Our text this morning, Numbers 13:25–33, is the report they brought back to Moses.

The Report of the Scouts

I want you to notice three things that stood out in their report. The first thing they spoke about was richness of the land. In verses 26 and 27, the scouts showed pieces of fruit that they had picked, and said, "The land flows with milk and honey." Unlike the dry and parched desert, there is nothing that this land cannot produce.

The second thing they spoke about in their report was the people who inhabited the land. Verse 28 reads: "But the people who live there are powerful, and the cities are fortified and very large. We even saw descendants of Anak there. The Amalekites live in Negev; the Hittites, Jebusites, and Amorites live in the hill country; and the Canaanites live near the sea and along the Jordan." As the Israelites begin murmuring about how difficult, if not impossible, it would be to conquer these people and possess the Promised Land, Caleb shocked them with his optimistic challenge: "Let us go up and take possession of the land, for we can certainly do it."

The third and most important thing I want you to notice about the report is found in verses 31 to 33. Caleb must have been the only optimist in the bunch. The other eleven scouts immediately threw cold water on his appeal to move forward: "We can't possibly attack those people. They are stronger than us. All the people living there are giants." The last part of verse 33 really illuminates their true feelings: "We seemed like grasshoppers in our own eyes, and we looked the same to them."

Do you hear what the Israelites were saying? "God, I know that several months ago you rescued us from the chains of slavery. I know that you parted the Red Sea and provided us with food in the desert. You don't understand; we've got bigger problems now. We're too small and we don't have adequate resources to take the land that you've already promised us."

According to chapter 14, the Israelites grumbled against Moses, wishing they were back in Egypt. Their own fear of inadequacy stopped them from moving forward and left them wandering in the wilderness for forty years.

Humanly Inadequate, Divinely Empowered

What was wrong with Israel's response to her inadequacies? Her fear or feeling of inadequacy could have been a source of discouragement or the beginning of a new courage.

As Israel stood camped just before the Promised Land, her fear of inadequacy did not have to lead to rebellion and despair. She could have realized that her source of strength was not within herself, that the God who had been faithful to her in the past would remain faithful.

God's word is full of examples of people who felt inadequate to the task that they were assigned but who were empowered with courage and strength from God.

Moses, as he stood barefoot beside the burning bush, confessed to God that he was inadequate to serve as his spokesperson to Pharaoh. He even offered Aaron as his substitute before the Lord.

David, a little shepherd boy armed with a leather sling in his hand, probably felt inadequate as he looked across the valley and saw Goliath draw his huge sword.

A little boy came home from Sunday School and his mother asked him about the morning's lesson. He proceeded to tell her the story of David and Goliath. He recounted how the giant was over nine feet tall, and that David had nothing to fight with except a slingshot and a few stones. Finally, he concluded, "that big giant got hit in the head with a stone from David's slingshot and fell over dead."

"Now, what does this lesson teach us?" his mother asked. The lad thought for a moment and replied, "I guess it teaches us to duck!"

No, the story doesn't teach us to duck. It teaches us that even during the times when we feel most inadequate, God is able to do his greatest work. Moses and David were humanly inadequate, but they were divinely empowered.

What are your feelings of inadequacy keeping you from doing? Maybe they're keeping you from teaching a Sunday School class? Maybe they're keeping you from accepting a promotion at work? Maybe they're keeping you from witnessing to a neighbor or a friend? Maybe they're keeping you from accepting God's unconditional grace? Maybe they're keeping you from growing a church?

There's an ancient legend that comes from India. It tells about a mouse who was terrified of cats until a magician agreed to transform him into a cat. That took care of his problem—until he met a dog, at which time he again became afraid. So the magician changed him into a dog. The mouse-turned-cat-turned-dog was content until he met a tiger. But then the once-mouse-now-tiger came complaining to the magician that he met a hunter of whom he was afraid and said he wanted the magician to help him again. The magician refused, saying, "I will make you into a mouse again, for though you have the body of a tiger, you still have the heart of a mouse."

God has a purpose and plan for each and every one of us. That plan and purpose includes us in an abundant and eternal life that God has made available to us through his Son, Jesus Christ. God has a purpose and plan for this church, too.

As we pursue God's purpose for our lives, may he give us the courage to admit our human inadequacies and accept his divine empowerment. Eleven of the scouts said, "We can't possibly attack those people; they are stronger than us. . . . We seemed like grasshoppers in our own eyes, and we looked the same to them." But Caleb said, "Let us go up and take possession of the land, for we can certainly do it."

NOTES

1. Harold Levinson, *Phobia Free* (New York: M. Evans, 1986), 17.
2. Doug Hall in *Leadership* 8 (Spring 1987): 19.
3. All quoted in Warren Wiersbe, *Meet Yourself in the Psalms* (Wheaton, IL: Victor, 1983), 111.

VI. DEVOTIONAL

34. What Keeps Us Going
Charles B. Bugg

Luke 24:28–35

In his book *How Prayer Shapes Ministry,* John Biersdorf coins an
arresting phrase, "holy despair." It is the despair that at the end of
ourselves opens us to something beyond ourselves. Read the words
of the text, and much of it sounds like unholy despair. On Sunday
afternoon two followers of Jesus make their way from Jerusalem to
the village of Emmaus. Rumors have reached them that the tomb
of Jesus is empty. They don't know whether to believe the reports.
(Besides, it's not enough to build our lives on something that's *not*
there.)

Late in the afternoon these two followers meet a stranger on
the road. Luke tells us the stranger is Jesus. As the readers, we
know the stranger's identity, but to the disillusioned disciples, he's
still a stranger. As night falls, the stranger is inclined to continue on
the road. The disciples say, "Stay with us." That night around the
table their eyes are opened. The stranger is the Savior. The one on
the journey is the one they had called Jesus. These followers now
had more than the memory of an empty tomb and a missing body.
They had a Risen Lord. Unholy despair became holy around the
table.

What happened at the table that opened these disciples' eyes?
What caused them to see who this stranger really was and to remember his words on the road? Was it his words of gratitude at
supper? Luke says, "When he was at the table with them, he took
bread, gave thanks . . ." How like Jesus. Here in this moment when

Charles B. Bugg is pastor of Providence Baptist Church in
Charlotte, North Carolina, following service as the Carl E. Bates
Professor of Christian Preaching at Southern Baptist Theological
Seminary. Dr. Bugg holds degrees from Stetson University and
Southern Baptist Theological Seminary, where he received a Ph.D.
He is the author of *Getting on Top When Life Gets Us Down.*

gratitude seemed distant, he gave thanks. If ever there was a moment not to give thanks, it was this moment. Back in Jerusalem the young Galilean had died, and so had the dream of his disciples. Dreams die hard. We want something so much—a job, a marriage, an invitation. We dream about it, and then one day, it's dead. What do you do when that happens? Give thanks?

I was jogging one afternoon when a school bus stopped nearby. Out stepped a boy, and I could tell immediately that he was physically challenged—shuffling as fast as he could toward a house. I saw a woman waiting for him on the front porch. I assumed it was his mother. My thoughts were, "How sad." Did she ever say, as most of us have, "If only my child were healthy?" When he reached the sidewalk leading to the house, he was met by his mother. She embraced him, kissed him; it was a party, a celebration. She seemed wonderfully grateful for her son. Why wasn't she spending her life saying, "If only it had turned out differently"?

Gratitude—it turns up in surprising places. At sundown on Sunday night in a house in Emmaus, a stranger says, "Thanks," and perhaps the disciples remembered the one who had taught them to live out of gratitude. Or maybe it was his hands. The stranger took the bread in his hands and broke it. Hands reveal much about us—nail-scarred hands; gnarled, twisted hands; delicate hands. Hands communicate a lot—an open hand, a clenched fist. Hands tell much of our story. When my mother died in 1992, I noticed her hands gently folded across her chest. I remembered the day that she walked me to kindergarten. Hand in hand we walked up to a building that seemed bigger than anything else I had ever seen. After a few minutes my mother let go of my hand, kissed me, and left me there to make my way in this new world. Now I looked at her hands folded across her chest and remembered how those hands had sometimes held on and sometimes let go. Did the disciples remember when they saw the stranger's hands? The story of our lives—look at the hands.

Or were their eyes opened because Jesus took charge of the supper and served them. Luke is clear. The house may not belong to the stranger, but the supper does. He "began to give it to them" (Luke 24:30b). The bread represented life, and when Jesus took it and gave it to them, it may have been a reminder that this is the Lord who holds all life in his hands. That was important to these disciples. With their leader dead, these men had no center, nothing to give life any real purpose. The divine dimension was dead, and life was little more than helter-skelter. The only benediction that we can give when there is nothing beyond us is: "Make the best of it." In a world where good people like Jesus get nailed and children die and the cruelty of war strikes the innocent and dreams turn to ashes, that's all that we have to offer: Make the best of it, because there's nothing beyond us to give any sense to things. No wonder these followers were gripped by despair. But in the room their eyes were opened by something. In the place to which they had invited the stranger, they were invited by him to the table. It was his table, his bread, his life; and knowing this, they could live again.

The fact is that we don't really know what opened these men's eyes and gave them new vitality. But something happened in the room around the table that revealed the stranger's identity and gave his followers new identity. At this point, Luke's Gospel records a most remarkable thing: "They [the disciples] got up and returned at once to Jerusalem" (Luke 24:33). They didn't even spend the night in Emmaus! They went back to Jerusalem—the place of pain and perplexity—but they went back with a new presence and power.

What is it that keeps us going? What is it that moves us back into the midst of life, to live with a sense of hope? Why don't we all take up residence in Emmaus, which is the place to go when everything seems like "unholy despair"? When these two followers returned to Jerusalem, they found the other disciples still together, and the first words out of their mouths were: "It is true! The Lord has risen and has appeared to Simon" (Luke 24:34).

A few hours before, it had seemed as if nothing was true except that life was terribly uncertain. Now there was a new truth: "It is true! The Lord has risen. . . ." Does this mean that there is no more uncertainty? That there are no more crosses? No more valleys? You and I know better, and the disciples knew better. As long as they lived, they would never forget that Friday when the best of people had the worst of things done to him. This was a part of their lives. The truth of the Resurrection is not that there are no more deaths and tombs, no more suffering and sadness. We know better, don't we? Try preaching that to the families at the Children's Hospital. Tell them that if they have enough faith, their children will get well, and the doors of the hospital will be closed. That is a dangerous theology, preying on the vulnerable and creating even more despair. We live in Jerusalem, and even after the Resurrection, we live in a Good/Bad Friday kind of world.

But something else also became true for these disciples. The stranger was the Savior. He is risen. At the end of themselves, the pilgrims to Emmaus found someone beyond themselves. Life was not just flat and horizontal. The ordinary table in the room became the place of extraordinary transcendence. This is what keeps us going. This is holy despair. We do have the strength in Christ to face Jerusalem or whatever life may bring.

35. Is God As Good As Our Friends?

Ronald W. Higdon

Luke 11:5–13

I read from an author who talked about his student days at the University of Glasgow and his worship on Sundays at the church where George Morrison was pastor. He noted that almost every Sunday at least one person would make this observation: "The sermon was good but it's the prayer I'll remember."

And then the writer added: "When George Morrison said, 'Let us pray,' you knew that before long, if you had any spiritual sensitiveness at all, you would be ushered into the Holy of Holies."[1]

I think something similar must have been experienced by Jesus' disciples. They were awestruck by his miracles, they marveled at his sermons and parables, but when he prayed they knew they had been ushered into the Holy of Holies.

That may be why we are told in Luke 11:1: He was praying in a certain place, and after he had finished, one of his disciples said to him, "Lord, teach us to pray. . . ." Jesus then proceeded to give them a model prayer, what we call the Lord's Prayer. But in the next verse Luke writes: "*And* he said to them . . ." What he said to them is the parable that is our lesson for the day.

The context of this parable is a part of Jesus' response to the request "Teach us to pray."

The story sounds strange to us, but in the culture of the time it was readily understood. In those days people often traveled at night to avoid the heat of the day. And, of course, most travel meant that the traveler walked.

Ronald W. Higdon is pastor of Broadway Baptist Church in Louisville, Kentucky. He holds degrees from Georgetown College and from the Southern and Southeastern Baptist Theological Seminaries.

The parable Jesus tells is about the traveler who arrives at midnight at the home of a friend and the friend is embarrassed because he has nothing to feed his guest. Bread was baked daily so that it would be fresh. The traveler must have taken his friend by surprise, because there had not been enough bread baked that day for a visitor.

It was a disgrace not to be a proper host, and so the man whose guest arrived at midnight went to his neighbor, knocked on the door, and asked if he could borrow some bread. As one would expect, the door of the neighbor's house was shut. During the day the door was usually left open, indicating accessibility; when the door was shut it was a sign that the occupants did not want to be disturbed. Certainly they did not want to be disturbed at midnight.

From within the house on the other side of the closed door the neighbor calls, "Do not disturb me, please, we are turned in for the night." This may not mean much to us until we realize that the house was a one-room house and in the evening when the family was tucked in, some livestock were also brought inside. So the man and his wife and his children and various animals are all bedded down for the night and this neighbor is pounding on the door. If the household gets up, everybody and everything will be awakened, and who knows how long it will take to get this menagerie settled down again?

But Jesus says that the man in need of bread just keeps on knocking and, finally, simply because of his persistence the neighbor gets up and gives the man some bread. Jesus used this simple story to teach some amazing lessons about prayer.

The first lesson is the obvious one: the lesson of persistence. The moral of the story Jesus plainly states: So I say to you, ask, and it will be given you; search, and you will find; knock, and the door will be opened for you.

Here it is important to know the sense of each of these verbs. What Jesus literally says is: Keep on asking . . . keep on searching . . . keep on knocking. Jesus says the man finally got bread from his neighbor because he just wouldn't stop knocking on the door. The first lesson in prayer is: Just keep it up. Don't stop asking, don't stop seeking, don't stop knocking.

I know how strange this sounds in the culture in which we live; we're not used to waiting. *Instant, quick,* and *no waiting* are the words by which most of us live. The tone of our times seems aptly summed up in these words from Carrie Snow: "I prefer Hostess fruit pies to pop-up toaster tarts because they don't require as much cooking."

Some things require cooking and simmering and attention and time and waiting. Prayer is one of those things. This doesn't mean that God doesn't immediately hear a prayer when it is offered. But Jesus says that the key to the kind of praying he did, and the kind of praying the disciples wanted to learn something about, was persistence and time and effort and waiting. It was not something that opened to the casual inquirer.

A lot of things are available to people who just stumble on them or casually inquire or just have an interest, but the kind of praying Jesus did is not ever going to be unearthed by folks with that approach.

In a play by Maxwell Anderson two men, Biggs and Skimmerhorn, find themselves in grave danger. A part of their conversation runs like this:

> Biggs: "Say, do you know any prayers?"
> Skim: "I know one."
> Biggs: "Say it, will you?"
> Skim: "Matthew, Mark, Luke, and John. Bless the bed that I lie on."
> Biggs: "That's not much good, that one."
> Skim: "It's the only one I know."[2]

The problem wasn't that Skimmerhorn didn't know another prayer; the problem was, he didn't know anything about prayer. You don't just flip out a quick prayer and stumble into the presence of God. Jesus says that for prayer to really do you very much good, there has got to be a conscious and determined persistence.

In fact, camouflaged in this story is something that I think is one of the most important elements in prayer. The full meaning of the Greek word for knocking on the door of the neighbor doesn't show up in any English translation I have found. The Greek word means "to knock with shameless persistence." Jesus says, "That's the way you pray." If the man had been hesitant or cautious in knocking on his friend's door, he would have gotten no bread. He shamelessly and persistently kept pounding and saying, "I've got to have some bread for my guest."

Shock upon shock! Jesus says, "You wanted me to teach you how to pray. This is the way to do it!" I think the disciples probably just wanted a model prayer. Most rabbis gave their disciples model prayers. Jesus gave them a model prayer but then added, "When you pray this model prayer or any prayer you must be shamelessly persistent. Knock on the door. Pound on the door."

Most of us are too cautious and too polite in our praying. I agree with the idea that it would do most of us good to read and pray the Psalms in order to overcome our reluctance and learn how to be shamelessly persistent. What strikes us as we read the Psalms is how these people pounded on God's door. They threw caution to the wind. They accused God of being asleep; they accused him of being off somewhere on a journey. They fussed at Him. They held back no feeling or request. They just let 'er rip.

Jesus tells his disciples that when they pray they are to be like a desperate man who just keeps pounding and calling at the door of his neighbor because he has just got to have some bread for his hungry guest. Jesus says the first lesson in prayer is: Keep on! Don't stop.

A big question this parable answers is one that some people today still ask: When we pray, is God like a reluctant neighbor whom we have to convince of our need? In other words, is God the problem in prayer? Do we have to get God's attention or God's interest or God's sympathy?

Children can teach us a great deal, partly because they are so open and so plain. I read a dialogue between a mother and a child, and, after I got through, it was obvious to me that the child had a better concept of God than the mother did—although this is easy to miss. Listen to the dialogue:

Mother: "Did you know that God was present when you stole that cookie from the kitchen?"

Child: "Yes."

Mother: "And he was looking at you all the time?"

Child: "Yes."

Mother: "And what do you think he was saying to you?"

Child: "He was saying, 'There's no one here but the two of us—so take two.' "[3]

My question to you is: Is the better image of God that of a policeman who is constantly watching and keeping tabs on all you do, or that of a friend who would say, "Oh, go on, have another cookie"? Of course, I don't want to make this the total concept for the image of God, but I believe the child had a much healthier concept of God than the mother!

Jesus had a healthy concept of God. Jesus did *not* say that God was like a reluctant neighbor whom you had to beg, or even like a good earthly parent. What Jesus did say was: "Ask . . . search . . . knock. If you as an imperfect parent know how to give good gifts to your children, how much more will your heavenly Father give . . . !"

Jesus' whole point is, if persistence can finally persuade a reluctant neighbor, think of what our sincerity and persistence can do with our heavenly Father who loves us and cares for us more than we can imagine. God is not reluctant! The problem in prayer is never with God! If there is a problem in prayer, that problem must always have to do with me because God does not have to be persuaded to love me or care for me. God is already *for* us (Rom. 8:31).

I think the key words in what Jesus says are the words *how much more*. If a child asked for a fish, no parent would give a snake instead. If a child asked for an egg, no parent would give a scorpion instead. Jesus says, "If you know how to give good gifts . . . think of *how much more* your loving heavenly Father will give good gifts to those who ask him."

Although I knew the minister, I had not heard the story. Dr. Edward Pruden was for many years pastor of the First Baptist Church of Washington, D.C. This story is about his son, Eddie, who, as a four-year-old, had this conversation with his mother:

Eddie: "Mother, I wish we could have another little boy at our house."

Mother: "Where in the world would we find one?"

Eddie: "Maybe some other mother would give you her little boy."

Mother: "Oh, no, Son. I would never give you to anybody."

Eddie: "Well, you might, when you get through with me."

Mother: "But son, I'll *never* get through with you."[4]

That's the kind of Father to whom you are praying: He'll never get through with us. For me, that is the lesson about the father in the story of the prodigal son. He never got through with his son. And God is never going to get through with you. He's committed to you. I know we need to talk about our commitment to God, but sometimes we need to be reminded of God's commitment to us. One who is committed to us in love—forever. In Romans 8, Paul reminds us that nothing will ever be able to separate us from God's love. My hope is not that I have a hold on God; my confidence is that God's love will never get through with me.

In spite of all this good stuff we know about God, C. S. Lewis has written something about prayer that is disturbing. Near the end of his *Letters to Malcolm,* Lewis said that he decided to come clean. He admitted that for most people prayer is a duty, and an irksome duty at that. He observed that we are reluctant to begin and delighted to finish.[5]

I reluctantly agree that this is all too true for most of us. We want to pray, but we find we have to almost force ourselves to do so. Perhaps we need to change our idea about what prayer is. Suppose for a moment you discarded all the ideas you have ever had about prayer and just thought of prayer as the opportunity to talk with the loving heavenly Father, the one who loves you more than you can imagine. And your praying is just this: You tell him about your day, you talk to him about your disappointments, you talk to him about your dreams, you talk to him about your burdens and the burdens of others. You don't hold back anything you think or feel. You just have a long talk with God as you would with someone who is interested and cares about every detail of your life. I wonder what difference that would make in praying. I think that is the way Jesus prayed. I think that is why he could pray all night.

The plain teaching of Scripture is that when we pray, if we keep on asking, we will receive; if we keep on searching, we will find; and if we keep on knocking, the door will be opened to us. Persistent prayer yields results. But what will we get? What will we find? What doors will be opened to us?

When Matthew records this parable, his wording at the end is: ". . . how much more will your Father in heaven give good things to those who ask Him!" Whereas Luke records: ". . . how much more will the heavenly Father give the Holy Spirit to those who ask him!" I maintain that there is no contradiction in these two statements.

C. S. Lewis thought the question "Does prayer work?" was a bad question. So do I. This makes prayer sound like a vending machine and all you need is right coinage—the proper words—and out pops the treat of your choice. The question makes prayer sound like something magic.

If we must talk about prayer working, I think one writer says it best:

> Prayer works in that it is a personal contact
> between ourselves, incomplete as we are, and the
> one utterly concrete Person. Confession and
> [repentance] are the beginning, adoration is the
> main part, and enjoyment of the presence of God
> is the highlight. Asking for things is a correct and
> important part of prayer, but it is not the most
> important part. Prayer works when God shows
> himself to us—and that is not always as we expect
> or desire.[6]

When Luke says that the heavenly Father will give the Holy Spirit to those who ask him, he just believes that the very best thing God can give us is his presence. So do I. What a gift! What an answer to prayer! If you could sense that God is with you in the presence of his Spirit, think how many questions would be answered, how many searches would be over, and how many doors would stand open.

Matthew and Luke are both correct. Jesus promised that prayer would result in good gifts from the Father, along with the best gift of all—the assurance of his presence.

I don't think Jesus simply told his disciples how to pray; I think he told them how he prayed. He prayed persistently. He prayed shamelessly; he didn't hold back anything. He poured out his heart to his loving heavenly Father whom he trusted—implicitly.

Oh, by the way, I do want to answer the question of the sermon: Is God as good as our friends? The answer: God is better than the best friend you can ever imagine having. When you pray—remember this.

NOTES

1. Robert McCracken, *Questions People Ask* (New York: Harper, 1951), 58.

2. Quoted in McCracken, *Questions People Ask*, 79.

3. Anthony de Mello, *The Heart of the Enlightened* (New York: Image Books, 1991), 52.

4. Edward Pruden in *Homiletics* 5 (2): 45.

5. Kathryn Lindskoog, *C. S. Lewis: Mere Christian* (Wheaton, IL: Harold Shaw, 1987), 128.

6. Ibid., 119.

36. Thanks Giving
Steven P. Vitrano

In Luke's Gospel, chapter 17, verses 11 to 19, we read that Jesus was traveling one day toward Jerusalem on a road that ran between Samaria and Galilee:

> And as he entered a village, he was met by ten lepers, who stood at a distance and lifted up their voices and said, "Jesus, master, have mercy on us." When he saw them he said to them, "Go and show yourselves to the priests." And as they went they were cleansed. Then one of them, when he saw that he was healed, turned back, praising God with a loud voice; and he fell on his face at Jesus' feet, giving him thanks. Now he was a Samaritan. Then said Jesus, "Were not ten cleansed? Where are the nine? Was no one found to return and give praise to God except this foreigner?" And he said to him, "Rise and go your way; your faith has made you well."

Now, what does this story say to us in terms of what it means to be a Christian? A number of things perhaps, but one seems quite obvious: Gratitude is a Christian virtue. Note the emphasis Paul gives to this virtue: "Be thankful. Let the word of Christ dwell in you richly, teach and admonish one another in all wisdom, and sing psalms and hymns and spiritual songs with *thankfulness* in your hearts to God. And whatever you do, in word or deed, do everything in the name of the Lord Jesus giving *thanks* to God the Father through him."

(Col. 3:15–17; emphasis supplied)

Steven P. Vitrano is Professor Emeritus of Preaching, Worship, and Evangelism at the Seventh-Day Adventist Seminary in Berrien Springs, Michigan. His published works include *How to Preach* and *God's Way of Righting Wrong*. Dr. Vitrano was a contributor to *Best Sermons 4*.

But gratitude is more than saying, "Thank you." This is seen clearly in a parable Jesus told, recorded in Luke 18:10–14:

> Two men went to the temple to pray, one was a
> Pharisee and the other a tax collector. The
> Pharisee stood and prayed, "God, I thank thee that
> I am not like the other men, extortioners, unjust,
> adulterers, or even like this tax collector. I fast
> twice a week, I give tithes of all that I get."
> But the tax collector stood some distance away
> and, beating his breast, prayed with downcast eyes,
> "God be merciful to me a sinner!"
> (Luke 18:11–12)

What a contrast between these two characters! Who would dare to say that the Pharisee's prayer was characterized by *gratitude*? He was nothing but a pompous religious bigot. You know his kind, don't you? (He's always the other fellow!)

But then there's the tax collector. You know his kind, too, don't you? (How dare he come to church!) And yet he had something the Pharisee badly needed. Christ's appraisal of the situation would not surprise us: "I tell you, this man [the tax collector] went down to his house justified rather than the other; for every one who exalts himself will be humbled, but he who humbles himself will be exalted" (Luke 18:14).

Into the fabric of gratitude are woven the threads of humility. It is hard for a proud person to be truly grateful.

Have you heard of Zacchaeus? He's that "wee little man" the children sing about. He had heard a lot about Jesus and wanted to see him. So when he learned that Jesus was coming he joined the crowd. But the crowd was tall and he was small. What to do? Looking around, he spied a sycamore tree, climbed it, and waited for Jesus to come by. He didn't want to be noticed; he just wanted to see.

But when Jesus came near and saw him, he looked up and said, "Zacchaeus, make haste and come down; for I must stay at your house today" (Luke 19:5).

The text says, "So he made haste and came down" (v. 6). More than likely he came close to falling down in getting out of that tree.

This teacher, this healer is going to his house! "By all means, Jesus, come on in!"

Now this might strike you as being a bit humorous and unusual, but certainly not objectionable. He was a little man. And yes, he climbed a tree to see Jesus—a rather unusual thing to do. But you can't fault him for being resourceful. But he was a *sinner!* Everyone knew that. He was not just a tax collector, he was a *chief* tax collector (v. 2)! And to think that Jesus would go to the home of a chief of tax collectors! Now, this is the stuff that scandal is made of, especially among the respectable in society. Hence their response: "And when they saw it they all murmured, 'He has gone in to be the guest of a man who is a sinner' " (v. 7).

Surely Zacchaeus knew he was not popular. He wasn't a tax collector because he wanted to be popular, especially with the pious and holy in his neighborhood—the chief priests and Pharisees. He was a tax collector because he wanted to be rich! So when Jesus confronted him with acceptance, it blew his mind. Here was a man of whom he had heard much—how he had blessed people, and healed people, and how good he was. And *he* was coming into *his* house! Caught within the circle of Christ's love, he was changed and changed radically. (Christ's love has a way of doing that, you know.)

"And Zacchaeus stood and said to the Lord, 'Behold, Lord, the half of my goods I give to the poor; and if I have defrauded any one of anything, I restore it fourfold' " (v. 8).

Now, that was going to cost him something. He knew who he was and what he had done. But it was different now; he was different. His response was a measure of his gratitude for what Christ had done for him. *Into the fabric of gratitude are woven the threads of generosity and unselfishness.* It is hard for a selfish or greedy person to be truly grateful.

This time Jesus is in the home of a Pharisee by the name of Simon. Jesus has taken his place at the table when a woman walks in with an alabaster flask of ointment and proceeds to anoint his feet with her tears and the ointment, kissing his feet and wiping them with her hair. This was more than Simon could take. First of all he questioned Jesus' integrity, saying to himself, "If this man were a prophet, he would have known who and what sort of woman this is who is touching him, for she is a sinner" (Luke 7:40).

Oops, that was a mistake. Not only did Jesus know who the woman was and who Simon was, but, unfortunately for Simon, he also knew what Simon was thinking. It just doesn't pay for a Pharisee to patronize Jesus.

But Jesus is not contentious at this point. He responds by telling a parable: "A certain creditor had two debtors; one owed five hundred denarii, and the other fifty. When they could not pay, he forgave them both. Now which of them will love him more?" (v. 42).

Simon answers, "The one, I suppose, to whom he forgave more" (v. 43). Good answer, Simon, but it leaves you rather vulnerable.

Perhaps we should stop short of saying that Jesus had just set him up for the kill, but Jesus had a way of rebuking hypocrisy. The truth can hurt, but it also can heal.

Turning toward the woman, he says to Simon, "Do you see this woman? I entered your house, you gave me no water for my feet, but she has wet my feet with her tears and wiped them with her hair. You gave me no kiss, but from the time I came in she has not ceased to kiss my feet. You did not anoint my head with oil, but she has anointed my feet with ointment. Therefore I tell you, her sins, which are many, are forgiven, for she loved much; but he who is forgiven little, loves little" (vv. 44–47).

The response to love is love, and love begets gratitude. *Into the fabric of gratitude are woven the threads of love.* It is hard for an unloving person to be truly grateful.

Once a year we celebrate Thanksgiving, but Christian generosity knows no season. How often do we see it today? In our grasp for things—the four-bedroom house in suburbia, two cars in the garage (at least one a Mercedes or a BMW), the furs, the gowns, the suits—or in our quest for position, power, and respectability, is there room for gratitude? Or must gratitude be preceded by adversity? Must we be knocked down so that we can be grateful when we can stand again?

I have taught preaching for many years to seminary students. I have found it a joyful and blessed experience and I have also found it to be one of the hardest courses to teach. There is nothing about which seminarians are more sensitive than their preaching. If they can't preach, they're dead in the water. After all, this is something they will be doing for a lifetime, professionally.

How nice it is when the task is done well! How bitter when done poorly! How nice it would be if we could just praise the good and ignore the bad! But this will not do. The student does not become professional without having the rough spots rubbed off, without having surgery when it is needed. Talk about pain!

And yet, the worst of times have been the best of times. When I have had to be brutally frank with a student, even when I have sandwiched the criticism in between praise and affirmation; when I have had to take his or her sermon apart and put it back together; when I have had to watch him or her squirm and sweat while watching the video of his or her own sermon; when it is all over, to have the student turn to me and say, in all sincerity, "Thank you, that was helpful"—what can I say? That is a revelation of true Christian gratitude! It is born of humble, unselfish love.

We cherish all of the Christian virtues. We want to be what he wants us to be. We can be if we let him teach us. *He will make us humble, unselfish, and loving—the fabric of Christian gratitude.*

37. Two Christmas Meditations

Eugen Bannerman

What's Special About Christmas?

Glory to God in the highest heaven,
and on earth peace among those whom he favors!

—Luke 2:14, NRSV

What's special about Christmas?
What sets this day apart from other holy days?
There are many reasons that the soul finds
to celebrate Christmas.

On no other day of the year
do we experience such deep longing for peace and security.
We hear the words of the angels to the shepherds,
and we want the peace and goodwill they proclaimed
in our lives.

At Christmas, our memories go back to our own childhood,
to the time we experienced the safety and security
of our own family.
But as the years progressed and our families separated,
sometimes by distance,
sometimes by choice,
sometimes by death,
the longing for the togetherness of early years remained strong.

That is why at Christmas
we try hard to contact those people who are close to us,
and to tell them how much we love them,
and we ask that they, too, love us.

Eugen Bannerman is a psychology professor at Ryerson Polytechnical Institute in Toronto, Ontario. Dr. Bannerman is also a part-time minister in the United Church of Canada.

We need this feeling of security and comfort,
of togetherness and friendship,
which Christmas awakens in all of us.

Because of this need for intimate community,
we make a great effort to be worthy of love.
Hence we spend so much money and time preparing our presents.

But it is paradoxical.
The more expensive and time-consuming our gifts,
the more desperately we attempt to reach our goal of love,
the more we fail to grasp the essence of our need.
Our deepest desire is to be accepted as we were
when we were children,
unconditionally and cheerfully, by those that matter.

What people in every age have craved
is somebody, somewhere, somehow,
who can touch their inner soul
and respond to them in a way that few have ever responded.

Our secular culture has promised more than it can deliver.
We've been taught there are ready-made solutions for every
    problem,
even ageless, human problems;
that we must always be positive and feel good,
otherwise something is wrong with us.

But life is not so simple;
it is difficult, and sometimes tragic and overwhelming.
Real life always contains the unexpected,
the leap, the reversal of fortune,
the sudden change of heart,
the indiscretion and blunder,
the crippling effects of guilt and shame,
and always the baggage of unfinished business.

Real life is a mystery for which secular culture
has not provided sufficient solutions.

This is where the story of Christmas finds a focus,
for it offers us the mystery of God in human circumstances:
Mary's unexpected teenage pregnancy,

and the delivery of the child in a strange city
in a stranger's barn;
the helpless infant, needing love and milk,
yet wrapped in the divinity of God.
And we who contemplate the mystery find our own faith in life
    enlarged.

At Christmas, we see the imaginations and fears of all people
focused onto one child,
a child whose destiny included
the hopes and fears and suffering of all humans.

This is why Christmas is so important,
for it awakens the mystery of love,
a mystery only love can teach us to understand.

Love alone makes our eyes shine,
as we watch the shepherds kneel in adoration
before the hour-old infant.

"Eyes seeking the response of eyes
Bring out the stars, bring out the flowers,
Thus concentrating earth and skies."
(Robert Frost)

These are but a few of the reasons Christmas is special
wherever it is celebrated:
It awakens our need for peace and security,
and it offers us the love of God.

Amen.

A Live Nativity Scene

> While they were there, the time came
> for her to deliver her child.
> And she gave birth to her firstborn son
> and wrapped him in bands of cloth,
> and laid him in a manger, because
> there was no place for them in the inn.

Luke 2:6–7, RSV

There is something very compelling
about a live nativity scene.

It is as if the sanctuary setting of straw and manger,
of proud parents and newborn child,
telescopes the past into the present
and opens our eyes wide to new vistas of meaning.

Watching the modern mother and father and child,
we are compelled to wonder about the first mother and father
and holy child.

How did Mary and Joseph feel that night,
surrounded by straw and animal smells,
and strangers peering through the door,
as Mary labored to give birth to the helpless infant?

Were there tidal waves of pain and pushing during labor,
and then indescribable joy as the child was born?

Was the birth a transcendental experience for Mary,
as it is for so many mothers today,
one where, against all odds,
the physical demands give way to the mystical moments,
as the infant emerges into the light?

Our Christmas cards and carols do not do justice
to the realism of the birth,
but describe a pain-free, miracle birth,
like the arrival of some supermagical apparition.

But the live nativity scene brings us back
to a more convincing human arrival,
and connects the past in Bethlehem
with the realities of our own experience.

The live nativity suggests there is every reason to suppose
Jesus was born in the normal, human way;
that Jesus was a real baby, and Mary was a real mother,
and the birth a real event.

The live nativity tells us that God reveals himself
in the very midst of ordinary life,
and in ordinary human circumstances.
Nothing is more common or more human than childbirth;
and God chose to be born a child.

Yet something uncommon was going on;
a special consciousness of the child's messianic destiny
was planted in Mary's mind,
but kept secret until the child's manhood and mission
were revealed.

The live nativity scene gives us a momentary glimpse
into what the scene in Bethlehem may have been like,
and what it may have meant to Mary and Joseph.

Finding the extraordinary in the midst of the ordinary,
finding God in a child,
in our child,
is what Christ and Christmas is about.

Amen.

38. The Pleading Widow
Mary Harris Todd

Luke 18:1–8

There is an old Japanese saying that if a sick person makes one thousand folded paper cranes, then she will be made well. Lots of people believe that prayer works that way: If enough people pray enough prayers to God, then God is bound to grant their request. Prayer is a way of getting God to do what we want.

That's a mechanical way of understanding prayer: If you put x number of prayers in the prayer machine, then you'll get the result you want. If you don't get the answer you want, then you haven't prayed enough.

That understanding of prayer may stem in part from the parable that we just read. The conclusion people draw is that if a judge who doesn't care will finally relent under pressure, surely God, who *does* care, will give justice when his people ask.

But this parable leaves me uncomfortable. Can we conclude from the story of the widow that prayer is a way of putting pressure on God, or that we should nag God? Is God somebody who must be nagged before he'll do something? I suspect that there is a deeper teaching about prayer in the parable, one that doesn't imply that God needs to be nagged like the unjust judge.

Mary Harris Todd is pastor of Morton Memorial Presbyterian Church in Rocky Mount, North Carolina. She is a graduate of the University of Richmond, Presbyterian School of Christian Education, and Union Theological Seminary (all in Virginia), from which she received her B.A. (1982), M.A. (1987), and M.Div. degrees (1988), respectively. From 1985 through 1988 she was a W. T. Thompson scholar at Union Theological Seminary, and she received a Friends of the Seminary Fellowship in 1984.

Think of the folks in the early church to whom Luke told this story. They were worn out from the struggle to be faithful to Jesus in hard times. People around them misunderstood them and rejected them, plus they had the same struggles with illness and tragedy that we have. They had been praying faithfully, fervently seeking the Kingdom of God, but it hadn't come yet. They hadn't received the answers they wanted. The world was still in bad shape, and they were still hurting. They were tempted to lose heart. They needed more than the simple advice to "just keep praying. Pray harder." There must be more help than that to be found in the parable.

Let's picture the story in our minds. In a certain city there is a judge who has no respect for God or for people. How a person like that got to be a judge, I don't know. But it seems to me that there is plenty of that sort of attitude in the world, plenty of folks to whom God means nothing. There are plenty of folks who have no regard for anybody but themselves and their kin.

Now, in this city, there is a widow who needs to have a judgment rendered. She has taken someone to court. The story doesn't say why, but I think I can imagine why. In Jesus' day widows were often in a bad fix financially, and they needed special help to survive. That's probably the situation of the widow in the story. Someone *owes* her money, and she really *needs* that money to make ends meet. The situation is unjust. It's not right!

So the widow goes to the judge and pleads for her rights: "Help me against my opponent!" And the judge says, "No!"

Does she give up? No! Again and again she goes around to the judge's chambers and knocks on his door, seeking what is good and right.

Seeking, knocking, asking. That's what prayer is. Sometimes prayer is quiet and contemplative, or conversational. Sometimes prayer is feisty and active, like the widow going down to the judge's chambers day after day after day to plead for justice. This passage is a call to pray with our bodies and our actions as well as with our hearts, minds, and mouths.

Think of all the people like that widow who live out their prayer and keep knocking on doors: folks who need and want healing, who pray for it in words, and who pray for it by actively getting help. Folks who have a hard time getting around, but who struggle and sacrifice in order to come to worship in the congregation on Sunday. Feisty folks just like that widow seeking justice. They are in our congregation.

Think of the folks who are earnestly and patiently seeking a cure for cancer. Day after day they go to their labs and pray with their minds and hands. They knock on the door again and again, seeking what is good.

Think of parents who act on their prayers for their children. I remember a story in *Good Housekeeping* magazine about a mother who knew that there was something wrong with her daughter. Something about the child's forehead just didn't look or feel right. This mother went from doctor to doctor asking for help for the child, but one right after the other pooh-poohed her concerns. But she persisted, and finally she found a doctor who could diagnose and treat the problem. The child *did* have a bone malformation, and she needed surgery! And she got it! That feisty parent relentlessly went after what was good and right for her child.

Many teachers are like the widow in the story. Tiny little children come to them with heartbreaking life stories. These young folks don't enjoy the many, many advantages that we do. They don't have folks who are interested in them, and who will support them, read to them, check their homework, give them guidance, and show them how much potential they have wrapped up inside. These faithful, persistent teachers struggle to maintain hope for their students.

Like the widow, the 1992 Nobel Peace Prize winner, Rigoberta Menchú, pleads for justice. She is thirty-three years old, and for her whole adult life she has been crying out for justice in Guatemala. That Central American country has a terrible human-rights record, especially against native Americans—the peoples who were here before Columbus arrived. Rigoberta is a native American. The government has killed her mother, father, and brother. She has been pleading for the abuse and killing to stop. Rigoberta keeps knocking on doors, seeking what is right, even though it places her in danger.

Again and again, the widow went around to the judge's chambers and knocked on the door. And for a long, long time he refused to help. She kept on until her knuckles bled. It was discouraging. I'll bet she did come near to giving up at least once. It *is* tempting to give up when it seems as though you're not making any progress and your hands are bruised and bleeding from the effort. It's painful and hard to hang in there. I'm sure any of the folks I have just mentioned could tell you about times when it was like that for them.

After he told the parable, Jesus said, "Now will not God judge in favor of his own people who cry to him day and night for help? Will he be slow to help them?" How does God help people who have knocked on the door until their knuckles are bleeding?

Well, isn't *that* what *God himself* does all the time? "Behold, *I* stand at the door and knock," God says (Rev. 3:20, RSV). *God* prays without ceasing. *God* seeks and knocks and works for what is right all the time. God's Holy Spirit constantly prays and groans with "sighs too deep for words" (Rom. 8:26, NRSV). Behold, *God* stands at the door and knocks.

God is not just sitting back twiddling his thumbs and leaving everything up to us until that great day comes when God's reign is complete, and the kingdom comes in all its fullness. God is knocking on the door, crying out for justice now! God is like that relentless widow who won't rest until justice is done. God keeps on confronting a world that is like the unjust judge who doesn't have any regard for God or others.

There God is, demanding justice in former Yugoslavia, where some groups of people are trying to wipe out others, where people are crying out, "How long, Lord, before you save us from violence?" (Hab. 1:2, NRSV). God is knocking on the door in Somalia, and he won't give up until his children are provided for there.

God is knocking on the door in South Africa, where, if your skin is black or even slightly brown, for a long time you couldn't vote; and in Japan, where, if you're Korean, you have to have a special ID card.

God is knocking on the doors of troubled and abusive homes. God is knocking on the doors of churches that silently look the other way while injustice goes on in their midst and around them. Behold, *God* stands at the door and knocks!

God knocks on the door even until *his* hands *bleed*. In Christ, he knocked on the door, and pleaded for what was good and right, until his hands bled on the cross.

Jesus said, "Don't be afraid, little flock, for it is your Father's good pleasure to give you the kingdom." In his name I say to you, "Don't be afraid, little flock" (Luke 12:32, NRSV). God *is* going to bring in the kingdom. That great day is coming. It seems slow, to us, but it is surely coming.

In the meanwhile, God does come quickly to *help* us. He is with us in the place of the widow. *This* is what prayer is: Prayer means seeking solidarity with God as we *talk* with him and *act* with him. Prayer is something we do together with God.

Through prayer, God talks with us and walks with us, and knocks on the doors of the world with us. The one who sagged in exhaustion on the cross can help us when *we* sag with exhaustion, and when *we're* tempted to lose heart. The one whose hands bled on the cross can bind up our wounded hands. He takes them so gently in his. We place them in his through prayer.

With hearts, minds, voices, and bodies, we *can* pray without ceasing, like stubborn, relentless widows, because the most steadfast, stubborn pray-er of all, *God,* prays in us, with us, for us.

Praise God for his steadfast love and faithfulness! Praise God for every act of justice, for every taste of his kingdom! Praise God for the day when his kingdom finally comes for good!

39. Barabbas
MEMOIRS OF A THIEF
Nancy D. Becker

Mark 15:6–11

Barabbas and me, we go way back. I first met him when we were both fighting in the underground movement—trying to get a revolution going that would kick those Roman dogs out of our country.

We were freedom fighters. The people called us zealots. Of course, the Romans called us terrorists. We were good, too! They never knew when we would strike. Sometimes a couple of those Roman soldiers would be walking down the street like they owned it. One of our gang could pick off two or three of them from a roof.

My specialty was the slingshot. I was pretty good at it, if I say so myself. Silent and deadly those slingshots. When they least expected it—bam!—one of our gang was waiting for them.

So they were always tense, always on the lookout for us. But we knew the land a lot better than they did. They couldn't even begin to guess where to look for our hideouts.

Nancy D. Becker has been associate pastor of churches in Connecticut and Illinois and is currently pastor of Ogden Dunes Presbyterian Church in Indiana. She received her M.A. from Bridgeport University (1976) and her M.Div. from Union Theological Seminary (1981). She also received the Maxwell Fellowship of Union Theological Seminary in 1981. She has published articles in several periodicals, including the *Christian Century* and *Preaching Today,* and she was a contributor to *Leadership Handbook of Practical Theology* (1992, 1994).

Those days were some of the best times of my life—living out in caves in the desert or hiding in rooms in the middle of the market streets of Jerusalem. Nobody could tell us what to do. Least of all those arrogant Romans.

Barabbas, though, he wanted more than just scattershot terrorism. He wanted to go after the top guys—even the governor himself.

We were having a hard time getting enough of the people to go along with the idea of a revolution. I suppose most of them wanted the same thing we wanted—to be free of Roman imperialism. But most of the people were just so scared.

And they had good reason. Anybody who got caught in a plot against the Romans usually ended up nailed to a cross. You can bet nobody wanted to be at the wrong end of their so-called justice system.

But Barabbas, he was practically fearless—a real daredevil, always pushing the rules and risking his neck. I never met a better freedom fighter.

Anyway, it was his idea to try to make a run on Pilate's stronghold and either capture or kill the governor himself. That's how Barabbas got caught.

He made this almost foolproof plan to sneak into the palace and kidnap the governor. He drew a model of the governor's palace in the sand next to the campfire one night.

He knew where the doors in and out were, and he knew where the guards were posted. Four of our front-line soldiers, including Barabbas, were going to work their way through the back hallway and into the central room where Pilate usually met with his generals and doled out sentences to prisoners.

My job was to stand guard at the gate in front of the palace.

We decided to go on a night before the Passover, when the moon would be dark.

It was a good plan, but it ended up they had to kill the palace guards to get into the central control room. Then, when they got in, Pilate wasn't there; but his personal guards were, and they got the drop on Barabbas and the front line.

To this day, I don't know if Pilate was tipped off or if he just got lucky.

Like I said, I was standing guard at the gate, so when Barabbas was arrested and thrown into the brig, I escaped back into the hills.

Some of the front line got away, too. They said that Pilate's men were really only interested in Barabbas, and once they knew they had him they didn't care much whether the others got away.

All of us who escaped ran like rabbits back into the hills. We figured Pilate might send out a century or two of soldiers to search out the hills, and try to smash the movement entirely now that they had our leader.

I lay low for a while, but by a few days later my curiosity got the best of me, and I went back into the city to see what was happening.

There was a big crowd of people gathered around the governor's palace. A lot of them were the Pharisees and the chief priests. I kind of eased into the crowd and tried to find out what was happening. Finally, I worked my way up to the front and I could see the Roman governor getting ready to make some kind of speech. So I ducked back where he couldn't see me. Just in case.

Pilate made this fancy speech about how, since it was the Passover, he would let the crowd choose one prisoner to be pardoned and set free. It was just a phony public-relations gimmick. He always knew which prisoner he wanted to let go, and he usually got the crowd to go along with him.

This time he had already handpicked the guy he wanted the crowd to choose. A guy name Jesus, who had been picked up on suspicion of blasphemy. Some of his followers were apparently claiming that he was the Messiah.

I figured that's why the chief priests and the elders and the Pharisees were out in such numbers. Pilate wouldn't have thought blasphemy was such a big deal, and it was certainly no threat to him. What did he care what the Jews argued about among ourselves?

It suddenly dawned on me that if the Pharisees wanted this Jesus to be convicted, it would make sense to them to help see that Barabbas was chosen to be the released prisoner. So when Pilate asked who the people wanted to be released, I spoke right up and shouted, "Give us Barabbas."

I knew I was probably taking my life in my own hands, but the Pharisees got the idea right away, and they took up the cry too. Before the crowd could think of asking for Jesus, they said, "Give us Barabbas."

From there on it was easy as skinnin' a rabbit. The rest of the people thought we knew something they didn't, so they went right along with us.

"We want Barabbas," they said.

Pilate sure didn't like the way things were going, and he tried to get them to vote for Jesus. So he yelled out, "What do you want me to do with Jesus then?"

But by this time the people had their blood up and weren't about to take any advice from that Roman dog.

"Crucify him," they shouted.

Pilate was getting mad then. Of all the prisoners he had taken that month, Barabbas was the one he *least* wanted to let go. So he got arguing with the crowd: "Why? He hasn't done anything wrong."

But there was no changing their mind, now. "Crucify him," they shouted again.

Hah! Pilate looked at that crowd like he'd like to arrest the whole lot of them! But there wasn't anything he could do but let Barabbas go. He went inside the palace, and the next thing I knew there was Barabbas free as a bird, walking out of the palace.

I whistled to him, and he saw me there. We waited behind a shop in the market until the crowd had gone.

We were afraid the guards would follow us and find the hide-out, so we found a place to sit and wait until it was dark. That would be a while, since it was just midmorning by then.

I was elated, but Barabbas seemed quiet. I thought he would enjoy the joke of having put one over on the Roman dog—beating him at his own game. He was glad about that, all right, but I could tell there was something bothering him.

We had just gotten some figs and bread at a shop and sat down to eat when there was a commotion out in the street. It was the other prisoner, the one that didn't get released. The Romans were all around him. We just got a glimpse of him through the crowd. He was carrying a big wooden cross, and the Romans were beating him with a whip to make him move faster.

The prisoner looked over at where we were eating and saw Barabbas. For a minute it looked almost as if he sort of—smiled. It wasn't a real smile exactly, but it was like you might look at a friend. It was only for a minute, and I might have been wrong.

When they had passed, I said to Barabbas, "You sure had a close call. That could have been you carrying the cross. But God seems to be looking out for you, today."

He didn't answer for a long time. He just sat, looking at the place where the guy with the cross had passed by. Finally, he said, "Jesus. His name is Jesus. I talked to him some in the guardhouse. He's a very unusual man. Some of the Jews think he is the Messiah. Did you know that?"

I shook my head and bit into another fig. But Barabbas wasn't eating, and he still had this odd, kind of serious look on his face. He wasn't really acting like his old self.

"How could he be the Messiah?" I asked. "The Messiah wouldn't be under the whip of some Roman dog. You can bet the Messiah would be on the opposite end of the whip. With the power of God behind him.

"The prophet said he would come in clouds of glory with a flaming sword to take care of all the enemies of the Jews. The last I saw, this guy, he sure didn't look like the power of God. In case you didn't notice, he was dragging a cross to the hill for his own crucifixion."

But Barabbas wasn't convinced. "I don't know," he said. "There was something about him. In the guardhouse I was bragging a little about the rebellion, and asked him if he'd ever killed a Roman. He said he came to save life, not to destroy it.

"And then, while we were waiting for the crowd to choose one of us for Pilate's little public-relations stunt, he seemed to know that he wouldn't be chosen. And he wasn't very bothered about it. In fact, the way he talked, it was almost as if that was the way it was supposed to happen according to some kind of a plan.

"Then he asked if I wanted to follow him—to be one of his disciples. Now, under the circumstances, one of us was not going to be following anybody. One of us was headed for the cross. But, like I say, he seemed pretty sure that that was what he was going to do. And that I wasn't going to have to."

Barabbas had never been much of a talker, but he couldn't seem to let up about this Jesus. He went on talking:

"Even though he knew about the guards I killed when we were trying to get to Pilate—I wish I hadn't done that—Jesus still seemed to think it was right that I should go free and he should go to the cross. Almost like he wanted to die in my place, like he was willing to die to save me; and he never met me before."

Well, I have to tell you, that kind of talk from Barabbas made me a little nervous. I didn't like to hear him feeling repentant about killing some Romans. It wasn't like him at all. Like I said, he was the best terrorist I ever knew.

I wanted to get out of there, and I suggested that since the Romans were busy with this crucifixion thing, maybe we could get out of the city without being followed and get back to the hide-out.

Barabbas didn't answer for a long time. Then he said, "I think I'd like to follow along behind Jesus for a while and see what happens."

"Follow him? Follow him where? He's headed for death!" But Barabbas felt real strong about this, so we went along the path that Jesus had taken with the cross and ended up outside the city on a hill. By the time we got there the Roman soldiers had already nailed him on the cross and stood it up on the hill.

There was a good-sized crowd. A lot of the priests and Pharisees were there. I recognized some of them from the crowd at the palace. They were still yelling at him and mocking him because he had claimed to be the Messiah.

I couldn't see it, either; a Messiah should be powerful enough to free us from the Romans. But here this guy was, pretty much defeated by the system.

There were some others there, too, the followers of Jesus—mostly women. They were praying and crying.

Barabbas couldn't seem to take his eyes off the guy on the cross. He said, "You know, there was another thing he said in the guard room yesterday. Something about knowing the truth; that only truth can make you free. Yet there he is on the cross and I'm the one that's free. But somehow I have this strange feeling that he is more free than I am. He seems to know a kind of peace and freedom that I don't think I've ever had."

While we were watching, Jesus died.

A lot of the people lost interest then. The Pharisees and the priests left. Most of the Romans left. The only ones left were the followers of Jesus. They were still there, crying and grieving and comforting each other.

The next thing I knew, Barabbas was going over to this group of Jesus' followers. He walked right up to one of them and said, "This Jesus, was he the Messiah?"

One of the women said, "We believe he is. We don't know why this has happened, but we still believe that God sent him to us. To save us."

Barabbas told them, "I should have been the one on the cross. He died so that I might live. He asked me to follow him. But I don't know how."

The woman was very kind. She said, "None of us knows quite what to do or how to follow him now. He taught us to treat all others with love and with peace, and we hope to learn to live so. We must wait for God to show us how. But if you would like to join with us, you are welcome."

Barabbas thanked her and without another thought said he would be pleased to join with the disciples of Jesus. He looked at me and asked if I wanted to go with him.

But I didn't want to go with them. How could I follow someone who didn't want me to kill the Romans? How could I follow someone who didn't even have enough power to beat them? Who didn't even have enough aggressiveness to stand up for himself? None of it made any sense to me.

I left Barabbas there with them and went back to the hideout in the hill country.

It was three or four days later that Barabbas came back. I saw him riding up and thought he had probably come to his senses. But instead he had news. He started talking before he even dismounted. Jesus, the guy who had died on the cross, was alive again.

"He is the Messiah!" Barabbas said to me. "But it's a different kind of power that he has. God's power isn't the power of hate—it's the power of love! And that kind of power brought him back from the dead. We had the wrong idea—that the Messiah would come to wipe out the Romans. The Messiah came to wipe out death!" He kept shaking his head, saying, "It's incredible. It's incredible."

When he realized I wasn't saying anything, he said, "You've got to come back with me. This is the greatest revolution I've ever been a part of. A revolution of peace and love. Think of it! Think of the power of it!"

Well, in the end I went with him. I didn't really understand what he was talking about then. To be honest, I don't fully understand even now what it is all about. But it is the most amazing revolution. There is amazing power in it.

I believe that the evil Roman government will be overcome someday too. Not with the slingshots or the knives, but with the power of God's love.

It was the best move we ever made, me and Barabbas, that day we decided to follow Jesus up the hill. We follow him now, too. Wherever we go we follow him.

40. Trivial Pursuit

Gene Wilder

Matthew 6:16–24, 33

Today, I want to begin my sermon by testing your knowledge with a few brief questions. If you think you know the answer, simply raise your hand. Ready? Here we go.

Who made George Washington's false teeth? (The answer: Paul Revere.) What sport features small hops called pitty pats at the end of a run of plinkers? (The answer: stone skipping.) What happens if you get pepper in your proboscis? (The answer: You sneeze.) And last but not least, who knows the name of Mrs. Jumbo's son? If you guessed "Dumbo," you are absolutely correct.

Do you know the source for all these questions? That's right, the questions came from a board game called Trivial Pursuit. The name says it all, because the object of this game is to spend hours on end seeking trivial answers to extremely trivial questions. Yes, over the last few years, Americans have amused themselves by diligently searching for the insignificant.

But to many Americans, trivial pursuit is more than just a board game. To many Americans, trivial pursuit is a way of life. For in our land of ladder-climbing, money-grabbing, society-seeking yuppie beings, most of us get blindly caught up in a dili-

---

Gene Wilder is pastor of the First Baptist Church in Fitzgerald, Georgia. He has a B.A. in music and received his M.Div. and D.Min. from Southern Baptist Theological Seminary. He has published several articles and was a contributing author for *Time Out for Men*. He has received the Pastor of the Year Award from the Macon Baptist Association (1988) and the Golden Pen Award from the *Macon News* (1990), and he was featured in *Who's Who in Religion* (1992). He and his wife, Patricia, have two children, Jeffrey and Ginger.

gent search for the insignificant. Even before thinking, we become absorbed in spending our money, our time, and our energies pursuing goals that don't mean a thing.

A pastor friend of mine told me about a woman he saw at the checkout register of Macy's. Her purchase consisted of fifteen Izod belts—you know, those stylish yuppie belts with the little alligators embroidered on them. As both of them waited in line, my pastor friend jokingly commented, "Ma'am, you sure must have an awfully big family." Her not-so-joking reply was, "Oh, these are not for anyone in my family. I don't know who will wear them. I just found them on sale for one dollar apiece and I couldn't pass up the chance to buy them."

Imagine that! Fifteen dollars to buy a bunch of fashionable belts that no one will ever wear. If that's not a trivial pursuit, I don't know what one is.

The words of Jesus in today's text forcefully indict those of us who are living our lives in trivial pursuit. Jesus is speaking to you and me. Jesus is speaking to those of us who are diligently pursuing cars and houses, shirts and blouses, positions and ovation and advance social stations. Yes, today's text beckons the attention of all who tenaciously seek the kingdom of man while scarcely noticing the Kingdom of God.

What does Jesus say to those of us who are caught up in the hoax of our trivial pursuit? First, Jesus addresses:

The Pitiful Reward of Our Trivial Pursuit

In verse 16, Jesus addresses the trivial pursuit of the scribes and Pharisees. They were in pursuit of public attention. They wanted to be noticed. They wanted to be admired and would stop short of nothing to pursue the attention they desired. In fact, the scribes and Pharisees would often rub white makeup all over their faces before going into public on Jewish days of fasting. They did this to make people think they had fasted so long and so hard that their skin had become pale.

In verse 16, Jesus points out the pitiful reward of their trivial pursuit. He says, "And whenever you fast, do not put on a gloomy face as the hypocrites do, for they neglect their appearance in order to be seen fasting by men. Truly I say to you they have their reward in full."

And what was their reward? The reward was being seen, and that was all. A pretty pitiful reward for all that trouble, don't you think? But that's the way it is with one's trivial pursuit. Trivial pursuits always pay off with pitiful rewards.

In verses 19 and 20, Jesus elaborates on the pitiful rewards of man's trivial pursuit. He states: "Do not lay up for yourselves treasure upon earth, where moth and rust destroy, and where thieves break in and steal. But lay up for yourselves treasure in heaven, where neither moth nor rust destroys, and where thieves do not break in or steal."

Yes, Jesus is warning those of us who tenaciously pursue the trivia of the world. Jesus instructs us to forget our pursuit of cars and houses, shirts and blouses, positions and ovations and advanced social stations. He directs us to forget our pursuit of the things that won't last, because the rewards of such pursuits are pitiful indeed.

In his album *The End of Innocence,* lyricist Don Henley pictures the pitiful reward of pursuing the things that won't last after death. He states:

> From Main Street to Wall Street to Washington,
> From men to women to men.
> It's a nation of noses pressed up against the glass.
> They've seen it on the TV and they want it pretty fast.
> You spend your whole life just pilin' it up there,
> You've got stacks and stacks and stacks.
> Then Gabriel comes and taps you on the shoulder
> But you don't see no hearses with luggage racks.

Yes, Henley's right. "You don't see no hearses with luggage racks." So if you're pursuing those things that will not last past death, the reward of your pursuit is trivial indeed. For death is the great definer of that which is truly significant. That which is truly significant is that which survives when we die. If what you're pursuing can't last past death, then what you're pursuing is ultimately trivial.

Let me ask you: What significant things about you will people miss when you die? When I die, I hope none of you stand by my casket and say, "I'm gonna miss Gene's brightly colored ties and his Italian shoes. I'm gonna' miss the way Gene drove a golf ball and manicured his lawn." If those are the things you'll miss about me, then my life's been lived with little significance. Instead, I hope you'll miss my hugs and my smiles, my words of encouragement, my friendship, my fellowship, my love and concern. For ties, shoes, and manicured lawns will never last the test of time, but hugs, smiles, and the love of a friend can never be erased—not even by death.

We've seen how Jesus addressed the pitiful reward of our trivial pursuit. Now let's see what he says about:

The Problem Result of Our Trivial Pursuit

In this text, Jesus shows us that we incur a serious personal problem whenever we get caught up in pursuing the trivial. The problem we experience is a problem of sight. When we fix our eyes on the trivial, we soon become blind to that which is significant. In verses 22 and 23, Jesus states it this way: "The lamp of the body is the eye; if therefore your eye is clear your whole body will be full of light. But if your eye is bad, your whole body will be full of darkness. If therefore the light that is in you is darkness, how great is the darkness!"

Yes, when we stare at the darkness of the trivial long enough, we soon lose our ability to distinguish the light. We soon lose the ability to distinguish the trivial from the significant.

In his book *Actions Speak Louder Than Verbs*, Herb Miller relates the story of two Kentucky farmers who owned racing stables. Over the years a keen rivalry had developed between the two farmers. One spring, each of them entered a horse in the local steeplechase. Thinking a professional rider might give him an edge on his friend, one of the farmers engaged a crack jockey.

Minutes into the race, the two horses were neck and neck, with a large lead over the rest of the pack, but as they came around the last turn, both suddenly fell, unseating their riders. The professional jockey remounted quickly and rode on to win the race.

When the winning jockey returned to the stable, he found the farmer fuming with rage. "What's the matter?" the jockey asked. "I won, didn't I?" "Oh yeah," roared the farmer. "You won all right, but you crossed the finish line on the wrong horse."

Only then did the jockey realize he had jumped on the competitor's horse after the fall. He was so preoccupied with reaching the finish line that he was blind to the horse on which he rode.

Some of us are like that. We stare so hard at the finish line of our trivial pursuits that we become blind to the significant things that surround us. When we stare too hard at career success we often become blind to the needs of our family. When we gaze too longingly at material wealth we often become blind to the value of relationship. When we fix our sights solely on social status we often become blind to the values of integrity, mercy, faith, and love. Yes, a trivial pursuit is a dangerous thing, for when we stare too long at the trivia of life, we soon become blind to that which is significant.

So far in this text we have examined the pitiful reward of our trivial pursuit and the problem result of our trivial pursuit. Finally, let us examine:

The Proper Placement for Our Trivial Pursuit

As Jesus talks about those who pursue the insignificant, trivial things of life, he offers a word of advice. He says, "Let's make a deal. If you'll replace pursuing the trivial with pursuing the significant, then I'll throw in the trivial as a divinely added bonus." Listen to his words in verse 33: "But seek first the Kingdom of God and His righteousness; and all these things shall be added to you." Jesus tells us that if we'll spend our time, our talents, our energy, and our money pursuing that which is of divine significance, then we'll get the trivial things of life as an automatic bonus.

Several weeks ago, a local office-products store opened here in Macon. In their advanced advertisement they sent a coupon, redeemable for a big tin of sugar cookies. The only catch to the coupon was that you had to buy ten dollars' worth of merchandise before you got the cookies.

One day, I took my coupon and went to the store. As I was shopping around for some office supplies, I overheard the conversation between a customer and one of the sales clerks. The customer had his coupon in hand and was complaining because the sales clerk would not redeem it for his tin of sugar cookies.

"But sir," the clerk said, "the coupon is only valid when you buy ten dollars' worth of merchandise." With a huff, the man walked out mad and empty-handed.

Later, when I took my merchandise to the checkout counter and presented my coupon, the sales clerk cheerfully handed me my tin of sugar cookies. No problem at all.

Now why did I walk out with the cookies while the other man walked out empty-handed? The answer is obvious. I got the cookies because I realized the cookies were only secondary to the principal product—office supplies. The other customer tried to make the office supplies secondary to the cookies, and of course the store wasn't ready to do business that way.

Many people in our society try to cash in on God's cookie coupon without first investing their lives in God's significant product. They want the money without investing in the ministry, the houses without investing in the homes, the careers without investing in God's purpose, the popularity without investing in the relationships. Yes, many of us want the worldly tin of God's sugar cookies without investing in God's principle product of righteousness. But God doesn't do business that way. If you are seeking first the things of this world and then expecting God to just hand them out, you've turned things around. God's cookie coupon is redeemable only for those who first buy into his plan. You don't get the cookies before the kingdom. Instead the coupon reads: "Seek ye first the kingdom of God, then all these things shall be added unto you."

Recently, a group of sociology students surveyed twenty adults who had reached the age of ninety-five. One question they asked produced amazingly similar responses. The question was: "If you could live your life all over again, what would you do differently?"

They responded with these three things: They would risk more; they would meditate more; and they would spend more time and energy pursuing things that would survive after they died.

Isn't it a shame most of us have to live ninety-five years before we can distinguish between the trivial and the significant? Isn't it a shame most people come face-to-face with death before realizing that their life has been little more than a trivial pursuit. It doesn't have to be that way for you. You can choose to replace the pursuit of the trivial with the pursuit of the divine. You can choose to invest your life in things that will quickly fade away, or you can choose to immerse your life in a cause that is bigger than life itself.

Which is most important anyway, knowing the name of Mrs. Jumbo's son, or knowing the life of God's dear Son? Never forget: Anything less than a pursuit of the divine is nothing more than a trivial pursuit.

EPILOGUE:
ESCHATOLOGICAL

41. A Word for All Seasons
James W. Cox

Romans 8:26–39

This text is one of my favorite passages in all of Holy Scripture. I am sure that many of you have found that it speaks to your heart in many circumstances of life. If you have not discovered its riches, I believe that as we proceed you will see why many of us turn to these words again and again, read them over and over, perhaps even repeat them from memory.

I can hardly think of any condition of our existence that is bypassed in these words. From the underside of this text we can find a laundry list of the grimmest words imaginable. Listen to some of them stated or implied here:

anxiety
 despair
  fear
   meaninglessness
   helplessness
    weakness
    defeat
    opposition
   accusation
   condemnation
  death
 life itself
unseen negative forces

James W. Cox is Senior Professor at The Southern Baptist Theological Seminary, Louisville, Kentucky, where he taught homiletics for thirty-four years and from which he received M.Div. and Ph.D. degrees. He has served as pastor of churches in Tennessee, his native state, and in Kentucky. He has written and edited thirty books and has been editor of *Pulpit Digest* and *Review and Expositor*. He has served as president of the Academy of

I.

Over against all of these chilling words stands one word, a word that does not appear in the text. But the word is there incognito. It is nowhere in the text; it is everywhere in the text. The word is *hope*. This word is a slippery one. Ambrose Bierce, in his *Devil's Dictionary*, defined *hope* as "desire and expectation rolled into one." That's not bad, as far as it goes. The psychiatrist Karl Menninger called hope "an adventure, a going forward—a confident search for a rewarding life." That's better. Hope, as taught in the New Testament, is *nothing* like the idea of Mr. Micawber, in *David Copperfield*, for whom hope was a matter of waiting for his ship to come in, a ship that never arrived because it was nothing more than wishful thinking unconnected to planning or working or anything real. Hope, as taught in the New Testament, is nothing like the nervous belief that you may win the lottery.

What the New Testament calls hope is an assurance that reaches two ways. It reaches back in faith to what Jesus Christ did in his cross and resurrection, and it reaches forward in trust to the promise of the Christ event and its fulfillment in the future, as God brings all things to a glorious consummation in Christ. Hope is the work of God from first to last. While we may be predisposed to it, it is nevertheless what God intervenes to bring about. In the eighteenth century, the Enlightenment and the Age of Reason offered the world, along with many good things, the counterfeit hope of inevitable progress. But two world wars and other factors have blasted the idea that every day in every way the world is getting better and better. The word *hope*, to the contrary, is looking better and better.

Dr. George Buttrick told about a man who was converted when he considered the miracle of gravity—that we are able to live on this planet and not be flung off into space. This man came to realize that there is something solid, reliable, and predictable that we can depend on, that there is *someone* out there, in there, down

---

Homiletics, a professional society of teachers of preaching, and has lectured on preaching at numerous institutions, including Princeton Theological Seminary and Episcopal Theological Seminary in Virginia. This sermon was preached at Crescent Hill Baptist Church, Louisville, and is included in this volume by request.

there, up there, everywhere that we can depend on. What he saw in nature was a sign pointing beyond nature itself to God. And that is precisely what John indicated was the purpose of the miracles of Jesus: They were signs. And John stated as the purpose of his Gospel: "that you may come to believe that Jesus is the Messiah, the Son of God, and that through believing you may have life in his name."

Many thinkers have observed that in every culture there are expressions of either a wish for or an expectation of a future life in which this life is completed, expanded, or glorified. I recall hearing President Ellis Fuller of Southern Baptist Theological Seminary say that hunger and thirst for food and drink are indications that something exists to satisfy such hunger and thirst and that likewise the universal desire for a life beyond is a sign that there is something beyond this life to satisfy the desire for immortality. In recent years we have read of near-death experiences in which people have come back to tell of celestial sights that they have seen, sights so real that they have come back to live lives transformed by what they experienced at the frontier. Even Robert G. Ingersoll, the famed agnostic, as he stood at his brother's grave, said that "hope sees a star, and listening love hears the rustle of a wing." William James, the Harvard philosopher and psychologist, said:

> If this life be not a real fight, in which something
> is eternally gained for the universe by success, it is
> not better than a game of private theatrics from
> which one may withdraw at will. But it feels like a
> real fight—as if there were something really wild
> in the universe which we, with all our idealities and
> faithfulness, are needed to redeem; and first of all
> to redeem our own hearts from theisms and fears.

One of the most triumphant biblical statements on hope is to be found in the First Letter of Peter, where he says: "Blessed be the God and Father of our Lord Jesus Christ. By his great mercy he has given us a new birth into a living hope through the resurrection of Jesus Christ from the dead, and into an inheritance that is imperishable, undefiled, and unfading, kept in heaven for you, who are being protected by the power of God through faith for a salvation ready to be revealed in the last time" (1:3–5, RSV). Such a statement is what really defines hope for us. Other faiths and philosophies point somewhat in this direction, but the biblical declarations surpass them all.

II.

When genuine hope is at work in our lives, things happen. Positive and creative forces are released within us.

For one thing, we feel accepted, we feel that we belong to God, we feel that we have a place in God's kingdom.

When I was a first-year seminary student, I heard Dr. Charles Graham, who, as many of you know, was pastor of Crescent Hill Baptist Church. He was one of the finest preachers I have ever heard. He spoke to the seminary students at the Thursday-night prayer meeting in Mullins Hall on the theme of self-acceptance. Though I do not remember precisely what he said, he underscored for us something that all of us need to know—that we have to come to terms with what we are, failures and all, and go forward from there, confident in the grace of God. But how can we accept ourselves unless we are assured, first of all, that God is willing to accept us? A famous sermon of the theologian Paul Tillich bears the title "You Are Accepted." Tillich said—and how right it feels!—"We experience moments in which we accept ourselves, because we feel that we have been accepted by that which is greater than we. . . . For it is such moments that make us love our life, that make us accept ourselves not in our goodness and self-complacency, but in our certainty of the eternal meaning of our life."

Can you imagine how it would be possible for someone like Saul of Tarsus, later Paul the Apostle, to come to the place of self-acceptance without the assurance within his heart that the Christ whom he had persecuted had accepted him? He could in one breath call himself "the chief of sinners" and in the next speak of having been made an example to those who would come to believe in Jesus Christ for eternal life. The fact that you and I are accepted by God makes it possible for us to accept ourselves.

However, this is not "cheap grace." Anything so costly to God—namely, God's gift of his only Son, who suffered the cross and all the rest for us—ought to and will produce in us a type of life and character that corresponds to what God has done for us in Christ. In this same letter to the Romans, Paul tells us that character produces hope, but it is also true that hope produces character. John, in his first letter, tells us that "we are God's children now; what we will be has not yet been revealed. What we do know is this: When he is revealed, we will be like him, for we will see him as he is. And all who have this hope in him purify themselves, just as he is pure."

It is said that during the roaring twenties, Pablo Picasso was asked to paint the portrait of a young poet, Gertrude Stein. He worked for months and finally unveiled the painting. The painting looked like her, but she was years older, wise and strong. She was not the young, uncertain woman that her friends knew. Those who saw the painting said, "But that doesn't look like her!" to which Picasso answered, "It will one day!" The artist's vision of a yet unrealized future represented her own vision—a vision that helped her become what she actually did become. When Helen Keller was asked if, in her opinion, there was anything worse than being blind, she answered, "Yes. Having no vision."[1] Hope is our creative vision that makes us what we can and ought to become. We should consider that before we write off this world as hopeless.

Embedded in that hope and our proper response to it is the answer to the question, What does it all add up to? Many people today are saying about life, with Shakespeare's Macbeth, "It is a tale told by an idiot, full of sound and fury, signifying nothing." Everywhere you turn, even in the comic pages, the question of meaning comes up. It is an unavoidable issue, and sooner or later every intelligent person will likely ask, "What does it all mean?" A number of years ago, when Viktor Frankl of Vienna spoke in Louisville, he told of a grieving general practitioner whose wife had died two years before. He had loved her more than anything or anyone. Apparently no one had been able to help him out of his severe depression. Frankl wondered how he could help him. What should he tell him? Frankl refrained from telling him anything, but instead confronted him with the question "What would have happened, Doctor, if you had died first, and your wife would have had to survive you?" "Oh," he replied, "for her this would have been terrible; how she would have suffered!" Then Frankl said, "You see, Doctor, such a suffering has been spared her, and it was you who have spared her this suffering; but now, you have to pay for it by surviving and mourning her." The man said nothing, but shook Frankl's hand and left.[2] The man's life had meaning that he had not seen before, and the prospect of recovery was real. This is proximate meaning, something that you can almost measure, and it is genuine. But we reach out for ultimate meaning, that which enabled the apostle to say, "I consider that the sufferings of this present time are not worth comparing with the glory about to be revealed to us." No wonder Robert Louis Stevenson could say, "I believe in an ultimate decency of things; ay, if I woke in hell, I should still believe it."

In all of this—acceptance, character, and meaning—comes empowerment: "We are more than conquerors through him who loved us." Does it puzzle you a bit that Paul speaks of predestination? What is it all about? Why is God doing this and that for us? His eternal purpose for us is summed up in the words "to be conformed to the image of his Son." And that image is cruciform. He calls us to take up our cross and follow him, not in this life only, but into the life to come. In the words of Tennyson:

> . . . We trust that somehow good
> Will be the final goal of ill,
> That nothing walks with aimless feet;
> That not one life shall be destroy'd
> Or cast as rubbish to the void,
> When God hath made the pile complete.

The Apostle Paul stated his hope in these words: "I am convinced that neither death, nor life, nor angels, nor rulers, nor things present, nor things to come, nor powers, nor height, nor depth, nor anything else in all creation, will be able to separate us from the love of God in Christ Jesus our Lord."

NOTES

1. Quoted in Joan Delaplane in *The Living Pulpit* 1 (1): 15.
2. Viktor E. Frankl, *Man's Search for Meaning* (Boston: Beacon Press, 1959, 1962), 114–15.

Index of Contributors

Index of Sermon Titles

Index of Scriptural Texts